John Moore

Gretchen Peters has covered Pakistan and Afghanistan for more than a decade, first for the Associated Press and later for ABC News. A Harvard graduate, Peters was nominated for an Emmy for her coverage of the 2007 assassination of Benazir Bhutto and won a SAJA Journalism Award for a *Nightline* segment on Pervez Musharraf. She lives in the United States with her husband, John Moore, the Robert Capa Gold Medal–winning photojournalist, and their two daughters.

How Drugs,
Thugs, and Crime
Are Reshaping
the Afghan War

SEEDS OF TERROR

Gretchen Peters

PICADOR

———

THOMAS DUNNE BOOKS
ST. MARTIN'S PRESS
NEW YORK

Book design by Jonathan Bennett

The Library of Congress has cataloged the St. Martin's Press edition as follows:

Peters, Gretchen.
   Seeds of terror : how heroin is bankrolling the Taliban and al Qaeda / Gretchen Peters.—1st ed.
      p. cm.
   Includes bibliographical references and index.
   ISBN 978-0-312-37927-8
 1. Taliban.   2. Drug traffic—Afghanistan.   3. Heroin industry—Afghanistan.
I. Title.

HV5840.A23 P48 2009
958.104'7—dc22

                                                              2008044630

Picador ISBN 978-0-312-42963-8

First published in the United States by Thomas Dunne Books, an imprint of St. Martin's Press

First Picador Edition: May 2010

10 9 8 7 6 5 4 3 2 1

This book is for Isabella and Sophia.
Never believe it isn't possible.

And in memory of Abdul Samad Rohani (1982–2008).

CONTENTS

ACKNOWLEDGMENTS

This book would not exist today were it not for the brave and tireless efforts of six local reporters who have chosen, for their own protection, to get no public credit for their work. Blandly cited throughout the pages that follow as research assistants 1, 2, 3, 4, 5, and 6, they took extraordinary risks to help collect a detailed catalog of information. Any insights provided in this book are theirs and the mistakes all mine.

The danger they faced became painfully real when Abdul Samad Rohani, a BBC reporter in Helmand, was abducted and killed by unidentified gunmen in June 2008. Rohani, who also wrote poetry in his native Pashtun, had reported extensively on the drug trade. Friends who investigated his murder suspect a corrupt former provincial police official whom Rohani had implicated in the heroin trade.

Rohani was just one of eight journalists killed in Afghanistan and Pakistan during 2008 and 2009, according to figures tallied by the Committee to Protect Journalists. Dozens more were injured or had their homes destroyed. The Khyber Union of Journalists estimates that 50 percent of the local reporters in Pakistan's Northwest Frontier Province and the Federally Administered Tribal Areas fled to safer parts of the country during 2009. Others who could left the region entirely.

Those who stayed faced daily threats and intimidation amid a troublesome atmosphere of double standards between the local and foreign media. The deaths of Sultan Mohammed Munadi, a New York Times reporter killed in Kunduz in 2009, and Ajmal Naqshbandi, who was beheaded in Helmand in 2007, justifiably outraged Afghan reporters, who demanded to know why their friends died while the foreign journalists with whom they worked were rescued. It's no exaggeration to say that local reporters in Afghanistan and Pakistan are among the world's most vulnerable, taking daily risks to complete even the most mundane aspects of their work. At a time when the world needs regular and reliable information from Afghanistan and Pakistan more than ever, we must do all we can to support and protect the reporters who are our eyes and ears. They are a critical source of information.

Some may interpret this book as anti-Pakistan or anti-Afghanistan. Nothing could be further from the truth, and I hope my friends in both countries—both those who serve in government and those who do not—understand that I wrote this book because I think the great people of both nations deserve better. The international community talks about the importance of building a stable South Asia but seems to look the other way when it comes to the deeply corrosive issues of corruption and criminality. This must stop if we are to truly help this region.

As the ABC News reporter in Pakistan and Afghanistan, I had the great pleasure of working with Habibullah Khan, Nasir Mehmood, Islam Mujahid, and Aleem Agha. A woman could not ask for better travel companions along the border, and I thank them for patiently explaining their culture to me and for putting up with my frequent faux pas. I am also indebted to David Westin, Chuck Lustig, Chris Isham, and Rhonda Schwartz, who from early on supported my efforts to pursue this complex story.

My indefatigable agent, Helen Rees, devoted the same energy and zeal to my book as she does to life in general. Marcia Markland, my editor at St. Martin's/Thomas Dunne, has expertly steered the project through the publishing process. I'd also like to thank Sally Richardson, Tom Dunne, Steve Cohen, Joseph Rinaldi, Dori Weintraub, Kerry Nordling, Julie Gutin, Sam Douglas, and everyone else at St. Martin's who made this book possible. I am indebted to Frederick Hitz for his kind foreword and to Hannah Bloch, Niko Price, Warrick Page, and Michele Jaffe for their thoughtful edits.

An earlier version of this book was written as a report for the U.S. Institute of Peace, which generously awarded me a research grant. There, I'd like to thank Carola Weil, Kathleen Kuehnast, April Hall, Alex Thier, and Mauna Dosso for their help in administering the project. Robert Templer, Blair Murray, and Ulrike Hellmann at the International Crisis Group provided the project a nonprofit umbrella and were instrumental in helping me fulfill technical requirements. I am grateful to Samina Ahmed, William Olson, Barnett Rubin, Andrew Wilder, and Lisa Pinsley for providing commentary on early versions of the USIP report and for pointing out flaws. I'd also like to thank the staff at the National Security Archives at George Washington University.

Many sources for this book can't be thanked by name; hopefully you all know how grateful I am. In no particular order I would also like to acknowledge friends, journalists, diplomats, scholars, and other officials who have helped guide or support my research, shaped my thoughts, engaged me in lively argument, or listened to my tirades about the Afghan heroin trade: Ahmed Rashid, Ghulam Hasnain, Rahimullah Yusufzai, Zahid Hussein, Pir Zubair Shah, Rehmat Meshud, Arian Sharifi, Bilal Sarwary, Daoud Yaqub, Ryan Crocker, Elizabeth Colton, Beverly Eighmy, Ken Thomas, Doug Wankal, Bobby Charles, John Cassara, Steve Coll, William Maley, Ali Jalali, William Olson, David Smith, Raymond Baker, Hannah Bloch, Peter Tomsen, Jack Lawn, Richard Fiano, Seth Jones, Christine Fair, Chris Alexander, Joanna Nathan, Vikram Parekh, Michael Shaikh, Ali Dayan Hasan, Aamir Mansoor, Talat Massood, Adan Adar, Whit Mason, Rodolfo Martin and Susana Saravia, José María Robles Fraga, Anna Fumarola, Sophie Barry, Tim McGirk, Graeme Smith, Carlotta Gall, Kim Barker, Tamur Mueenuddin, Romano Yusuf, Fayesa Amin, Lulu Tabbarah-Nana, Mimo Khan, Phil Goodwin, Liz Cotton, and the great Afghan reporters at IWPR.

Thank you to my hiking buddies Zulfiqar, Lauren, and Bronwyn, because climbing up the Margallas kept me sane. And I'd like to mention Tariq Amin, because he is the only person who, when he found out I was writing a book about drugs, said, "Ooh, I hope there is a part about me in it."

My wonderful parents, who probably hoped I'd do something less risky with my life, have been nonetheless supportive and loving. Thanks also to my sister, Jenny, whom I adore and admire, and to my extended family: Leslie, Jan, Bud, and Casey. I am lucky to have you.

My fabulous husband, John, and near-perfect daughters, Isabella and Sophia, have put up with a wife and mother who has been exhausted and too often foul-tempered. I love you more than anything and thank you for your understanding. Hopefully, I will be less busy now.

Este libro nunca habría sido completado sin Socorro Espinosa Jiménez. Ella ha sido una segunda madre para mis hijas, y es una persona que hace todo en su vida con mucho amor y cariño. Este libro también es tuyo, Coco.

FOREWORD

On page 177 of this detailed and readable study of the poppy trade in Afghanistan, Gretchen Peters observes: "Eight years after 9/11, the single greatest failure in the war on terror is not that Osama bin Laden continues to elude capture, or that the Taliban has staged a comeback, or even that al Qaeda is regrouping in Pakistan's tribal areas and probably planning fresh attacks on the West. Rather, it's the spectacular incapacity of western law enforcement to disrupt the flow of money that is keeping their networks afloat."

By tracing masterfully the enormous success of the illegal heroin trade in the region, Ms. Peters means it, and she proves her case. It is a case that becomes more compelling as a reinvigorated Taliban challenges NATO and Afghan government troops more boldly each week.

Ms. Peters brings a wealth of area knowledge and experience to her report. She has worked as a journalist in Pakistan and Afghanistan for more than a decade. Her reporting shows a firm knowledge of Afghan history as well as the mountainous countryside. Her contacts appear to be with a broad range of U.S. and local officials, including those from the spy services.

Ms. Peters's well-written odyssey takes us through the economics of the poppy trade and points out the distinction and conflict between the Taliban's prohibition of personal consumption of heroin by Muslims and their need to grow and sell the poppy in order to finance their war against the government in Kabul. What is so compelling about Ms. Peters's story line is the simple and obvious equation she draws. Some regions of the world possess petroleum, uranium, or land that is ideal for the production of rubber or cocoa—Afghanistan has the poppy and has grown it for centuries. It is what pays the bills and cements the loyalties, individually and for ethnic groups.

To have imagined that the creation of an unproven, western-supported regime in Kabul would have the power to eliminate the traditional cash crop of hundreds of tribal chieftains without an enormous and lengthy struggle is once again the height of western hubris and ignorance.

Ms. Peters makes that point colorfully and clearly in this highly readable account.

—Frederick P. Hitz,
Inspector General of the CIA (1990–1998)

INTRODUCTION

People always ask me how I did it.

The line of questioning is usually about the same: How did you—a six-foot-tall blond woman—operate in the border areas between Afghanistan and Pakistan? Don't you kind of stick out there? Wasn't it really dangerous? How could you track down drug smugglers and Taliban?

Truth be told, it wasn't nearly as hard or scary as people often imagine.

There are two reasons why that is so. First, most Afghans and Pakistanis are incredibly friendly and helpful. Not only did I rarely face hostility, but the majority of people I encountered bent over backwards to make me feel welcome and to open their world to me. Even in villages mired in extreme poverty, complete strangers fed and put me up in their homes. Friends helped me make key local contacts, and drove me places I would have never otherwise found.

Sure, there were scary moments, like the time my local colleagues and I got chased off a poppy field by Kalashnikov-wielding men. And as security deteriorated, the realm in which I could safely operate shrank dramatically. Now there are many areas of Pakistan and Afghanistan where local reporters can't travel either.

But for most of the five years that I spent researching and

writing this book, the occasions when I was struck by people's hospitality and warmth far outnumbered the dangerous moments. And wherever I went, Afghans and Pakistanis expressed the same concerns: They wanted security, jobs, and a safe place to send their kids to school—the very same fundamentals we expect in our own communities.

As Greg Mortenson, the man behind *Three Cups of Tea*, put it in a recent talk we gave together: "Once you get down to basics, people on this planet are about 90 percent the same."

From what I know from my travels, he's absolutely right. And as Greg says, we ought to focus on finding that 90 percent of common ground between us, and stop fighting about the 10 percent that sets us apart.

The second factor working in my favor was that people involved in the drug trade were relatively accessible. Rampant corruption and ineffective law enforcement meant that smugglers operated with almost total impunity.

I made a policy of meeting people I considered dodgy only on safe turf: I drank tea with a trafficker in a busy Peshawar hotel lobby. I flew to Quetta to meet contacts who traveled down from the dangerous border town of Baramcha, a key opium hub.

With the help of local reporters and friends, I collected information from truck drivers, lab workers, and money launderers. They were all willing to talk about what they did in part because they didn't fear arrest.

Ironically, it was harder to extract information from western officials than the local community. Senior U.S. commanders initially scoffed at the notion that the Taliban were reaping extensive profits from drug smuggling and other criminal activity.

Leading experts dismissed my analysis as a misrepresentation of the facts. My editors back home listened with vague interest whenever I pitched stories on the subject, but they always got knocked off the air when something blew up in Iraq.

Meanwhile, the poppy fields grew larger and larger, while violence shot up in direct proportion. The opium trade became the thirteen-ton gorilla in the room—huge and threatening. No one wanted to talk about it, much less deal with it, but it was always right there in your face, the bright shining lie of the Afghan war.

For me, this conflict wasn't about religion, or a clash of civilizations. It was about criminal money, and lots of it. And it sometimes seemed like everyone—both America's allies and its enemies—were on the take.

Around the time this book was first published, the deteriorating situation in Afghanistan made the deadly mix of drugs, crime, insurgency, and corruption impossible to ignore.

On May 20, 2009, just four days after *Seeds of Terror* hit the bookstores, I was ushered into a super-secure conference room at the Pentagon known as "the Tank" to deliver a briefing on the Taliban's ties to drugs and other crime. I did further presentations for military intelligence, Special Operations forces, the DEA, and the State Department. As thousands more American troops poured into the poppy-rich south, this book flew off the shelf at the PX in Bagram and in Kandahar.

The war strategy shifted to target opium stockpiles and drug labs, taking the focus off impoverished poppy farmers. U.S. federal courts heard the first cases against heroin kingpins with links to the Taliban. An interagency task force was formed to track the criminal financing of the insurgents and terror groups.

There's a long way to go in this battle—and there continues to be resistance to the narco-jihadist link in some government circles. I still cringe whenever I hear a senior official claim the Taliban gets more money from "donations" than crime.

One day I was working on my laptop when a friend from Waziristan came online from Pakistan. He said his family had fled the tribal areas after a cousin got shot and killed in a shootout between rival Taliban factions.

He asked me how my work was going. I told him that I gave presentations every week around the country, but that I sometimes became discouraged by the difficulties in convincing skeptics of what he and I already knew: that the Taliban and al Qaeda were morphing into the world's new Narco-Mafia.

His simple response reminded me why I should carry on.

"There is no crime these gangsters have not committed," he wrote. "May Allah protect and guide you in this important mission."

SEEDS OF TERROR

1. THE NEW AXIS OF EVIL ∵ ∵

A TRIO OF MILITARY HELICOPTERS SWEPT IN LOW OVER THE cracked moonscape stretching toward the Pakistan frontier. Under cover of a graphite predawn sky, the choppers touched down, unloading a covert squad of British and Afghan paramilitary troops known as Task Force 333. The unit had been developed and trained to take out drug refineries processing opium into morphine base and crystal heroin. This was their first mission in southern Afghanistan. It was May of 2004.

The sixty commandos walked in silence for two hours, their boots crunching softly against the barren, hard-packed earth. They headed for Baramcha, a drug smuggling hub straddling the remote border between Afghanistan's Helmand Province and the Chaghi district of western Pakistan. Their target was a three-story refinery that processed raw opium into morphine base by night and fell silent by day. Big labs like this were capable of cooking hundreds of kilos of narcotics every week.

The British officers who planned the operation had kept their destination a secret; most Afghan paramilitary troops on the mission didn't even know where they were headed. The idea was to catch the chemists and lab workers at the plant off guard, just as they were finishing up their nightlong shift. But as the Triple-3 squad entered Baramcha, they passed a group of local militia fighters loyal to the district police chief who were standing guard outside another compound. Apparently those guards gave the lab workers a heads-up, because soon after, the trouble began.

The paramilitary troops approached the refinery, fanning out silently around the large walled compound. But before they even got into position, a fierce battle erupted. "Bullets were flying. There was RPG fire, snipers on the roof. It was total chaos," said a TF333 commander. An Afghan scout who reached the main building heard a lab worker shouting into a satellite phone, calling for reinforcements from the local Taliban. "Suddenly fighters on motorcycles were coming from all around," said the commander. "We tried to advance on the lab but the fresh reinforcements forced us into retreat. We were literally fighting for our survival."

The Triple-3 unit radioed the district police for help, but no local forces ever came to their rescue. Eventually, the British commandos called in American warplanes, which strafed the compound, sending Taliban fighters and lab workers fleeing over the border into Pakistan driving four-wheel-drive pickup trucks. When the counternarcotics unit was finally able to get inside, they found blood on the floor, but the chemists and the insurgents who provided security had escaped, apparently with most of the drugs that had been stored in the attached warehouse.

Task Force 333 was nonetheless stunned to discover large, silent generators that powered the building and sophisticated communications equipment, along with a basement garage holding fifteen SUVs, each of them equipped with a GPS system and a large radio antenna. The unit seized notebooks with codes for smuggling routes and lists of phone numbers in Afghanistan, Pakistan, Iran, Dubai, and India. The following day, a British signals intelligence team intercepted a call to one of the Afghan numbers on the list. Analysts suspected the cryptic message pertained to a raw opium shipment that may have been destined for the Baramcha refinery. "Don't move the camel from the house," the caller said.[1]

Today, it is widely accepted that the opium trade has played a critical role in destabilizing Afghanistan since 2001, both in terms of corrupting the Afghan government and police, as well as financing the Afghan Taliban's astonishing resurgence. The Taliban earns a large percentage of its operational funding from taxing and protecting southern Afghanistan's $3.4 billion poppy market, while insurgents across both Pakistan and Afghanistan engage in a wide array of criminal activities, ranging from kidnapping and human trafficking to extortion and highway robbery. Blunting their ability to fill their coffers while simultaneously improving local governance have become central pillars of President Barack Obama's revamped strategy toward Afghanistan. To that end, the bulk of the 30,000 U.S. troops deployed there as part of the 2010 surge headed for Helmand and Kandahar, the financial and spiritual base of the Taliban and the epicenter of the poppy trade.[2]

However, as recently as 2004, when Task Force 333 made its first bloody foray into Helmand Province, many western policymakers still rejected the notion that the Taliban was profiting off narcotics. Key players within the Bush administration, including Defense Secretary Donald Rumsfeld and top military commanders, would actually suppress evidence to support that reality. With U.S. attention focused on the bloody war raging in Iraq, indications that a drug-fueled Taliban could potentially stage a deadly comeback in Afghanistan represented an inconvenient distraction.

Wearing his signature lambskin cap, Hamid Karzai was sworn in as the country's first ever democratically elected president in December of 2004, an event the U.S. vice president hailed as the final nail in the coffin for the Taliban regime. "The dictatorship that harbored the world's most vicious terrorist group is now history," declared Dick Cheney at a press conference following the inauguration ceremony.[3]

Privately, however, a handful of frustrated western officials watching diplomatic cable traffic and intelligence reports from the region were becoming increasingly concerned that growing clusters of Taliban insurgents were profiting richly from protecting the opium trade, and gaining strength. More ominous still were the indications that international terror groups were helping to smuggle dope beyond Afghanistan's borders.

In December 2003, for example, when American sailors boarded two rickety-looking dhows in the Persian Gulf, they found wanted al Qaeda operatives sitting on bales of heroin worth $3 million.[4] A few months later, U.S. counternarcotics agents raided a drug smugglers' lair in Kabul, where they confiscated a satellite telephone. When CIA agents ran numbers stored in its memory, they discovered the telephone had been used repeatedly to call suspected terrorist cells in western Europe, Turkey, and the Balkans.[5] Suddenly, links between extremists and narco-traffickers began popping up across Afghanistan and Pakistan. It was the start of things to come.

Nine months earlier, just as the Taliban leadership had announced it was staging a comeback, opium cultivation had exploded across southern Afghanistan.[6] U.S. troops began finding multimillion-dollar drug stashes whenever they raided Taliban hideouts.[7]

American spy satellites tracked cargo ships leaving Pakistani shores laden with Afghan heroin, and returning with weapons and ammunition for the insurgency.[8] The U.S. Department of Justice brought smugglers with ties to Taliban leader Mullah Mohammed Omar and Osama bin Laden to the United States to face justice.

Despite growing evidence of their links to drug smuggling, the widely accepted stereotype of the Taliban and al Qaeda has continued to portray them as fanatical holy warriors waging jihad against the West from caves in the mountainous border region. Washington and the militants alike both tout this characterization, which suits each side for different reasons. Just nine days after hijacked airliners smashed into the World Trade Towers and the Pentagon, President George W. Bush famously claimed that those responsible for the 9/11 attacks "hate our freedoms." Launching his Global War on Terror, and pitching it as a cosmic battle between "freedom and fear, justice and cruelty," Bush told the American people: "Al Qaeda is to terror what the Mafia is to crime. But its goal is not making money."[9] The militants, meanwhile, developed their own sophisticated public relations campaign, complete with Web sites, audio/video releases, and even ringtones that could be downloaded onto cell phones. In it, they cast themselves as poor mujahideen living off the alms of ordinary Muslims and fighting under the flag of Islam, willing to lay down their lives in order to drive Western infidels from Afghanistan and reestablish their rigid vision of sharia law.[10]

No doubt this stereotype has some basis in reality: A large percentage of Taliban foot soldiers are poor, devout, and illiterate in the ways of the world. However, characterizing the Taliban and al Qaeda as medieval fanatics caused the United States and its allies to both underestimate their enemies (at least at first) and to almost completely ignore the multibillion-dollar criminal economy that helps support them. This book will lay out evidence that Afghan militants and al Qaeda have collaborated closely with powerful smuggling cartels and money-laundering groups for decades. It's important to recognize the astonishing feat this union of traffickers and terrorists has accomplished since 2001: Working together in one of the planet's most remote and mountainous regions, where there is no major road network, Wi-Fi, or even widespread literacy, they have successfully integrated an agricultural product into the global economy. Just like their predecessors in remote parts of Colombia and Southeast Asia, they have come to dominate the global market share, and now supply more than 90 percent of the world's opium.

There are numerous reasons why poppy has flourished in the current environment in Afghanistan. It's a drought-resistant crop that neither bruises nor rots while making its way to market. And even though a glut in production has caused the farmgate price of opium to drop precipitously, it still retains a higher value than most licit crops. Corruption and poor governance opened a space for the insurgency and traffickers to operate, and drug production always gravitates toward insecure regions. But there's another factor at play that often gets overlooked: From importing precursor chemicals to getting loans to thousands of small farmers, from running drug labs to providing security for heroin shipments, coordinating and managing Afghanistan's mammoth opium trade is an organizational feat of the highest order. It is not being run by fanatics who live in caves.

Businessmen who traffic drugs remain the masterminds behind

the opium trade and they reap the greatest profits from it, but this book will show how Taliban commanders who work with them have expanded their ties to crime, integrating themselves vertically through the opium market and seizing new opportunities to earn funds in other criminal ventures.

This phenomenon should come as no surprise. In hot spots around the globe, today and throughout history, terrorists, insurgents, and other anti-state groups have forged symbiotic relationships with dope runners and the criminal underworld. Of the State Department's forty-two designated terrorist groups, eighteen have ties to drug trafficking, according to the Drug Enforcement Administration. And thirteen of the smuggling organizations the DEA believes to be primarily responsible for America's illegal drug supply have links to terrorist groups.[11] "In the new era of globalization, both terror and crime organizations have expanded and diversified their activities," Michael Braun, then the DEA's chief of operations, said in 2005. "As a result, the traditional boundaries between terrorists groups and other criminal groups have begun to blur."[12]

They flourish around the globe in places where good governance does not. The players may change by region, but the script remains largely the same. Whether it's the Irish Republican Army moving ecstasy into Northern Ireland, Maoist insurgent groups in Nepal running hash into East Asia, or Sri Lanka's Tamil Tigers moving Burmese heroin to the West, anti-state groups the world over have been linked to criminal enterprise, from drug smuggling to kidnap for ransom, credit card fraud, and extortion. Some, like Turkey's Kurdistan Workers Party, or PKK, got their start by taxing traffickers who pass through their control zones. Their engagement typically deepens over time into smuggling and drug processing. European law enforcement now estimates the PKK may control as much as 80 percent of the heroin smuggled into the Continent through Turkey.[13]

For some groups, drugs and crime provide an opportunity to break free from state sponsors whose support may be dwindling or politically conditional. Hezbollah, for example, appeared to start protecting drug production in Lebanon's Bekaa Valley around the year 2000 in order to fill a void when funding from Iran declined.[14] Terror groups have every incentive to seek financial independence. According to a Stanford University study that examined why some conflicts last so much longer than others, crime was a crucial factor. Out of 128 conflicts, the 17 in which insurgents relied heavily on "contraband finances" lasted five times longer than the rest.[15] "Drug money eventually trumps ideology, and becomes as addictive as the dope itself," said Antonio-Maria Costa, executive director of the UN's Office on Drugs and Crime. "Afghanistan is approaching this point. After years of collusion with criminal gangs and corrupt officials, some insurgents are now opportunistically moving up the value chain: not just taxing supply, but getting involved in producing, processing, stocking, and exporting drugs."[16]

As this metamorphosis occurs in Afghanistan, it's pertinent to step back and examine the origins of the world's most powerful organized crime groups. The Triads, a globalized network of Chinese gangs operating across Asia and North America, began as community-level secret societies founded to protect peasants from their corrupt rulers. While the early days of the Yakuza remain a matter of some debate, historians generally trace Japan's dominant criminal network to the peaceful Tokugawa era, when as many as half a million unemployed samurai warriors shifted their focus from community service to crime and violence.[17] The origins of the Mafia are also steeped in legend: By some accounts they started out as local Robin Hoods, defending the Sicilian people from invading Spaniards and northern Italians during the feudal age. Other historians suggest they were born around 1860 when Sicily was annexed by Italy, and made their mark by settling local disputes and protecting the lucrative citrus export industry.[18] All those stories sound eerily similar to the origins and changing nature of the Taliban, raising the possibility that today's Mullah Omar could morph into tomorrow's John Gotti. To be sure, this transformation won't happen overnight, but it's already underway. Compare the evolution of the insurgents in Afghanistan to rebels in Colombia, and worrisome patterns start to emerge. As one U.S. diplomat who shifted from South America to South Asia put it: "It's like watching a bad movie all over again."[19]

The Revolutionary Armed Forces of Colombia, known by the Spanish acronym FARC, formed in the 1960s. It joined communist militants and peasant self-defense groups that operated mainly in Colombia's south, ambushing military units and elite landowners. Strapped for funds and eager to win the support of landless *campesinos* growing coca in the Andean jungles, the FARC began levying tax on coca farmers and drug traffickers. In time, the Marxist rebels began using their soldiers to protect drug shipments and later took control of factories refining coca into cocaine. They also started kidnapping wealthy Colombians for ransom, and forced businesses to pay "war taxes" in exchange for protection. Still the oldest and most powerful insurgent group in Colombia, the

FARC eventually became financially self-sufficient and established a shadow government. A 2009 report by the U.S. Government Accountability Office said the FARC accounts for 60 percent of the cocaine exported from Colombia to the United States.[20]

The Taliban is undergoing a similar evolution—only much faster. During their time in power, the Taliban appeared to confine their role in the drug trade to taxing poppy farmers, opium markets, and heroin labs. When they reemerged in the post-2001 period, insurgent commanders also began charging money to protect opium shipments leaving the farm areas, as well as heroin refineries like the one in Baramcha. In their control zones, they reestablished their system of taxing poppy farmers, even handing out receipts in some areas to ensure no one gets charged twice. Spotting fresh opportunities for income, Taliban commanders in some districts helped organize farm output, while others began running their own heroin labs. Counternarcotics operations in 2009 provided indications that the Taliban is increasing its involvement in the processing and export phase of the opium trade, precisely where the opportunities to profit are greatest.

Meanwhile, outside the poppy belt, there are two other, separately commanded factions of the Afghan insurgency that also engage in crime to fill their coffers. The Haqqani Network in the country's southeast runs an elaborate kidnap-for-ransom network. Insurgents in the mountainous eastern zone, known as the Hizb-i-Islami Gulbuddin or HIG, protect timber and gemstone traffickers, and also tax poppy grown there.

Militant commanders from all three factions of the Afghan insurgency also have ties to human traffickers. They extract protection money from aid programs and development projects funded by the NATO-led coalition. Additionally, insurgents loot trucks bringing supplies to Western forces, extort shopkeepers and local businesses, and collaborate with smugglers who are pillaging the country's ancient sites. "The Taliban are acting like a broad network of criminal gangs that enables them to utilize different sources of income," said Ahmad Nader Nadery of the Afghanistan Independent Human Rights Commission.[21]

Across the border in Pakistan, where five distinct factions of the Pakistani Taliban operate, they engage in criminal moneymaking schemes, ranging from kidnap for ransom to good old-fashioned bank robbery. Arab, Chechen, and Central Asian militants linked to al Qaeda help smuggle drugs beyond Afghanistan's borders, and appear to facilitate criminal activities between the often-divided Taliban factions. Despite their deepening ties to crime, I do not suggest that any of these groups have completely shelved their ideological goals, as proved by soaring levels of terrorist violence on both sides of the border. But having studied their operations at the village level for more than five years, it is clear to me that in every single "AfPak" militant organization, the distinction between criminal and terrorist is blurring. When you examine the day-to-day activities keeping their networks financially afloat, and probe how they interact with local communities and with each other, the Taliban and al Qaeda start to look a lot more like *Mafiosi* than *mujahideen.*

As the Afghan Taliban gets sucked deeper into drugs and crime, the group is losing ties to its ideological roots, just as other anti-state groups have done throughout history. "There's a very small core of true believers still left in the Taliban," a top U.S. military official told me in 2006. "But our intel is that most of the guys are just in it to make a buck."[22] My research came to a similar conclusion. Using local reporters, I surveyed more than three hundred people who worked in or alongside the drug trade in twelve districts along the Pakistan-Afghanistan border where the insurgency holds power or significant influence.[23] Eighty-one percent of respondents said Taliban commanders' first priority seemed to be to make money, rather than to recapture territory and impose the strict brand of Islam they had espoused while they were in power from 1996 to 2001.

Again, the Taliban is following the same pattern as the FARC, becoming more ruthless and violent over time. But their violence now serves to further their financial ambitions as often as their political and strategic goals. "People should be concerned about the FARCification of the Taliban," said Doug Wankal, who headed the Counter Narcotics Task Force at the U.S. Embassy in Kabul until mid-2007. Individual commanders may have become corrupted by money, but the criminalized insurgents have nonetheless made significant territorial gains against the corrupt and ineffective Kabul government and the NATO coalition. Consider this: The FARC at its height controlled 40 percent of Colombia, and is still estimated to earn more than $500 million annually from exporting cocaine. By 2009, insurgents in Afghanistan held tight control over 30 percent of Afghan territory, and I calculate they earn about the same amount annually in criminal revenue.[24] This should certainly be a cause for concern. After all, as Wankal put it: "It does not take a lot of money to fund their operations."

But how much are they making from drugs and crime? Where does al Qaeda come into the picture? And what do they plan to do with all that extra cash? These questions continue to generate considerable debate.

The Taliban earn from the opium trade at four stages: They levy an agricultural tithe—usually 10 percent—on poppy growers, charging slightly larger percentages from small traders and truckers who transport raw opium from the farm areas. Taliban fighters collect protection fees to guard drug convoys, opium markets, and heroin labs. They also tax refineries cooking opium into morphine base and crystal heroin, collecting duties on imported precursor chemicals as well as the refined drugs once they are ready for export. Finally, the biggest source of drug money for the Afghan Taliban appears to be the regular payments made by large trafficking organizations to the Quetta Shura, the ruling council named for the frontier city in Pakistan where the Taliban leadership is believed to take refuge.

In addition to opium profits, there's that host of other criminal activities in which insurgents also engage, like shakedowns, extortion, and kidnapping for ransom. Since most of this crime never gets reported, it's virtually impossible to estimate how much money it generates for the insurgents. Muddying the waters further, insurgent commanders routinely take payment in the form of commodities useful to their war effort, receiving food and shelter, motorcycles, trucks and SUVs, weapons and ammunition, cellular phones and talk-time credit, even medical care and R&R. In many cases, there's no money trail to follow at all. In an August 2009 assessment of the war, General Stanley McChrystal, the commander of U.S. and NATO forces in Afghanistan, said the size and diversity of insurgent funding streams now made degrading them a huge challenge. "Eliminating insurgent access to narco-profits—even if possible, and while disruptive—would not destroy their ability to operate so long as other funding sources remained intact," he wrote.[25]

Estimating Taliban drug revenue remains an area of particular controversy. In the 2009 edition of this book, I calculated that the Taliban could earn as much as a half billion dollars annually from opium. I based my numbers off the 2008 opium yield in Taliban control zones, extrapolating from the taxes and the protection fees they charged, the estimated output from drug labs, the commodities they often received in place of cash, and the rumored value of the payments made by drug cartels in Pakistan. The UNODC came in with a lower figure, putting the Taliban's yearly drug earnings at somewhere between $200 million and $400 million.[26] Meanwhile, the U.S. intelligence community—which for years had denied that insurgents had any links to the opium trade at all—came up with a number at the low end of the spectrum—estimating in an August 2009 report that the Taliban took in just $70 million from the opium trade, and another $106 million from "donations." These figures—and the terms being used—warrant some unpacking.

Seven provinces controlled or dominated by the Taliban produced about 6,831 metric tons of opium in 2009, or about 99 percent of Afghanistan's total crop. After years of overproduction, farmgate prices sank to their lowest rate since 2001, a factor that would have reduced the income insurgents earned from farm taxes to about $40 million or less. At the same time, there was clear evidence the Taliban leadership moved itself *up* the value-added chain in the drug business, deepening its involvement in the lucrative processing and export stages of the opium trade, and for the first time using Taliban fighters to transport shipments across Afghanistan's southern and western borders, a point when the drugs double in value. Amid evidence that dozens more refineries were operating in Taliban control zones, and that a growing percentage of them were run by Taliban commanders, those shifts would have more than compensated for any loss in revenue at the farm level, and possibly even increased overall insurgent profits in 2009.[27]

When putting numbers on criminal earnings, even the best estimates are just ballpark figures, especially in such a fluid environment. But it's helpful to break down the range of potential earnings using just one drug seizure as an example. In October 2009, U.S. and Afghan forces confiscated 45 metric tons of opium during a single raid on a Taliban base in Helmand, along with 1.8 metric tons of crystal heroin.[28] Sold at the average wholesale market rate inside Afghanistan, that opium would have fetched about $2.9 million and the heroin another $4.3 million.[29] In recent years, that is probably what would have happened. It was common then for Taliban commanders to sell opium they collected at the village level to local agents, who would then resell it to refineries near the border. But that has changed. Now that Taliban commanders run labs and transport drugs across the border, they stood to earn far more off this one drug stockpile.

Smuggled across the border into Pakistan or Iran, the heroin alone would have sold for up to $7.5 million, or 10 percent of what the intelligence community estimates the Taliban took in all year. There's no way of knowing if the Taliban commanders at that specific base planned to smuggle those drugs across the border in

order to gain that key bump in profits, but we know that phenomenon is taking place, meaning it's a factor that must be considered when estimating the possible range of insurgent drug
revenue.

The UNODC estimated that the trafficking, lab processing, and
precursor chemical industry in Afghanistan was valued at $3 bil-
lion in 2009, and U.S. military intelligence found insurgents in
certain border districts to be collecting as much tax revenue off
precursor chemical imports as they earned from the opium itself.[30]
Trafficking and lab taxes appear to range from 10 to 25 percent,
meaning that segment of the business alone could have netted the
Taliban between $300 million and $750 million. For all these reasons, I stand by my estimate of the previous edition: The potential
sum of the various revenue streams could easily reach half a billion dollars a year.

In various conversations I had with U.S. intelligence analysts, I
asked for a precise accounting of how they came up with the figure of $70 million: Did it combine the farm tithe, transport and
lab taxes, protection fees, and the payments made by traffickers
to the Taliban leadership? Or was it just some of the above? The
responses I got were vague. "The reporting is not very good," one
senior official admitted. "We don't know the numbers with total
fidelity."[31] In another meeting I pressed further, saying $70 mil-
lion seemed very low to me. On several occasions, analysts told
me they were limited by what they could prove from known drug
seizures, rather than what they could extrapolate from those figures. "We have to use a number that skeptical policymakers will
believe," one senior analyst told me, to my utter surprise.[32] I had
believed it was the job of the intelligence community to tell policy-

makers what was actually happening, not just what analysts think our lawmakers wanted to hear.

I'm also troubled by the continued use of the term "donations" to describe money flowing to the militants. Say a drug kingpin gives Mullah Omar $5 million. Is that a donation or is it drug money? Personally, I'd file it under narco-proceeds. And actually, a lot of the cash that the Taliban receives could be more accurately described as "security investments" not donations. A Taliban commander in Ghazni explained how the system worked to one of my local assistants: "Many businessmen who smuggle precious stones, drugs, sculptures, and other historic artifacts pay dues to the Taliban to avoid trouble on the road. A businessman that I know from the past sent [$3,000] to my 135 men last year from Dubai."[33] In our surveys and interviews, my local colleagues and I heard this over and over: Traders and businessmen send money to protect their interests. This is not ideology or religion. It's the criminal way of doing business.

The Taliban may claim to live off the alms of the people, but ask ordinary civilians in Afghanistan and Pakistan about the money they hand over monthly to the militants and most will tell you they feel they have no choice in whether they "contribute" or not. When someone has a gun to your head, it's not called a donation: It's a shakedown. And increasingly, militants on both sides of the border are hitting up families who have relatives living in the Gulf or farther afield, forcing them to hand over a percentage of the monthly remittances their relatives send home.[34]

Nailing down how al Qaeda relates to the drug trade and other crime is even tougher than calculating Taliban criminal earnings, and the U.S. government complicates matters by changing its official mindset on this matter every few years. Some in Washington claim that evidence of al Qaeda's ties to opium is fragmentary. The argument goes like this: Bin Laden's two public statements on drugs indicate he, like Mullah Omar, is deeply opposed to the *use* of narcotics (Neither man has gone public with his opinion on *trafficking* drugs).[35] Captured al Qaeda operatives have reportedly told U.S. interrogators bin Laden warned his people to stay away from the opium trade, fearing it would expose them to greater risk. "Our reporting was they were very worried drugs would corrupt their movement," a senior U.S. counternarcotics official told me in 2007. "I have seen nothing to indicate that has changed."[36]

However, earlier in the decade, a number of very senior American officials claimed there *was* a clear link between al Qaeda and Afghanistan's dope trade. Back in the year 2000, then CIA director George Tenet testified to the Senate Select Committee on Intelligence that "there is ample evidence that Islamic extremists such as Osama bin Laden use profits from the drug trade to support their terror campaign."[37] Rand Beers, a former director of the State Department's Bureau of International Narcotics and Law Enforcement Affairs (INL) told the Senate's Judiciary Committee in 2002 that "Afghanistan's opiate trafficking . . . was reportedly advocated by Osama bin Laden as a way to weaken the West."[38] And a month later, Asa Hutchinson, the DEA administrator at the time, said his agency "received multi-source information that Osama bin Laden himself has been involved in the financing and facilitation of heroin-trafficking activities."[39] In 2003, Steven McCraw, the Federal Bureau of Investigation's assistant director of intelligence testified to Congress that "al Qaeda and Sunni extremists have been associated through a number of investigations with drug trafficking."[40]

Then suddenly, as the Bush administration ramped up for war in Iraq, the official permitted language on this issue took a 180-degree turn, to the immense frustration of officials who tracked it closely. "Suddenly I was only permitted to say that we had a 'high probability' of drug money going to the Taliban and 'the possibility' of it going to al Qaeda," said Robert Charles, another former INL chief.[41] It wasn't clear whether top aides to President Bush didn't know how to deal with the narco-terror threat, or if they simply worried the issue would distract the general public from their wider ambition to invade Iraq. Either way, the administration tried to stir up confusion over whether it was really happening. "It was kind of like déjà vu all over again," complained a senior Republican aide, recalling years of debate in Washington over whether the FARC in Colombia was involved in cocaine smuggling or simply getting funds from ideological sympathizers. "We lost precious years there not fighting drugs and terrorists simultaneously, and we [did] the same thing in Afghanistan."[42]

Now U.S. officials accept that the Taliban earns from drugs and crime, but continue to doubt that al Qaeda operatives help to move drugs out of the region or receive commissions for facilitating the trade. A 2009 report to the Senate Foreign Relations Committee, based on interviews with dozens of U.S. officials, was typical, concluding that "There is no evidence that any significant amount of [Afghanistan's] drug proceeds go to al Qaeda."[43] When leaders of the terror group issued four separate appeals in 2009 for money to bolster recruitment and training, American officials concluded the movement was struggling, and that an intensive two-year campaign of Predator strikes had killed key operatives and kept al Qaeda's senior leadership on the run.[44] "We assess that al Qaeda is in its weakest financial condition in several years, and that, as a result, its influence is waning," said David Cohen, the U.S. Treasury Department's assistant secretary for terrorist financing.

That might be what Washington *wants* to hear, and I honestly wish it were true. But locals in Waziristan and Bajaur, two agencies of Pakistan's tribal areas that are home to hundreds of Arab, Chechen, and Central Asian militants, say the foreign jihadists appear to be well supplied with sophisticated weapons and good uniforms, even if the increased number of drone strikes have prompted them to keep a lower profile than before.[45] Despite those strikes, al Qaeda's video production house, as-Sahab, released a new video every five days on average throughout 2009, according to IntelCenter, an Alexandria-based firm that monitors jihadist media. The group noted that the videos had improved in their level of production and included more regular appearances from senior al Qaeda leaders, including seven new statements by Osama bin Laden himself.[46]

In contrast to the notion that terror groups operate from caves in the tribal areas, the Islamic Movement of Uzbekistan, an al Qaeda–linked group, posted a video online featuring their official media wing, Jundullah Studios. It showed black-turbaned militants working on at least half a dozen laptops, with a video projector and a photocopy machine in the background. They clearly ran their public relations campaign from a well-supplied office using modern technology and reliant on a steady power supply.[47]

Additionally, al Qaeda and other allied militant groups appear to be attracting a steady supply of western-raised cadre, a phenomenon that has increased concern among American and European intelligence agencies that fresh plots are in the works against Western targets. American authorities in September 2009 arrested Najibullah Zazi, an Afghan-American shuttle driver later charged with conspiring to set off bombs blended with hydrogen peroxide–based hair products he purchased at beauty supply stores. German authorities believe that more than two dozen German nationals have been recruited to Pakistan for training, and that about ten of those individuals have returned to Europe.[48] In one 2009 propaganda video about the so-called German Taliban, the camera panned briefly over a bald and clean-shaven man identified onscreen as Abu Ibrahim al-Amriki (a moniker than translates "the American"), indicating there could be a U.S. national among the group. "In the past, such volunteers were largely self-motivated and had to find their own way to South Asia," *The Washington Post* reported in October 2009. "Today, however, al Qaeda and its affiliates have developed extensive recruiting networks with agents on the ground in Europe, counterterrorism officials said. The agents provide guidance, money, travel routes, and even letters of recommendation so the recruits can join up more easily."[49]

There are signs that al Qaeda is collaborating ever more closely with the Taliban both in Afghanistan and Pakistan, both in terms of planning and launching attacks and embedding foreign "experts" within local insurgent fighting units. Al Qaeda also appears to have co-opted some Pakistani extremist and sectarian groups that once functioned with the support of the Inter Services Intelligence, or ISI, Pakistan's spy agency. Pakistani officials and militants alike describe a faction of militants who are commanded by al Qaeda leaders, but made up of Pakistani nationals who once belonged to extremist groups like Lashkar-i-Jhangvi and Lashkar-i-Tayyiba, the group blamed in the November 2008 attacks in Mumbai, India. The ties to Pakistani sectarian groups give militants in the border areas new reach into the Punjab, Pakistan's most populous province, and the engine of the country's economy.

Pakistani officials suspect one reason the militants are building a nationwide network is to support criminal fund-raising activities, including smuggling. In August, police in Karachi arrested seven operatives from Lashkar-i-Jhangvi who had three suicide vests, fifteen kilos of explosives, ten assault weapons, and about two kilos of heroin in their possession. "It is often talked about that militants do drug business to finance their needs, but this is the first time we have arrested such a gang," said Fayyaz Khan, a Karachi police official. He said the raid had yielded intelligence about where the drugs were sold and how the profits made their way back through Pakistan to the Afghan Taliban. Part of the drug money was transferred to a Taliban commander based along the Afghan border, Khan said.[50]

Based on my research, al Qaeda and other foreign militant groups don't get involved in the opium trade inside Afghanistan, although there are sporadic reports of foreign jihadists working in the poppy fields at harvest time for extra cash. I accumulated multiple reports of al Qaeda operatives getting involved once the opium was refined into heroin and ready to be smuggled out of Pakistan, precisely the point where the profit margin is the highest, and where U.S. officials privately admit they have least intelligence on who is involved. Forty-one percent of respondents to my survey said low level al Qaeda fighters regularly helped to protect heroin shipments once they reached the Pakistan border. The data makes sense when you consider that western intelligence officials believe top-tier al Qaeda leaders are largely cut off from the day-to-day running of their organization, leaving lower level operatives to fend for themselves financially. "It's wrong to think you'll find Osama bin Laden with a bag of opium in one hand and a dirty bomb in the other," said a western official. "But the link is there. Increasingly, there are signs that al Qaeda fighters have learned to live off of drug money."[51]

That's certainly true among terror cells in Europe. "Crime is now the main source of cash for Islamic radicals [here]," said attorney Lorenzo Vidino, author of *Al Qaeda in Europe*. "They do not need to get money wired from abroad like ten years ago. They're generating their own as criminal gangs."[52] Take the terrorists behind the March 2004 train blasts in Madrid, which killed 191 people and left 1,500 wounded. They traded hashish for explosives and learned to construct bombs—all connected to Mitsubishi Trium T110 mobile phones—from Internet sites linked to radical Islamic groups. When police raided the home of one plotter, they found 125,800 Ecstasy tablets, making it one of the largest drug hauls in Spanish history. Eventually, investigators recovered almost $2 million in drugs and cash—far more than the militants needed to pull off the operation. Although a man who identified himself as Abu Dujan al-Afghani, and who said he was al Qaeda's "European military spokesman," claimed responsibility in a video released two days later, authorities never found any evidence al Qaeda's top leaders ever provided the Madrid bombers financing or direct guidance.[53]

European authorities have also linked drug money to the 2003 attacks in Casablanca, which killed forty-five people, and the attempted bombings of U.S. and British ships in Gibraltar in 2002. European police knew for years that Islamic fundamentalists— some through links to Afghanistan dating back to the anti-Soviet resistance—were peddling drugs around the continent.[54] "What is new is the scale of this toxic mix of jihad and dope," wrote author David Kaplan, who has reported extensively on the crime-terror nexus.[55] Investigators believe extremist groups have broken into as much as a third of the $12.5-billion Moroccan hashish trade, Kaplan reports, meaning they can not only reap enormous profits but also take advantage of extensive smuggling routes through Europe.

There's concern about what happens to money that "AfPak" terror groups raise from crime. By mid-2004, U.S. Treasury Department agents monitoring drug and terrorist finance started watching large sums of illicit money moving *out* of Afghanistan and Pakistan—a region that had traditionally attracted large *inflows* of cash, money that had been identified as donations from Islamic charities.[56] By 2009, it was widely agreed that the Taliban was earning far more money than it needed to fund its operations inside Afghanistan, and the new threat finance task force established by the U.S. military also identified huge outflows of cash from Afghanistan. Where those funds ended up—and just what they might eventually pay for—remains a mystery. One thing everyone agrees on: it's highly worrisome. The September 11 attacks cost al Qaeda only $500,000, according to the 9/11 Commission. Militants in Pakistan and Afghanistan are bringing in more than that from drugs and crime every week, even if you believe the CIA's $70 million estimate.

Unfortunately, there's little sign that extremists are spending their criminal earnings to live lavishly. So what are they saving up for?

A mysterious package received by my office in Pakistan just days before the 2004 U.S. presidential election always stuck with me as I researched this project. It was the videotaped statement of a man claiming to be a new spokesman for al Qaeda. His face was wrapped in a *kafiyya* and he spoke English with an American accent. He turned out to be Adam Yahiye Gadahn, the Orange County native turned al Qaeda front man who has since been indicted for treason. When the next 9/11 comes, he warned on the video, "The casualties will be too high to count." For years, western intelligence has documented al Qaeda's efforts to get its hands on weapons of mass destruction. Former CIA director George Tenet called it the issue that kept him up at night.[57] Extremists have widely disseminated assembly instructions for an improvised chemical weapon on the Internet, experimented with rudimentary biological-chemical attacks in their former camps in Afghanistan, and made several attempts to set off bombs that had a chemical component. Experts say it will be technically difficult for a terrorist group to successfully pull off an attack using weapons of mass destruction. But one thing would make their goal a lot easier to reach: lots and lots of money.

I hope it won't take another massive terrorist attack to focus the international community's attention on the vast criminal sums that militants are earning. Debate has by and large ended among senior U.S. policymakers about the Taliban's relationship to opium and other crime. But so far the international community has not responded coherently to the tempest brewing along the

Afghanistan-Pakistan border. The union of insurgents, drug smugglers, and terror groups is the world's new Axis of Evil, a perfect storm that has greatly destabilized that region, and which could threaten U.S. security as well. Despite these threats, months of debate over the end goal in Afghanistan and how best to reach it delayed President Obama's decision to surge another 30,000 troops there. There is growing clamor in much of Europe to pull out of the conflict entirely. And just as the 30,000 new American troops reach Afghanistan, Canadian commanders plan to start packing up, in order to have their 2,800 troops out by July 2011, the end date of Canada's military mission there as dictated by a parliamentary motion.[58]

Two core problems prompt some leading analysts to conclude—not without some reason—that the war in Afghanistan is not winnable, or not where the focus should be. One issue is corruption. The other is Pakistan. Why should the U.S. and NATO allies send our young men and women to fight and die in order to prop up a government that in 2009 the monitoring group Transparency International ranked the second most corrupt in the world? Can NATO actually have any effect as long as militants continue to enjoy sanctuary across the border in Pakistan? And if the militants are in Pakistan, shouldn't we be focusing our efforts there instead? And while I do not agree with those who say the United States should pull out of or draw down in Afghanistan, these are all valid questions. I do believe there must be continued rigorous debate over how to best move forward in a complex conflict with an elusive endgame.

There is no doubt in my mind that fighting drug-related graft will be as great a challenge in both countries as combating the

Taliban and al Qaeda. There has been considerable media attention to the corruption problem in Afghanistan, a country that U.S. Secretary of State Hillary Clinton defined as a narco-state. President Karzai's half-brother Ahmed Wali is widely reputed to be a key facilitator for Afghan traffickers—the man responsible for making sure cooperative police are in place when drug convoys arrive at checkpoints and border crossings. The Karzai brothers have repeatedly denied the accusations, and demanded evidence. Meanwhile, news reports citing documented evidence have also linked Karzai's running mate, Marshal Fahim, and his deputy counternarcotics minister, General Daud Daud, to safeguarding smugglers.[59] A Canadian reporter went undercover to detail the drug trafficking activities of Colonel Abdul Razik, who commands a tribal militia and border police force that extends across the poppy-rich provinces of Kandahar and Helmand provinces.[60]

President Karzai didn't improve his reputation when he pardoned five convicted drug traffickers just ahead of the August 2009 presidential election, including one who was the nephew of his campaign manager.[61] Despite widespread evidence of industrial-scale electoral fraud (some of the worst of which appeared to occur in Spin Boldak, Col. Razik's turf), Karzai nonetheless won a second term in office. His closest competitor dropped out of a U.N.-mandated runoff vote in protest. Unless this climate of impunity changes, progress in Afghanistan will remain sluggish at best. A counterinsurgency campaign is only as good as the government it supports. And at a time when White House and Pentagon officials claim they are trying to support rule of law in Afghanistan, it doesn't look good to have *The New York Times* publish a front-page story revealing that Karzai's half-brother Ahmed Wali is on the CIA's payroll.[62]

Then there's Pakistan, perhaps the most convoluted facet of the entire Afghan conundrum, and especially murky where opium is concerned. Like the insurgency itself, the command and control of Afghanistan's opium trade operates largely from Pakistan, out of reach of NATO forces. The poppy fields and the heroin labs may be located in Afghan territory, but the drug kingpins and the Taliban leadership appear to call the shots from Quetta and Karachi.[63] The U.S. State Department now designates Pakistan a major trafficking country, and there are indications that high-level officials in the Pakistan government and military safeguard heroin smugglers.[64] "If you think drug corruption's a problem in Afghanistan," said a senior western law enforcement official, "it's ten times worse in Pakistan."[65]

Two years of bloody fighting between the Pakistani Taliban and the Pakistani army, along with a relentless string of militant attacks that targeted markets, hotels, and sensitive military and intelligence compounds, have hardened public attitudes against the Pakistani Taliban. But the Pakistan military has demonstrated considerably less willingness to pursue Afghan insurgents who shelter in Pakistani territory, and indeed, there are indications that members of Pakistan's intelligence community still collaborate with all three factions of the Afghan insurgency.[66] Washington could deploy half a million troops to Afghanistan, but until that support ends, it's hard to see much room for improvement.

I have no doubt the war in Afghanistan will cost the United Stares dearly both in blood and treasure. However, just as the criminalized nature of the enemy presents enormous challenges, it also provides opportunities for restrategizing the conflict. Ordinary people on both sides of the "AfPak" border are the primary victims of the Taliban's criminal activities. Efforts to protect them from burgeoning crime could help win the public's support. As well, law enforcement strategies that follow the money up the command chain could help the military and intelligence community locate Taliban and al Qaeda leaders. Because traffickers and terrorists are collaborating closely, the way to find terrorists is to track smugglers. As one U.S. official put it to me, "When you run with the dogs, you're going to find fleas."

In the first part of this book, I will map out how the heroin trade has shaped the Afghan conflict since the 1980s. Recent history set the stage for today's mess and shows how the international community, and Washington in particular, has routinely repeated mistakes of the past. I'll examine how heroin money saved the Taliban from the brink of extinction in Chapter 4, and illustrate why this reincarnated, reloaded Taliban is a very different animal from the one that governed Afghanistan in the 1990s. I'll also trace how the criminalized Pakistani Taliban has spread across that country's northwest. Chapter 5 profiles a kingpin whose drug network allegedly moves quantities of dope that would put him in a league with world-renowned drug traffickers like Pablo Escobar or Mexico's Juarez Cartel. Now in jail in New York, he remains unknown to the general public, and even to many U.S. policymakers focused on Afghanistan and Pakistan.

I'll follow the money trail in Chapter 6, tracing links to the shadowy South Asian crime boss Dawood Ibrahim, who is tied to Pakistan's spy agency and powerful Arab sheiks. This is not fanciful conspiracy theory: individuals profiled in this book are listed in government indictments and most-wanted lists. "If you want to understand what Osama bin Laden is up to," said a former senior

CIA official, "you have to understand what Dawood Ibrahim is up to."[67] I'll follow muddled U.S. counternarcotics policy in Afghanistan in Chapter 7 and trace the complex case against Haji Bashar Noorzai, a major smuggler with links to the Taliban and al Qaeda who was sentenced to life in 2009. His long journey from the poppy fields of Kandahar to a New York prison reveals the challenges and complexities international law enforcement faces in bringing Afghan dope smugglers to justice.

I'll examine why earlier policy has failed in Afghanistan, and put forth ideas for a way forward in Chapter 8. One thing is clear: counternarcotics experts, long-time Afghan observers, and our own intelligence and law enforcement community sounded warnings and offered clear advice for preventative action. "The biggest tragedy of where we are today," said a U.N. official with years of experience in Afghanistan, "is that this was all so fucking avoidable."[68]

2. OPERATION JIHAD

UNDER THE SHADOW OF THE LARGEST COVERT U.S. OPERAtion in history, two American federal agents crept over the Afghan border in January 1988 on a top-secret mission.

Across the devastated countryside, the final chapter of the Cold War was drawing to a bloody close. For nine years Muslim guerrillas, secretly funded by the CIA, had waged jihad against their Soviet invaders. The conflict had united thousands of Islamic radicals (among them a young Osama bin Laden) who flocked to Afghanistan from around the globe to join what they considered a holy cause. Poppy fields and heroin labs had sprung up across the territory controlled by the rebels, who were known as mujahideen, Arabic for "strugglers." By the time the two U.S. agents snuck across the border, the American spies who ran the clandestine program to train and equip the Afghan rebels knew the mujahideen were winning.

A month later, Soviet leader Mikhail Gorbachev would stun the world by announcing plans to withdraw the hundred thousand Red Army troops from Afghanistan. It would be an astounding victory for the mujahideen, and a CIA triumph. But even before Soviet tanks began their long retreat over the Hindu Kush, there was growing unease in some U.S. government circles that a deadly mix of heroin smugglers and Islamic extremists would one day emerge

31

as a by-product of the conflict. With that concern in mind, Charles Carter and Richard Fiano, two DEA agents posted to the U.S. embassy in Islamabad, grew out their beards and wrapped themselves in the flowing robes of the mujahideen.[1] Riding in the back of a dusty truck, they rumbled up a smugglers' trail into Helmand Province, with a handful of Afghans as their guards and guides.

Alongside the CIA's multibillion-dollar campaign to bring down the Soviet army, the DEA had concocted a relatively modest effort using mujahideen informants to identify and destroy labs where raw opium was processed into heroin. Most labs were nestled in the Garmser district of Helmand Province along the Pakistan border. "We trained the mujahideen with cameras, and if they found a place that looked like a lab, they would photograph it," said Carter, then agent in charge of the Islamabad station. The camps weren't much—just a couple of rudimentary mud huts, often strewn with grimy plastic barrels for mixing precursor chemicals like hydrochloric acid and acetic anhydride. "This wasn't Bristol-Myers Squib," Fiano said. Together, DEA and CIA agents in Islamabad analyzed photos their informants brought back. When the agents concluded a site was producing crystal heroin, "then we would go in with the mujahideen and take out the lab," Carter said. They dubbed the program "Operation Jihad."

Both the DEA and CIA pitched in funds to destroy the labs, paying the mujahideen as much as $25,000 per site. It was a small outlay given the millions of dollars' worth of heroin each lab produced in a thirty-day cycle. "Some of those labs were doing five, even six hundred Ks a month," Fiano said. They destroyed drugs on site, keeping small samples for the DEA's global tracking registry known as the System to Retrieve Information from Drug Evidence, or STRIDE. "As far as we were concerned, whatever else they seized was theirs," Carter said. There was often buried treasure hidden in the ground around the labs—British pounds, German marks, Iranian dinars, and Pakistani rupees valued at tens of thousands of dollars. "The mujahideen would take the money and turn it back around into their war effort," Carter said.

Fiano and Carter's three-week journey into Afghanistan, traveling with a half-dozen mujahideen, was aimed at verifying that Operation Jihad was working as intended. At a time when Americans were officially forbidden from crossing the border, it would end up being one of the longest and most extensive journey inside Afghanistan by any U.S. agents during the war.[2] Seeing the labs firsthand brought home the scale of the problem for the two DEA agents. "Especially when you caught them off guard and the lab was flush— with like three hundred kilos just sitting there," Fiano recalled. "And you think, 'Holy smokes, this is a bathtub operation, and they are putting out this much?' That surprised the hell out of me." The group traveled on foot along smugglers' trails through southern Helmand, taking along a goat, which their Afghan companions killed and ate along the way. "The nights were freezing, and it was a hundred degrees by day," recalled Fiano. "And after two weeks, that goat didn't smell very appetizing." Those were the days before satellite phones and GPS. If they came under attack, Fiano and Carter knew there would be no air support. If they got sick or injured, there would be no rescue. "Out there," Fiano said, "we had no one to count on but those mujahideen."

Operating as it did on a wing and a prayer, Operation Jihad eventually ran into trouble, mainly since the holy warriors the DEA hired to roll over heroin labs got into the habit of tying up the lab workers and executing them. "I got a call one day, and they said, 'We have a problem,'" recalled Jack Lawn, the DEA administrator in those days. "I listened, and then I said, 'How about we come up with a Plan B?'" Before long, Lawn and his agents were brought before the Senate Intelligence Committee for a grilling. The lawmakers were incensed that the program had turned lethal. They asked why the DEA never got permission from the host nation, something Lawn pointed out was impossible given that Afghanistan was run by the Soviets. The DEA chief defended Operation Jihad, saying that labs along the border produced more than half the heroin sold on U.S. streets. His agents were just trying to do something about it, Lawn said. If you had to do it all over again, the senators wanted to know, would you do anything differently? "Not one bit," Lawn replied, to the delight of his men. Years later, Carter still recalled the moment fondly: "I think Jack has a gigantic set of *huevos*."

After all, it was one of the few times in those days that a senior U.S. official took the stand to say stopping Afghanistan's drug output mattered enough to take a risk or two. For much of the 1980s, the U.S. government acted like the problem didn't exist at all.

The United States' clandestine adventure in Afghanistan bears remarkable parallels to what happened after 9/11. It began in 1979, when Pakistan was ruled by Zia ul-Haq, a mustachioed general who took power in a bloodless coup in 1977, ousting a democratically elected leader. The international community at first isolated the ruling junta, and then abruptly reversed its policy when the Soviets invaded Afghanistan. Overnight, Pakistan became a frontline state in the Cold War, and the conduit for billions of dollars in military and other aid flowing to the Afghan resistance.

Washington embraced the mujahideen as valiant freedom fighters, and their jihad in the forbidding Hindu Kush became a cause
célèbre bursting with drama and intrigue.

Strategically, the goal was to give the Soviets "a black eye," as
one former U.S. official put it, and get revenge for the United
States' humiliation in Vietnam. But no one wanted to start World
War III or get sucked into Afghanistan's complex political quag-
mire. A "light footprint" approach was better, the CIA reasoned.
Using Pakistan's spy agency, the Inter-Services Intelligence (ISI),
as a proxy coordinator gave the United States deniability and
freed the agency from muddying its hands in local politics. The
downside to this approach was that it gave Pakistan free rein—
and unprecedented funding—to pursue its own Islamist agenda in
the region. Zia hoped that by waving the flag of Islam he could
stamp out ethno-nationalist aspirations among Pashtun tribes living along the 1,500-mile Pakistan-Afghanistan border.

Opium was hardly new to the region. Poppy has flourished along
the Golden Crescent—Afghanistan, Pakistan, Iran—throughout
recorded history. By some accounts, Alexander the Great first introduced opium to Persia and India in 330 B.C. Moghul leader
Zahiruddin Mohammad Babar wrote about smoking it (and then
vomiting) when he conquered Kabul in 1504. It was consumed so-
cially across Central Asia by the mid-sixteenth century. Through
much of the twentieth century, Afghanistan's opium trade was controlled by the ruling family, headed by Zahir Shah, and largely exported to Iran. Afghanistan became a popular stop on the "hippie
trail" in the 1960s because of its cheap hashish and striking scenery.
When King Zahir Shah was ousted in a 1973 coup, Washington
considered Afghanistan's drug trade worrisome, but Pakistan's

tribal areas, a lawless border region slightly larger than Rhode Island, was a far bigger concern.[3]

The opium poppy flourishes in warm, dry climates, like the one along the Pakistan-Afghanistan frontier. Its vivid flowers bloom three months after its tiny black seeds are planted. When the petals drop off, they expose a green pod containing a thick, milky sap—opium in its purest form. Farmers harvest the sap as they have for centuries, by scoring the buds with a curved scraping knife and collecting the sticky brown resin that dries on the buds. In rudimentary "laboratories," often nothing more than a mud hut with metal mixing drums and a brick stove, raw opium is mixed with lime, boiled in water, strained, and blended with ammonium chloride to make morphine base. Once poured into molds and sun-dried into hard bricks, it is reduced in weight and volume by a factor of 10, making it easier to smuggle.

More elaborate refineries cook the morphine bricks with acetic anhydride to create heroin base, a coarse granular substance. Referred to locally as "brown sugar" for its color and coarse consistency, this low-grade heroin is what gets sold on the streets of Pakistan and Iran. Injectable crystal heroin—highly potent and white in color—is what gets exported to the West. More complex to produce, it requires elaborate charcoal filtration and further cooking stages using hydrochloric acid, chloroform, and sodium carbonate. At the time, most labs along the frontier could only produce the so-called brown sugar, and normally exported partially refined heroin to more elaborate facilities along the Turkish border for the final stage of refinement, according to counternarcotics officials.

When the Afghan resistance began, Pashtun tribes in Pakistan's tribal areas grew more poppy than all of Afghanistan put together, and had been smuggling all sorts of commodities for centuries. A 1965 bilateral agreement allowing goods to be transported duty-free from Pakistan's coast to landlocked Afghanistan worked to the benefit of the tribes, giving birth to an elaborate network briskly ferrying commodities in and drugs out. This was known as the "U-turn scheme": Pashtun trucking companies carried goods ranging from refrigerators to foodstuffs from the port city of Karachi up to the tribal areas across the border, whereupon they would be smuggled back into Pakistan to avoid Islamabad's protectionist customs fees. The trucks would return to the coast laden with hashish, heroin, and other contraband. From time to time, Karachi authorities launched raids into the coastal smuggling dens at Sohrab Goth, a teeming Pashtun slum hugging the seaboard, where they uncovered massive underground narcotics bunkers.[4] After Jimmy Carter's administration signed off on the first secret aid for the anti-Soviet resistance in 1979, members of his own administration worried in a *New York Times* editorial that the United States was making a mistake by supporting Pashtun guerrillas who also smuggled dope. They wrote: "Are we erring in befriending these tribes as we did in Laos?"[5]

Their concerns were well founded. Reports filtering out of the war zone in the early years of the resistance asserted that rebel-held areas had begun growing poppy on an unprecedented scale.[6] Opium production more than doubled in Afghanistan between 1984 and 1985, from 140 metric tons to 400, according to U.S. government estimates at the time, doubling again in 1986.[7] Ali Ahmad, a young rebel commander from Sangin, in Helmand Province, said it was a matter of simple economics. He could sell a pound of opium for as much as $50—roughly one hundred times what other crops would bring in. "Everyone is taking it up," he said.[8]

The devastation the war inflicted on the countryside was largely to blame. Millions of refugees had fled over the border to Pakistan, leaving fewer people to work the land. Meanwhile, the Soviets' scorched-earth policy left far less land to work. Opium is a sturdy, drought-resistant crop that has few pests or ailments and doesn't rot. Afghan farmers found that there was an endless demand for it. "A farmer does not worry about selling his opium," said Daud Khan, another commander. "Dealers come from Iran with money in their hands. If a farmer thinks he can get a better price at the border, he can hire a camel for the trip."[9]

From early on, a system developed where farmers would hire rebel soldiers to protect their drug shipments, and the guerrillas would use the money to support the resistance. "If one of our soldiers is sick or wounded we must send money to his family," said Ali Ahmad. "We must also feed them and give them money for shoes and clothes."[10] When a *New York Times* reporter asked how strict Muslims could condone trafficking in narcotics, another mujahideen commander offered up a dubious rationalization that is still heard today across Afghanistan's poppy belt: Islamic law forbids *taking* drugs, but not *growing* them. (Leading Islamic scholars dispute this claim, saying the Koran unequivocally forbids the cultivation, trade, or consumption of narcotics under any circumstances.) "How else can we get money?" said Mohammed Rasul, whose brother, Mullah Nasim Akhundzada, was then regarded as the most powerful warlord in Helmand Province. "We must grow and sell opium to fight our holy war against the Russian nonbelievers."[11]

This trend would dominate the final years of the resistance, and become exacerbated by the inconsistencies in the way that foreign military assistance was distributed among the mujahideen parties, which created intense competition for funds and fierce infighting. The United States and Saudi Arabia were the central donors to the Afghan resistance, providing matching annual funds worth hundreds of millions of dollars. Britain, China, and various European nations also contributed. All the money was funneled through the ISI, giving the Pakistani spy agency tremendous control over which commanders and parties would benefit.

When the resistance began, there were more than eighty Afghan political groups clamoring for foreign money, each claiming to represent the Afghan people. "We told the ISI to bring this down to a manageable number," says a former U.S. official. "We said, 'You know the language and the culture, not us. You deal with this.'"[12] Pakistan's spy agency reorganized the groups into seven parties, which became known as the Peshawar Seven, since their leaders had to travel to the Pakistani frontier city to collect their funds and marching orders. Some of the parties were more loose amalgamations of regional warlords than functioning syndicates. "The loyalty of the commanders was often pretty fleeting," says Milton Bearden, the CIA's chief of station from 1986 to 1989.

Hundreds of millions in private donations also flowed in from wealthy Arabs, and tended to benefit mainly fundamentalist Islamic factions. The ISI also favored the fundamentalists, claiming they were more disciplined. In fact, Pakistan feared the rise of ethnic Pashtun nationalism—espoused by some of the moderate parties—along its border. The fundamentalists received more money, weapons, food, and medical supplies, while others struggled for money. The ISI would routinely withhold food and medical aid when they needed errant commanders to fall in line.[13]

Some commanders like Mullah Akhundzada sought early on to establish independence through the opium trade or other illicit activities, such as smuggling timber and gemstones.[14] "Akhundzada had his own power base," said Peter Tomsen, the State Department's special envoy to the Afghan resistance from 1989 to 1992. "A guy like that wasn't controlled by Peshawar."[15] Mujahideen commanders were generally satisfied to collect a 10 percent tax on the crops grown in their region. Akhundzada went further, setting production quotas and offering loans to farmers who planted poppy. Under the "salaam system," farmers would presell their crops at planting time at a price that was lower than its market value at harvest.

The system still functions today, and has trapped thousands of poor farm families into a crippling debt cycle.[16] Akhundzada also tapped into trafficking, opening an office in the Iranian town of Zaidan to manage his shipments west. By the time the Soviets withdrew, he ran Helmand like his personal fiefdom. In 1989, he demanded half the Helmand Valley farmland be planted with poppy.[17] He threatened farmers who did not comply with castration or death.[18] That year, the valley produced more than 250 metric tons of opium, earning Akhundzada the nickname "King of Heroin."[19]

Such abundances caught the attention of Gulbuddin Hekmatyar, a notoriously ruthless commander of the fundamentalist Hizb-i-Islami Party.[20] Hekmatyar was effectively a creation of the ISI and operated mainly along the Pakistan border. The power-hungry commander launched a two-year internal war against Mullah Akhundzada for control of Helmand's rich poppy fields.[21] By the end of the Soviet resistance, he reportedly invested in heroin labs along the border, working in partnership with Pakistani smuggling networks.[22] "All the big traffickers in those days tended to be from Hizb-i-Islami and that was principally because Hekmatyar was a border person," said Edmund McWilliams, another special envoy to the resistance who served from 1988 to 1989. "He was very much operating along the border because he was so dependent on Pakistani support."[23] Heroin money and ISI assistance helped Hekmatyar transform his network from a fledgling militia into a centralized military organization.

American officials assisting the war effort grudgingly acknowledged Hekmatyar's managerial prowess, but feared his rabid brand of Islam and vicious thirst for power. "He supported Saddam Hussein publicly. He was the deepest into drugs. He was killing modern Afghans and intellectuals. He had ordered his forces inside Afghanistan to kill westerners," said Tomsen. Yet repeated efforts by the Americans to cut Hekmatyar off failed because of his ISI connections. Years later, Bearden, the former CIA station chief, growled: "I always complain I should have shot that guy when I had the chance."

Yunis Khalis, who headed a breakaway Hizb-i-Islami faction, was a third fundamentalist commander deep in the heroin trade, according to ex-officials, historians, and mujahideen commanders. "Khalis was a drug dealer and a thief," says a former U.S. official. "He was also an effective fighter."[24] As with Hekmatyar, Khalis's rise to power was fully dependent on his manipulation of the heroin trade and his ties to Pakistan. Unique among the Peshawar Seven leaders, he came from a humble background, growing into a powerful businessman as his military strength swelled. According to one news report, Khalis ran a simple bicycle repair shop before the war; by 1989 he was operating a bus service with a fleet of fifty vehicles, and a huge auto parts store in Peshawar.[25]

Khalis worked systematically to gain power in Nangarhar, a province which had grown poppy for centuries. He reportedly skirmished with other mujahideen for control over poppy fields and roads leading to three heroin labs and hashish shops he ran on the border.[26] His party included the powerful eastern commander Jalaluddin Haqqani, who operated along the border and had close ties to both smuggling networks and the Arab fighters who would one day form al Qaeda. Another key associate was Haji Abdul Qadir, a Nangarhar commander nicknamed "Mr. Powder" who ran a rickety fleet of Antonovs that flew out of Jalalabad Airport under the flag of Khyber Airlines. The airline was widely believed to carry heroin on flights to the Gulf and return to Afghanistan loaded with electronic goods that would be smuggled over the Khyber Pass into Pakistan.[27]

The fundamentalist commanders weren't the only ones moving dope. Most Afghan resistance fighters got in on the exploding poppy market to some extent—mainly just taking a cut out of whatever passed through their region. "Drugs were behind everything," said a prominent former commander, who didn't want his name used, even years later. The extremist Islamic factions were more organized in their approach, however, integrating their operations horizontally across the narcotics trade, and investing in transport businesses and import-export schemes to conceal their shipments and launder money. Mujahideen leaders like Khalis and Hekmatyar never directly ran drug operations; a better comparison, say western officials, is the mafia overlord with his fingers in many pots of a diversified illegal empire. Lower-level commanders would actually do the dirty work, but the boss took a cut of every-thing. "Think of Tony Soprano and how he controls his guys," says a former CIA agent.

The next generation of Afghanistan's leaders would spring from the ranks of these fundamentalist commanders, and there are clear signs they were informed by this practice of fundraising. A young Mullah Omar fought from time to time under Yunis Khalis, while many senior Taliban officials served with Akhundzada.[28] It was Khalis who gave Osama bin Laden refuge when the Saudi national fled Sudan in 1994. Meanwhile, Jalaluddin Haqqani and Hekmatyar still operate along the border with Pakistan, today fighting the NATO-led coalition. U.S. military intelligence believes both Hek-matyar and Haqqani remain dependent on smuggling heroin and other commodities, including weapons, gemstones, and timber.[29]

If the emerging mujahideen links to the drug trade were trou-bling, more worrisome still were reports Pakistan's military govern-ment was deeply involved, too. By 1984, 70 percent of the world's supply of high-grade heroin was produced in or smuggled through Pakistan, according to European police estimates. There were also widespread reports the covert pipeline run by the ISI, which brought weapons and materiel to Afghan guerrillas, was carrying vast amounts of heroin in the return direction.[30] The secret mili-tary aid for the mujahideen arrived at Pakistan's seaport, Karachi, and traveled to the North-West Frontier Province (NWFP) in trucks run by the National Logistics Cell (NLC), a trucking com-pany wholly owned and staffed by the military. In 1985, a Pakistani news magazine, *The Herald*, reported the military trucks carried heroin back to the seaport. "The drug is carried in NLC trucks which come sealed from the NWFP and are never checked by police," the report said, quoting eyewitnesses. A senior Pakistani police official complained to another reporter, "If we want to investigate the NLC or military personnel who we may believe are involved we are told to 'keep out' by the army. If you push too hard, you are transferred. It's that simple."[31]

In a detailed memoir explaining how the pipeline worked, Brigadier Mohammed Yousaf, the ISI officer in charge of logistics, wrote that "the overall security of our methods" was helped by martial law. "The military was in complete control. They were both the makers and executors of the law."[32] Yousaf later insisted military trucks did not carry drugs, but even if that were so, it is hard to imagine Pakistani officers were not aware of and complicit in the huge amount of heroin crisscrossing the border region. The ISI controlled all traffic and inspected all cargo passing in and out of Afghanistan. Pakistan's spy agency also closely monitored vehicles plying roads into Iran.[33]

In fact, a number of incidents suggested the existence of a major heroin syndicate within the Pakistan military. In June 1986, an army major was arrested driving from Peshawar to Karachi carrying 220 kilograms of high-grade heroin. It was the largest heroin seizure ever made in Pakistan. Two months later, an air force officer was caught with an identical amount hidden in his car. He admitted to police it was his fifth mission. In both cases, military squads swiftly removed the men from police custody, shifting them to a high-security facility outside Karachi. Before any substantial investigation got underway—let alone a trial—the two officers made a highly suspicious "escape." In all, sixteen military officers were arrested in 1986 on drug charges. None were investigated.[34] A heavily redacted 1987 CIA analysis entitled "Narcotics Trafficking and the Military" concluded "corruption is widespread . . . and because of the generally low level of military salaries, it is likely to grow in the near term."[35] The late Baluch tribal leader Mohammad Akbar Khan Bugti put it more bluntly: "They deliver drugs under their own bayonets."[36]

Despite the growing evidence, U.S. officials working in support of the Afghan resistance largely ignored and even suppressed indications that America's allies were peddling heroin. *The Washington Post* reported in 1990 that U.S. diplomats had "received but declined to investigate" firsthand accounts that Afghan guerrillas and ISI agents "protect and participate" in heroin trafficking.[37] Lawrence Lifschultz, an American journalist who reported extensively on the issue, wrote that Afghan intellectuals who tried to alert the U.S. embassy to the problem were "politely noted but not acted upon."[38]

Years later, former senior officials at the U.S. embassy in Pakistan admitted they were aware of the rumors, but rarely followed them up, lest narcotics distract from the central focus. "We wanted to give the Soviets the biggest black eye and 'kick in the pants we possibly could," said Larry Crandall, who ran USAID operations from 1985 to 1990. McWilliams, the former special envoy, said: "You have to put yourself in the mind-set of the period. Raising issues like Hekmatyar and the ISI's involvement in the drug trade was on no one's agenda."[39] When President Ronald Reagan met visiting mujahideen leaders in the White House in 1987, he never mentioned heroin.[40] As Fiano from the DEA put it, "Reagan did not want the mujahideen to be involved in drugs."

Although there were widespread indications that Afghan rebels were neck-deep in the dope trade, proving the allegations was another matter, even if anyone wanted to do so. Former CIA agents interviewed for this book said they vetted mujahideen commanders with the help of the DEA, but found it nearly impossible to collect concrete evidence of wrongdoing. Agents were frustrated by the lack of information in general filtering out of the war zone. "Part of the problem is this mythical American interpretation that if you put enough money into something you will know what is going on," said William Piekney, a former U.S. Navy officer who ran the CIA's Islamabad station from 1984 to 1986. "We could never get a reliable estimate of how many mujahideen were under arms. No one even knew who was fighting, let alone if they were dealing in drugs." Because the logistics and training had been outsourced to the ISI, getting direct, reliable information was all but impossible. "Once you put the weapons in the hands of a bunch of tough fighters who owe their allegiance to their tribe first and foremost, the best you can do is try and find out what happened later," said Piekney.[41]

Officially barred from crossing into Afghan territory and largely prevented by the ISI from meeting mujahideen commanders directly, CIA agents say they developed various methods to try to gather independent accounts of what was going on. Along the way, they collected scraps of information about the drug trade: who was active in financing farmers, moving drug loads, and running labs. "I do not remember seeing too many commanders who were really heavily into drugs," said Bearden. "And there was never any reliable proof." When Carter and Fiano toured southern Afghanistan, destroying about sixteen labs along the way, they were able to identify individuals running the labs they hit, but gleaned little information on how their operations fit into larger networks. The DEA had a clear sense of who the kingpins were in Pakistan, but Afghanistan was a black hole. "Quite honestly, we did not even look for the major players," Fiano said. The DEA's Kabul office had been closed since 1979 when the Soviets invaded. "We had extremely limited information on how the trade worked inside Afghanistan," he said. "There was no way for us to know who was making a cut."

For senior administration officials back in Washington, the vague level of understanding was useful. When U.S. lawmakers brought up media reports suggesting U.S. allies were peddling heroin, the lack of finished analysis provided plausible deniability. One could acknowledge that individual mujahideen commanders might be lining their pockets, but still deny evidence of a systemic smuggling effort. The haphazard nature of the drug trade in Afghanistan made it easy for everyone to describe the problem as circumstantial rather than a matter of mujahideen policy.

A May 1986 statement by Robert Peck from the State Department's Bureau of Near Eastern Affairs was typical. In a hearing before the House Foreign Affairs Committee, Peck testified that there "was no evidence of organized resistance involvement in narcotics production or trafficking."[42] In 1987, Ann Wrobleski, then assistant secretary of state for international narcotics matters, actually went so far as to defend the Afghan rebels for dealing in "the only currency they have."[43]

In dozens of declassified documents and interviews with former officials, the pattern of behavior becomes clear: despite a wealth of evidence and intelligence reporting that showed mujahideen fighters were engaged in drug trafficking, there was never any systematic effort to map out the scale of the problem. At least one former CIA official is disparaging about former colleagues who claim there was no clear evidence. "We all knew what was going on," he said. "The people who could do something about it wouldn't hear about it, or they would listen and do nothing."[44]

Rather than trying to investigate the heroin trade inside Afghanistan, U.S. diplomats and counternarcotics officials in Islamabad busied themselves stamping out poppy cultivation in Pakistan's tribal belt. This was arguably an equally critical concern since more of the heroin produced there ended up on U.S. streets.[45] Between 1979 and 1986, a carrot-and-stick approach combining alternative livelihood projects and forced eradication succeeded in reducing the area planted with poppy by almost 80 percent. It was a Herculean effort that often erupted into violence. In 1985 alone, twelve poppy farmers and one law enforcement officer lost their lives when tribesmen attacked eradication teams arriving to destroy their crops.[46]

The Pakistan government repeatedly claimed stamping out poppy in the tribal areas demonstrated Islamabad's commitment to fighting narcotics. But actually, the program did little more than kick the poppy fields over the Afghan border, which local Pashtun tribes didn't recognize anyway. "Moving it five hundred meters in either direction hardly made much of a difference up there," said Teresita Schaffer, a former deputy secretary of state for South Asia.[47] The fields being planted may have shifted slightly, but for the smugglers based in Pakistan, it was business as usual. And business was better than ever.

The new cross-border nature of the trade made it even harder to track. Pakistan rapidly became a net importer of opium, and annual heroin production rocketed from six tons in 1984 to thirty tons by 1988. By then, more than one hundred labs were operational, most of them located just inside the Afghan border, in the tribal areas.[48] Pakistani authorities proved to be much less enthusiastic about stamping out trafficking than stopping poppy cultivation. They routinely arrested truck drivers moving drugs and rounded up tens of thousands of drug addicts every year, but high-level traffickers and lab owners operated with almost total impunity.

In October 1990, for example, troops with the paramilitary Frontier Corps (FC) near the Afghan border in Baluchistan stumbled upon what was then the biggest heroin seizure in world history, a shipment of nearly two tons of crystal heroin and nine tons of hashish. According to a State Department cable on the seizure, quoting a "highly accurate" local investigative news report, the incident was buried after calls to "high-placed federal officials" by a cartel of Pakistani heroin dealers referred to as the "Quetta Alliance." So powerful was the tribal alliance, according to the report, that three men accused in the seizure were granted bail by a local court before they were even arrested; the eight top counternarcotics officers in Quetta simultaneously applied for four months' leave of absence and the inspector-general of the FC immediately transferred.

The news report described a massive flow of opium and cannabis from guerrilla-controlled parts of Afghanistan to Baluchistan, where Pakistani smugglers processed it and moved it west. "The problem is now out of official control," said an unnamed FC officer quoted in the U.S. cable.[49] A DEA report said U.S. counternarcotics agents had identified forty major smuggling groups operating in Pakistan. Agents estimated as little as 5 percent of the heroin produced in or shipped through the country ever got caught.[50] When Wrobleski complained about that issue during a September 1987 meeting with

General Zia, the military ruler refused to budge, replying blandly that "current problems" limited action unless a "massive force" could be raised.[51]

In fact, there were indications that Pakistani drug syndicates had penetrated the highest levels of Zia's administration. In 1983, a young Pakistani smuggler arrested in Norway carrying 3.5 kilos of crystal heroin identified Hamid Hasnain, President Zia's personal banker, as a key player in a major heroin syndicate moving drugs into Europe. Zia's pilot, Major Farooq Hamid, was arrested on separate drug charges in 1988 following the president's death. And the man widely believed to provide protection for the heroin trade along the Afghan border was Lieutenant General Fazle Haq, the powerful chief minister of the North-West Frontier Province and one of Zia's closest advisers. Efforts by the Pakistani police to investigate Haq's activities were repeatedly blocked by top officials, according to news reports at the time. Haq, often referred to as "Pakistan's Noriega," once described heroin as a valuable "mineral."[52]

Inside Afghanistan, the heroin explosion was taking its toll on the Russian troops, according to a Rand study commissioned by the U.S. Army. The report detailed a staggeringly low level of morale among the occupying force and reported that "a majority, perhaps even a substantial majority, of the Soviet soldiers in the DRA [Democratic Republic of Afghanistan] used drugs on a fairly regular basis." Almost all the soldiers interviewed in the project freely admitted having used narcotics—mainly hashish—saying getting high helped them escape the horrifying drudgery of their existence on the Afghan front. "Most people smoked," read a typical response, "but in 1986 many started shooting with the needles that we have in our first-aid kit." Soldiers described going into battle while stoned, trying to maneuver military convoys down Afghanistan's treacherous highways under the influence, and looting Soviet military stores to trade weapons for heroin.[53] A *New York Times* reporter who separately interviewed Russian defectors to the resistance wrote that "Russian troops in Afghanistan have turned to drugs for the same reasons that many Americans did in Vietnam: They are young, away from home constraints, bored, frightened and under fierce pressure to prove themselves."[54]

Perhaps it was no accident that Soviet soldiers got hooked on heroin. The former French spy chief Count Alexandre de Marenches wrote in his memoirs that during a 1981 Oval Office meeting he proposed undermining Soviet morale by flooding them with hard drugs, Russian-language Bibles, and fake copies of Soviet newspapers full of demoralizing stories. Reagan and CIA director William Casey loved the plan, according to Marenches, who dubbed it Operation Mosquito, "because one tiny mosquito can drive a bear crazy." In his memoirs and in later interviews, the Frenchman claimed he subsequently pulled out of the plan because he wanted the Americans to promise it would never end up on the front page of *The New York Times.* Sorry, Casey reportedly told him, Washington leaks like a sieve.[55]

Brigadier Yousaf, the ISI agent, claimed years later that Casey floated the idea of "flooding the Russian troops with heroin" to the ISI chief, General Akhtar Abdul Rehman Khan, during a brainstorming session that Yousaf also attended. The meeting took place at ISI headquarters when Casey made his second visit to Pakistan in late 1984, Yousaf said.[56] Casey died of brain cancer in 1987 and Akhtar perished alongside President Zia in a 1988 plane crash, but Piekney, who was the CIA station chief at the time, rejects Yousaf's story as absurd. "I remember the visit," he said, "I certainly don't remember that idea coming up in conversation."[57]

Author Steve Coll, also quoting Yousaf, writes in *The Ghost Wars* that another proposal was also mulled at the same meeting: covertly backing uprisings by the Muslim population in Central Asia, then part of Soviet territory.[58] Both proposals would have been highly illegal under U.S. rules of engagement, and Yousaf is hardly the most accurate of historians. In his book *The Bear Trap*, for example, Yousaf rejects allegations of corruption among ISI officers who ran the notoriously leaky arms pipeline, insisting "nothing much went astray."[59] But, as Coll writes of the covert attacks inside the Soviet Union, Casey's floating such proposals to the ISI would have given the American spy chief "the perfect cutout" and total deniability.[60] Both phenomena—heroin use among the Soviet troops and Muslim uprisings inside the USSR—later became reality.

A former Soviet foreign service officer posted to Kabul in the 1980s said his government pieced together clear evidence that the United States and Pakistan intentionally tried to make addicts of their soldiers. "It was well known that they had a plan to spread drugs among Soviet troops and we indeed had a problem," said Zamir Kabulov, today Russia's ambassador to Afghanistan.[61] The issue raises the question of how much the CIA knew about the ISI's ties to the narcotics trade and when. This has remained one of the most closely guarded secrets of the Soviet-Afghanistan war. Most U.S. government documents from the era have been meticulously excised whenever the twin subjects of ISI and heroin come up.

Years later, former U.S. agents say they believed some of their Pakistani counterparts were deeply involved in the heroin trade, but concluded it was more a case of individual officers trying to enrich themselves rather than a government-wide policy. "You have to understand it's a totally corrupt outfit," said one former CIA agent.[62] While American spies did make efforts to figure out which mujahideen commanders were moving heroin, there was never any official investigation on how Pakistani officials tied in to the trade. "We heard things," said another American spy. "And it certainly looked like the ISI was involved in drug smuggling. But proving it was another matter."[63]

Since Langley never asked them to probe the issue further, no one took it up, agents said. "There were no requirements to collect on what the ISI was doing," said a former Islamabad station chief. "My sense is that no administration really wanted to know."[64] Other former officials at the U.S. embassy felt the agency blocked investigations into the issue, lest it discredit a crucial, though admittedly faulty, ally in the region. "One of my great frustrations at the time was that the CIA would not give us information on narcotics," said the former ambassador to Pakistan, Robert Oakley. "My belief was then and still is that they wanted to protect their contacts in Pakistani intelligence. We were convinced the ISI was involved but we could not get any hard evidence on it."[65]

From Laos to Nicaragua, the CIA's tendency to get into bed with rebel groups prone to illegal drug smuggling repeatedly landed the agency in hot water and spawned no end of fanciful conspiracy theories. Following news reports that the CIA-supported Contras were subsidizing their activities by smuggling crack cocaine into the United States, the agency launched an extensive investigation into the role its agents played in the matter. A subsequent analysis written by Frederick P. Hitz, the CIA inspector general who led the

Iran-Contra investigation, concluded that the problem—at least with regard to the Contras—came down to a lack of concrete guidance rather than the grand conspiracy so often imagined to exist. Until 1986, no relevant statutes within the agency governed the conduct of CIA agents who received information that people they worked with or funded were also smuggling drugs. Nor did individual agents act in a consistent manner when they received such allegations, Hitz wrote.[66] It's not clear if this glaring policy omission was left out by design or by mistake, but it did give CIA agents working with the Contras the ability to dismiss the drug issue if they did not want to deal with it, Hitz wrote. Similarly, at the Islamabad station, a "see no evil" approach defined the CIA's response to the swelling narcotics problem. It wasn't that the agents didn't know it was happening, but probing it too closely would have interfered with their central mission.

Overall, the policy of the U.S. embassy was to itemize and prioritize the various issues considered critical to American interests, rather than to try to create a holistic approach to the region's many overlapping problems. DEA agent Rich Fiano recalled his first meeting with then U.S. ambassador Deane Hinton when he arrived at the post in June 1986. The U.S. envoy asked him, "Mr. Fiano, what do you think our biggest priority is out here?"

Fiano answered, "Drugs, sir?"

No, the ambassador replied curtly. It was fighting the Soviets. "Do you know what our second biggest priority is?"

Fiano took another shot, "Drugs, sir?"

Again, wrong. "It's stopping nuclear proliferation," the ambassador said. "Can you tell me what our third priority is here?"

By this point, Fiano was stumped.

"Guess what," said Hinton. "It's drugs."[67]

To the frustration of Fiano and the rest of the DEA team, the fight against narcotics would remain off center stage for another two years, during which time two subsequent ambassadors would be posted to the region and more than $1 billion in military aid would be allocated to the Afghan resistance. "Until we were sure the Soviets would go in 1988," explained Crandall, who was USAID chief at the time, "we basically put drugs on the back burner."[68] By then a powerful and well-connected drug mafia had taken root on both sides of the Pakistan-Afghanistan border.

Mujahideen leaders competing for a stake in the new Kabul government turned their guns on each other as Russian forces began their pullout that spring. The vicious civil war that erupted would continue into the 1990s, dividing the country and the capital itself into warring fiefdoms. Afghan commanders would come to depend ever more heavily on opium profits. The lack of U.S. oversight into drug smuggling by the mujahideen had set up the preconditions for the complete integration of narcotics—and reliance on drug money—into the politics of the region.

Just as the war was shifting course in Afghanistan, a plane crash would set Pakistan in a new direction, too. On August 17, 1988, a C-130 transport plane carrying President Zia, U.S. Ambassador Arnold Raphel, and ISI Chief General Akhtar went down shortly after takeoff, killing everyone on board. Mirza Aslam Beg, the army chief who succeeded Zia, announced general elections and ordered the army to retreat from politics, ending eleven years of military rule. Benazir Bhutto, the Harvard- and Oxford-educated daughter of the ex–prime minister who Zia had ousted and later hanged, was swept into power. She was just thirty-six years old, completely inexperienced in government, and deeply distrustful of the ISI. She pledged immediately to make the fight against narcotics one of the priorities of her administration.[69]

Robert Oakley, the U.S. ambassador posted to Islamabad to replace Raphel, also embraced the counternarcotics cause, addressing how crucial the issue had become in a prophetic December 1988 cable:

> Widespread Pakistani belief that Afghan war has caused major upswing in narcotics traffic is well founded. Not only has war resulted in a flow of large amounts of weaponry to Pakistan, it has also led to increase in heroin traffic into and through Pakistan, through the hands of Afghan refugees as well as Pakistanis. We and the Pakistan government believe the situation will become much worse in terms of both heroin and arms entering Pakistan from Afghanistan as the war winds down unless urgent, effective measures are taken right away. The fight against "heroin-Kalashnikov culture" is almost as critical to the future of Pakistan's security as the fight against Soviet domination of Afghanistan has been.[70]

The cable warned that opium output in Afghanistan—estimated at 750 metric tons in 1987—could surge another several hundred tons when millions of refugees living along the borders of Pakistan and Iran returned home in need of a cash crop. Afghans in camps along the border were already refining opium into heroin, storing it in the refugee camps, and then shipping it onward, Oakley wrote. There were increasing reports of massive heroin shipments traveling west to Iran in heavily armed convoys, "and observers in the area say both the Afghan resistance parties and ISI are directly involved."

That same year, USAID launched its first counternarcotics pilot program for Afghanistan. "In 1988, I made the call," said Crandall, then chief of the USAID mission in Pakistan. "Since it now looked like we were going to win this thing, we couldn't countenance a situation where we were supporting a group of people who were freedom fighters but also drug traders." The embassy hired a U.S. contractor to develop a program it hoped would mirror earlier successful programs in Thailand, where the poppy crop had been reduced to almost zero, Crandall said. They hoped to blend forced eradication with support for alternative crops.

A CIA assessment circulated in September 1988 took up the narcotics problem on the Pakistani side of the border. Islamabad was "losing ground to an expanding drug industry," the report said, blaming "major increases in production in landlocked Afghanistan." Massive hundred-kilo heroin cargos were "moving routinely through Pakistan" and being smuggled west by boat from Karachi. The partially redacted document described a system that functions in much the same way today, according to police and counternarcotics officials: trucks coming from the NWFP deposit drug shipments at drop-off points along the main highways into the southern port city. Private vehicles then ferry smaller packages into the port.

"The size of such smuggling operations is, in fact, reflected in . . . a police investigation of a Pashtun-dominated section of the city—Sohrab Goth—that uncovered 11 underground storage facilities, each capable of holding up to one ton of heroin," it said.[71] At any given time three tons of heroin were "awaiting shipment to the United States or western Europe," the report said, adding that Pakistan's own addict population had tripled since the Afghan war began. Citing widespread corruption and a reluctance on the part of Pakistani authorities to tackle the problem, the CIA predicted "the narcotics situation in Pakistan will probably get worse before it gets better."[72]

Just as the drug issue leapt into the limelight, so did concern over the future aspirations of Afghanistan's holy warriors, many of them hostile toward the United States and now heavily armed and battle-hardened. The 1980s had witnessed a disturbing rise in terrorist attacks by Islamic radicals, from the 1983 bombing of the U.S. embassy in Lebanon to the 1985 hijacking of the *Achille Lauro*. In Washington and within the U.S. embassy in Islamabad, American officials were deeply divided over the best course of action for Afghanistan's post-Soviet future.

In October 1988, Special Envoy Edmund McWilliams clashed with Milton Bearden, the CIA chief of station, by suggesting in a classified cable that the United States needed to distance itself from the ISI and its ruthless protégé, Gulbuddin Hekmatyar. McWilliams's interviews with mujahideen leaders and Afghan intellectuals left him deeply alarmed about Afghanistan's future. As soon as the Soviet pullout had begun, Hekmatyar had launched a systematic campaign to wipe out his rivals in the resistance, butchering dozens of liberals, academics, and royalist politicians who might have stood against him in the political arena. Liberal Afghans worried what the fundamentalists would do if they ever got control of the country. "For God's sake," one warned McWilliams, "you're financing your own assassins."[73]

Bearden worked to maintain a balance of funding to the commanders by making unilateral payments outside the ISI's control to rival commanders like Ahmed Shah Massood and Abdul Haq.[74] But this effort was offset by the steady flow of Arab donations to the fundamentalist mujahideen and a shift in ISI policy from supporting the Peshawar Seven parties to supporting individual commanders, mainly Hekmatyar. It was a course of action that contradicted the international community's goal of strengthening a central council of leaders who would eventually share power. It also put the various resistance leaders under new pressure to raise funds any way they could.

With the Soviet army gone, agriculture and trade began to recover in the Afghan countryside. "Much of this renewed production took the form of opium growing, heroin refining, and smuggling; these enterprises were organized by combines of mujahideen parties, Pakistani military officers, and Pakistani drug syndicates," wrote historian Barnett Rubin.[75] Hekmatyar built up his forces into a conventional army and increased his involvement in the poppy trade, probably realizing that U.S. and Saudi funding was about to end. Other commanders shifted policy to shore up their military and financial positions, behaving more like feudal lords than allied members of a rebel army. Another new factor was the Arab radical Islamist fighters who arrived in eastern Afghanistan, bringing their own regional and global ambitions to the conflict.[76]

In the west, massive, heavily armed drug convoys were streaming out of Helmand, snaking their way across Pakistan's Baluchistan Province into Iran and on to Turkey. In March 1989, a confidential cable based on McWilliams's interviews with Afghan refugees reported: "The trafficking route entails cooperation of the mujahideen, Kabul regime, and GOP [government of Pakistan] officials and some elements inside the Iran government." It identified officials from the Pasdaran, Iran's Revolutionary Guard, as the main players in the illegal drug trade. "The convoys consist of approximately 30 specially equipped *Pajeros*. Each convoy is armed . . . and carries up to 10 armed Afghans." Stinger missiles, which had been provided to the mujahideen by the CIA to down Soviet helicopters, were now being used to protect heroin shipments, it said. "Convoy operators have been known to warn police checkpoints ahead of time," the cable said. "The police, who are thoroughly outgunned, arrange to be elsewhere."[77]

The partially excised document went on to describe the battle for control of Helmand's poppy fields between Nasim Akhundzada and Hekmatyar, accurately predicting that their internecine conflict was about to explode. In the course of the coming year, this war within the war would receive scant attention. The Soviet troops were completing their withdrawal from Afghanistan, and the ISI was busy cajoling the main rebel commanders into a shaky coalition that would set its sights on the vulnerable pro-Soviet regime still in power in Kabul. Without the Soviet troops there, the CIA predicted its imminent collapse. The moderate Sibghatullah Mojaddedi, one of the Peshawar Seven leaders routinely marginalized by the ISI, was selected to lead a new interim Afghan government in exile. Washington warned Mojaddedi to curb soaring opium production in mujahideen-held areas or face a cut in U.S. support. In meetings with Ambassador Oakley and President George H. W. Bush, Mojaddedi pledged to issue a religious fatwa banning opium. But he was powerless to move further on the issue and in any case would remain the titular head of government for just months.[78]

Beset by rivalries and infighting from the start, the rebel coalition mounted a spring 1989 attack on the western town of Jalalabad, hoping to install Mojaddedi's government there and proceed swiftly to Kabul. It would not go as CIA and ISI planners predicted. Bloody fighting dragged on for months, with casualties numbering in the thousands. Meanwhile, a separate turf war raged between Hekmatyar and Ahmed Shah Massood, a powerful commander from the Panjshir Valley who relied on smuggling gemstones to fund his operations. Historian Alfred McCoy later blamed the battlefield chaos on a diffident attitude among mujahideen commanders too busy fighting over spoils of Nangarhar's brisk opium trade to bother with the march on Kabul.[79] In the 1989–1990 planting season, Nangarhar Province produced a whopping 355 tons of opium.[80]

The situation out west was similar. By mid-1989, the U.S. embassy was reporting "chronic fighting" in northern Helmand over control of the production areas and trafficking. Several thousand families had been displaced, U.S. diplomats cabled in June, and the brutal Akhundzada had ordered those who remained to grow poppy. With more than four thousand troops under his command, villagers had little choice but to obey. Akhundzada sent massive drug convoys out to Pakistan every four to six weeks, the cable reported.[81]

A senior official at the U.S. embassy decided it was time to try to do something about the problem. He flew to Quetta, the capital of Baluchistan, and put out word he wanted to see Mullah Akhundzada. "I told him he was a disgrace to his people, calling himself a mullah and dealing drugs," said the former official, who did not want to be identified. "The good mullah said he needed narcotics to support his fighters, so I offered to help set up new ways to pay the fighters and build health clinics."[82] Akhundzada wanted a personal guarantee from Ambassador Oakley. So they set up a meeting, and, to everyone's surprise, Afghanistan's biggest drug dealer turned up at the U.S. mission in Islamabad a week later. He proposed to cut opium production by half in Helmand if the United States would invest $2 million in alternative development programs and help restart the Kajaki Dam, which provided hydroelectric power to the entire southwest region.

"I talked to him and he said, 'Look, we'd like to get the dam working again,'" Oakley recalled. "It was all rural development stuff—nothing outlandish."[83] Washington wanted a guarantee Akhundzada was going to deliver on his side of the deal before it handed out the cash. "The next year we had covert aerial reconnaissance, and we also sent ground teams with Nasim [Akhundzada]," Oakley said. "Both came back and reported the poppy was gone." But by then USAID in Washington had gotten cold feet, said former officials closely tied to the project. "Washington came back and said, 'You can't do deals with a known drug dealer,'" Oakley said.

Six months later, in March 1990, gunmen opened up their automatic rifles on Mullah Akhundzada as he and five subordinates walked out of a meeting in Peshawar. "They emptied a banana clip on him, literally cut him in half," said a former U.S. official. The bold assassination was widely blamed on Hekmatyar. With the cut in production in Helmand, raw opium prices had more than tripled, making it far more costly to supply Hekmatyar's refineries in Koh-i-Soltan. "Whoever did the killing, Nasim's death pretty much threw a wet blanket on anyone's willingness to cooperate on anti-narcotics for a while," said the U.S. official. "It showed everyone what a down and dirty business it had become." Akhundzada's brother, Ghulam Rasul, swiftly took over in Helmand. He ordered farmers in Helmand to return to "full production."[84]

The war in Afghanistan entered a new phase, as bloody and complex as ever. With the dawn of a new decade, Washington faced a new era of global geopolitics. Iraqi leader Saddam Hussein invaded Kuwait in August 1990, and the Soviet Union collapsed a year later. These two seminal events shifted the United States' focus away from Afghanistan, a cause that had fallen from grace anyway. Allegations of drug running and concerns about Islamic extremism suddenly made the mujahideen seem distasteful, if not downright worrisome. Indications that money had been funneled to the rebels using the disgraced Bank of Commerce and Credit International (BCCI), and that up to 70 percent of the money never even reached them, added the stench of scandal.[85] When William Gray, then chairman of the House Budget Committee, asked the General Accounting Office to look for the missing cash, they were rebuffed by the CIA, saying there would be "phenomenal security implications" if the GAO probed too closely.[86]

Just at a time when reconstruction funding might have provided poor Afghan farmers with an alternative to poppy farming, U.S. funding for the mujahideen, and Afghanistan in general, dropped off sharply. "The minute an issue becomes unpopular in Washington, interest in it dries up totally," said a U.S. official who worked on Afghanistan in the early 1990s. "That's what happened here. Everyone turned on it." Amid predictions that the pro-Communist government of Najibullah was about to disintegrate, the U.S. Congress allocated just $280 million in fiscal year 1990 for the final push on Kabul. It was a 60 percent cut over the previous year's grant.[87] Arab nations continued to kick in money—mainly to Hekmatyar and other fundamentalist commanders—until the Kuwait invasion distracted them, too.

In June 1991, the administration of George H. W. Bush approved an "off-budget" transfer of just $30 million in captured Iraqi weapons to the mujahideen. Although private Arab donations—mainly profiting fundamentalist parties—would continue to the tune of hundreds of millions of dollars, the secret U.S. program to aid the mujahideen was terminated in 1992.[88] "Overnight, that left 135,000 armed Afghans and their families with no way to support themselves," said a former CIA officer. "And what do you expect happened? The commanders turned to gun running to make money, and in no short time, most of them turned to drugs too." The agent realized then that what little influence the United States ever had on the rebel commanders had just evaporated. "I thought, hell, I am going to lose all my Afghan sources," he said.[89]

In April 1992, Najibullah's regime collapsed. Hekmatyar and his Panjshiri rival, Ahmed Shah Massood, entered Kabul and began to fight each other for control. Just a month earlier, Najibullah had begged the West to help cobble together a moderate new government. "If fundamentalism comes to Afghanistan, war will continue for many years," he told the *International Herald Tribune.* Otherwise, he warned, "Afghanistan will turn into a center of world smuggling of narcotic drugs. Afghanistan will be turned into a center for terrorism."[90]

But no one was listening. Shortly after shutting off military aid to the mujahideen, the Bush administration slashed relief and reconstruction aid to Afghanistan by more than 60 percent. The UN had just calculated that $1 billion would be needed to rebuild the devastated Afghan countryside.[91] The outgoing U.S. special envoy, Peter Tomsen, sent a confidential 1992 cable suggesting that the "drastic reduction" to the USAID budget would strip Washington of the "only political leverage we have with Afghanistan" and give the Afghans the impression the United States was abandoning them. It was in the interest of the United States, he warned, to stop Islamic radicals from using Afghanistan as "a training/staging base for terrorism."[92] It was the last serious effort a senior U.S. official would make to keep Washington sincerely engaged in Afghanistan.

When the new administration of President Bill Clinton took office in 1993, it zeroed the USAID budget for Afghanistan, according to former officials. As far as Washington was concerned, the country fell off the map entirely until 1998, when al Qaeda bombed the U.S. embassies in Kenya and Tanzania. "The Soviets left and America just lost interest," said Beverly Eighmy, who ran a counternarcotics pilot program for USAID that got shut down with the budget cuts. "Personally, it broke our hearts," she said. "We left them all high and dry." Added Bearden, the former station chief, "We just walked away, walked away from it all."

In the coming years, mujahideen forces would reduce Kabul to a pitiable state of rubble and ravage the countryside as they fought for dominance. Smuggling routes, before mainly limited to Pakistan, Iran, and Afghanistan, now snaked up into Central Asia, where the Soviet Union's collapse left a law enforcement vacuum and a population desperate for hard currency.[93] Commodities ranging from Iranian oil to Firestone tires and Sony televisions wound their way over the Afghan border, taking advantage of Pakistan's transit trade agreement and loose regional tax enforcement. By 1997, the World Bank estimated the illegal trade in legal goods to be worth $2.5 billion.[94] Afghanistan was by now the world's leading opium producer, having outpaced Burma. As author Michael Griffin wrote in *Reaping the Whirlwind*:

> The concentricity of the drugs, arms and smuggling rings around a single imploded state created the conditions for the birth of a unique, post-modern phenomenon: an illegal trading empire that defied customs, frontiers and laws . . . controlled by scarcely literate warlords living hundreds of miles from the nearest bank or fax.[95]

Next door, the heroin trade was now worth an estimated $8 to $10 billion, more than the government's annual budget and as much as one-quarter of Pakistan's entire GDP.[96] It had created a class of billionaire tycoons with tremendous influence over the new civilian government.[97] The leading smuggler was Haji Ayub Afridi, a tribal chief who ran a massive heroin empire from a luxury fortress in the Khyber Pass. Afridi worked closely with Zia's government to help smuggle weapons to the mujahideen and was believed to coordinate shipments of heroin smuggled out in NLC trucks.[98] Following Zia's death, he allied himself with the Punjabi politician Nawaz Sharif, actually winning himself a seat in the National Assembly in the 1990 general elections.[99] The second most powerful Pakistani trafficker, also tied to moving Afghan heroin, was Mirza Iqbal Baig, a Punjabi cinema owner with close ties to Benazir Bhutto's People's Party and a tendency to ruthlessness.

When two BBC reporters showed up at his office to interview him for a 1986 documentary, they were soundly beaten by a gang of thugs.[100]

Despite the huge amount of narcotics crossing their country, Pakistani officials for years blithely rejected American warnings that heroin addiction would one day become a domestic crisis. "Their attitude was always, 'We are sorry you Americans have this problem, but it's your problem,'" said Teresita Schaffer, the former deputy secretary of state for South Asia. By the early 1990s, Pakistan had more than 1.2 million heroin addicts. Suddenly, Schaffer said, there was "this dawning awareness" that they, too, had a major social problem on their hands.

Declassified U.S. documents reveal a high level of frustration among American diplomats over Islamabad's refusal to go after big-league drug lords like Afridi and Baig. An undated DEA analysis had especially sharp words for Islamabad's "weak policy" toward heroin lab owners in the federally administered tribal areas (FATA):

The GOP has now and then arranged for the surrender of some equipment (pots and pans) used at heroin manufacturing sites in the FATA and extracting formal promises from the operators that they will nevermore engage in heroin manufacturing. These surrenders and promises have been used by the GOP to fool itself and the international community into believing that at least something is being done against heroin manufacturing in Pakistan. Nothing could be farther from the truth. Never have these surrenders included seizures of heroin, morphine, opium or precursor chemicals in any significant quantity, and never have any important lab owners, profiteers or financiers been arrested, prosecuted and imprisoned in connection with these lab surrenders.[101]

But as it had done with the mujahideen, Washington began taking a tough line with Islamabad over drugs only once it became clear that the Soviets were withdrawing from neighboring Afghanistan. Legislation passed by the U.S. Congress meant Washington "certified" countries where narcotics were produced to signal they were making efforts to fight drugs. A confidential list of "talking points" distributed in September 1988 instructed American diplomats to warn their Pakistani contacts to "cooperate fully" with the United States on counternarcotics "in order to avoid the threat of decertification and the loss of most [U.S.] assistance to Pakistan." A handwritten note on the incoming telegram calculated that Pakistan stood to lose $228 million in military aid, economic assistance, and loan forgiveness for fiscal year 1989 alone.[102]

The pressure appears to have worked. By the following year, the Bhutto administration launched an aerial spraying campaign in the tribal areas, created an elite counternarcotics police force, and raided a notorious Afghan refugee camp, capturing one hundred kilos of opium and a large cache of gold and weapons.[103] In March 1989, Ambassador Oakley cabled that Pakistan "appears finally to be getting its act together on narcotics." He asked for a $5 million increase in the counternarcotics aid budget for Islamabad, writing: "We have poured a great deal of money into Pakistan over the years to fight narcotics and we are just beginning to see some important results."[104]

But by the end of 1990, Pakistan would get left out in the cold, too. Just as the CIA was disentangling itself from its decade-long partnership with the ISI over Afghanistan, American agents monitoring Pakistan's nuclear ambitions discovered Islamabad had recently approached Tehran about technological cooperation.[105] By October 1990, the Pressler amendment kicked in, cutting off most U.S. assistance to Pakistan. Relations between Islamabad and Washington plunged. CIA agents in Islamabad suddenly found themselves in the position of trying to get weapons back from the ISI and the mujahideen. "We actually had to destroy seven hundred tons of ammunition at one point," said a former intelligence official. Fearful that fundamentalist commanders might use the shoulder-fired, heat-seeking Stinger missiles for terrorist attacks, Washington launched a program to buy back the weapons. It provided U.S. agents the only cash leverage they had left to get information out of Afghanistan. The Stingers were now being put to use guarding two-hundred-vehicle convoys ferrying heroin west across the Iranian border. When U.S. agents found a way to put an informant on a convoy, the Department of Justice quashed the plan, ruling that it would mean the CIA was participating in the drug trade.[106] In just two years, the region had gone from being a central focus of U.S. foreign policy to falling off the radar screen almost entirely.

On its own, the region seemed dangerously adrift. A study commissioned by the CIA and leaked to the media in 1993 stopped just short of calling Pakistan a narco-state.[107] Since the cutoff of U.S. aid to Islamabad, the CIA report said heroin had become "the lifeblood" of the country's economic and social systems. Known drug lords held seats in the national and provincial assemblies, and had access to Prime Minister Nawaz Sharif's "inner circle." Drug mafias regularly paid off Pakistan's corps commanders and senior military officials, it said, citing an "underworld source." Many experts, the report declared, said Pakistan's military—and specifically the ISI—was "significantly involved in narcotics, and perhaps even using heroin money to finance covert operations and weapons purchases." The report also noted:

> Many believe the ISI allowed the Afghan resistance groups to trade in narcotics after the cut-off of U.S. assistance and that individual ISI officers participated in the trade, either as part of sanctioned operations or to enrich themselves. The ISI is also deeply involved with Sikh militants, who use Pakistan for sanctuary and who do use heroin for arms purchases. At the very least, the ISI tolerates Sikh involvement in heroin. The Kashmiri insurgency may also be partly funded by heroin. The strongest pro-Pakistan group, the Hezb-ul Mujahidin, is backed by the ISI . . . and the Hezb-i-Islami of Gulbuddin Hekmatyar.

The Pakistan government stoutly rejected the CIA report—a spokesman at their embassy in Washington called it "stupid . . . totally baseless."[108] But a year later, Nawaz Sharif himself, who by then had been kicked out of office after having been accused of corruption, would suggest it had been accurate. In September 1994, he told *The Washington Post* that in 1990, three months after his election as prime minister, General Aslam Beg, then army chief, and General Asad Durrani, then ISI chief, told him the Pakistan military needed money for covert foreign operations and wanted to raise it through large-scale drug deals. "I was totally flabbergasted," he claimed.[109] By the time the *Washington Post* story ran, Sharif had developed a reputation as a troublemaker, and the information was widely discredited (not least due to the former premier's alleged connections to heroin syndicates). Later, when he returned to power in 1997, Sharif denied the meeting ever took place. However shaky the information, it was another disquieting indication that a murky web of Pakistani intelligence agents, Islamic extremists, and international drug traffickers were cooperating, at least on some level.

Next door in Afghanistan, the situation was yet more disturbing. By the early 1990s, Jalalabad Airport, in eastern Nangarhar Province, had become a central clearing station for massive shipments of drugs, gemstones, electronic goods, and other contraband being smuggled to and from the Persian Gulf, according to former workers there. Mujahideen working for Yunis Khalis and Haji Qadir would arrive on the tarmac with truckloads of carpets laden with heroin powder. "We could always tell which carpets had heroin, since they were so much heavier than normal," said a cargo loader, still terrified to be identified two decades later. "They would shake out the carpets once they reached their destination, and the heroin would fall out."

Another trick, said a senior airport official, was to smuggle powder out in timber shipments—the logs would appear solid but have holes drilled inside, stuffed with heroin. Airport staff earned up to $2,000 a week—far more than they would normally take home—to pack and load drug shipments, both men said. Arab fighters often appeared alongside Khalis or his top deputies, boarding flights without clearing immigration and returning days later to hand out dates, a delicacy in the Gulf. Airport workers didn't see the "Arab

Afghans," as they came to be known, actively engaged in the heroin trade, but described them as "fellow travelers" on frequent heroin flights to the Gulf.[110] Along the border, smuggling mushroomed further. "By this point, the entire jihad was funded by drugs," said a senior Pakistani police official then based in the border area.[111]

As Pakistan and Afghanistan sank further into chaos, a handful of former American officials continued to defend U.S. involvement there, saying the principal objective of bringing down the Soviet Empire outweighed continued instability in the remote mountains of Southwest Asia. "What was more important in the worldview of history?" asked Jimmy Carter's national security advisor, Zbigniew Brzezinski, in a 1998 interview. "A few stirred up Muslims or the liberation of Central Europe and the end of the Cold War?"[112]

Far away in Kandahar, a few stirred-up Muslims who called themselves the Taliban were about to set their war-shattered nation on a collision course with the West. In the bloody new chapter of the Afghan saga, heroin would play a central role.

3. NARCO-TERROR STATE ∴

THE TALIBAN DROPPED A BRUISED, SHIVERING WRETCH AT our feet, his legs in shackles. "This is what we do to addicts," declared Abdul Rashid, head of their anti-drug force in Kandahar.

It was spring of 1997. I had traveled to the southern Afghan city—then the Taliban's de facto capital—with the Pakistani journalist Ahmed Rashid. I was writing a story about the opium trade for the Associated Press. Ahmed was researching his book *The Taliban*, which would become an overnight bestseller after the 9/11 attacks.

We met the counternarcotics chief in his shoebox-sized office. I made a joke about how the two men might be related, since they shared the same last name. Neither man found it funny. Ahmed was meticulously turned out in an Italian sports coat. His namesake picked bits of food from his greasy beard while he explained the Taliban's unique approach to curing drug addiction. First, he said, addicts got beaten until they confessed the name of their supplier. After that, they were thrown in jail. "Then we dunk them in ice-cold water for two or three hours a day," Rashid explained, adding brightly, "It's a very good cure." To prove his point, he ordered his minions to drag out Bakht Mohammed, a local shopkeeper recently caught smoking a joint.

"When they put me in that cold water, I forget all about

hashish," said Mohammed, slumped on the floor before us.[1] Normally I discount interviews with prisoners when their jailers are present, especially when it's clear they have been tortured. However, I was pretty sure this guy was telling the truth. As they dragged him off, Ahmed and I exchanged looks of horror.

A day earlier, we had driven to Arghandab, a fertile suburb of Kandahar where poppy fields stretched as far as the eye could see. "We could not be more grateful to the Taliban," a toothless farmer named Wali Jan told us, crediting the bearded crusaders with bringing security that allowed him to tend his crops in peace. Even though the Taliban cracked down on hash smoking, they gave full support to the poppy trade, farmers and Taliban officials told us. The next day, when Ahmed and I asked Rashid, the anti-drug cop, about this apparent contradiction in drug policy, he just smiled. "Opium is allowed because it is consumed by infidels in the West and not by Muslim Afghans," he said.

Largely because of its one-year ban on poppy cultivation, there is a widespread misperception in the West that the Taliban regime opposed drugs. Nothing could be further from the truth. The Taliban meted out harsh penalties to anyone caught using intoxicants: They crushed bottles of whiskey under tanks and beat up pot smokers. However, Mullah Omar's movement—almost from its inception—was highly dependent on and intertwined with the opium network spanning the Pakistan-Afghanistan border. Drug traffickers and tribes growing poppy were critical to the Taliban's swift and astonishing rise to power. Later on, the opium trade provided vital tax revenue, which kept the pariah state afloat despite global economic sanctions. It also funded the military campaign against the Northern Alliance and supported the global ambitions of Osama bin Laden, who plotted the 9/11 attacks at terrorist training camps he ran in southern and eastern Afghanistan. Fueled by drug money and joined at the hip with al Qaeda, the Taliban turned Afghanistan into the world's first fully fledged narco-terror state.

Three years of vicious fighting between various mujahideen warlords had put a chokehold on Afghanistan's multibillion-dollar transit trade. Rival commanders erected roadblocks—often just a few hundred yards from each other—where they extorted fees for safe passage along the highways. Roadblocks were especially numerous in southern Kandahar Province, where there was no clear strongman. The Pashtun trucking mafia controlling most shipping from Karachi, Pakistan, which passes through Quetta and into Kandahar Province at the Chaman border, was taking huge losses. Trucking firms wanted to end the intolerable situation.

When the Taliban first appeared on the scene, most assumed—not entirely incorrectly—that the new fighting force was a creation of Pakistan's security agencies. ISI officials had watched with dismay as their fundamentalist offspring Gulbuddin Hekmatyar got repeatedly trounced on the battlefield by his rival Ahmed Shah Massood. Benazir Bhutto, the newly reelected Pakistani prime minister, wanted to open up trade routes into the now independent Central Asian states. Islamabad was in the market for a new protégé across the border.

The origins of the Taliban are steeped in legend, aimed at elevating the group's barely literate, one-eyed leader to a semidivine status among Afghanistan's uneducated masses. The story begins in mid-1994 when rival warlords were ravaging the Afghan countryside and terrorizing the public. Neighbors came to Mullah Omar, then a teacher in a small religious school, or madrassa, outside Kandahar, to tell him that two young girls in their village of Maiwand had been abducted by a local warlord and repeatedly raped. Horrified, Omar raised a force of thirty madrassa students (or Talibs), armed with half as many rifles, and attacked the commander's base. They freed the girls and hanged the commander from his tank barrel.

A few months later, Omar's force intervened again when two rival commanders fought over a young boy both men wanted to take as a lover.[2] "Commanders were looting people, raping women and boys for days, and then killing them," said Mullah Roketi, a former mujahideen fighter who later joined the Taliban and now sits in the Afghan parliament. "Mullah Omar raised his voice against these people and said, 'I am going to fight them.'"[3] As Omar's reputation as a local Robin Hood grew, Afghanistan's war-weary public embraced the Taliban, which swept across the country, capturing many towns without a shot being fired.

Although Omar was inarticulate, reclusive, and barely able to write his own name, his supporters believed he was possessed with a profound, God-given wisdom. They spread the perception that his campaign to stabilize the nation was backed by divine forces. Later, in 1996, to legitimize the notion that he had been chosen by Allah to lead Afghans, Omar gathered supporters in front of the Shrine of the Cloak of the Prophet, one of Afghanistan's holiest sites. He took out the ancient relic and wrapped himself in it, whereupon the tumultuous crowd ordained him Amir-ul-Momineen, the Leader of the Faithful. It was a ranking in Islam nearly second to the prophet Mohammed himself.[4]

Like all good myths, aspects of the tale were true. Many who encountered the Taliban at their outset say the group was well-intentioned, even if their behavior was medieval. In their initial meetings with foreigners, the Taliban appeared to be village simpletons—unkempt, naïve, and utterly devout. On my first visit to Kandahar, senior Taliban officials I met had piled furniture in the corners of their offices and received guests sitting cross-legged on the carpet, their seating area inevitably adorned with a vase of dusty plastic flowers. "My God, these people don't even know how to sit on chairs," I thought. The Taliban publicly stoned women accused of committing adultery and whipped men caught trimming their beards. They were ignorant of the outside world and had little understanding of international diplomacy, modern technology, or how to run a bureaucracy.

According to people who witnessed the early movement, the Taliban initially made commitments to stamp out the poppy trade—but only acted on them a handful of times. These commitments were swiftly dropped as political realities and need for funds overcame their original objectives.[5] Despite their good intentions and efforts at myth making, the Taliban's rise to power in Afghanistan had little to do with the grace of Allah, as they claimed. In fact, from its inception, the movement relied on the financial backing of a distinctly unholy alliance with drug smugglers and trucking companies. During their first year in power in Kandahar, the Taliban issued a book outlining what was permissible under their strict brand of sharia law. Most forms of simple entertainment, like music and television, were banned; alcohol and cannabis were "absolutely forbidden." But on one issue Kandahar's new leaders were conspicuously ambiguous: "The consumption of opiates is forbidden, as is the manufacture of heroin," the book said. "But the production and trading in opium is not forbidden."[6]

By the end of 1994, diplomats at the U.S. embassy in Pakistan were scrambling to determine who exactly was backing the Taliban, according to declassified documents. The Islamabad mission sent a rash of cables debating whether the ISI had created this new fighting force, or as one report suggested, if an alliance of northern Afghan warlords was trying to mount a unified Pashtun opposition against the ISI-backed Hekmatyar. The Saudis had taken an interest in the student movement, American diplomats noted, as had Maulana Fazal-ur Rehman, who ran the Jamiat Ulema-i-Islam (JUI), a leading Pakistani fundamentalist party providing fighters from its chain of madrassas.[7] Probably, the U.S. diplomats concluded, the Taliban enjoyed a combination of backers. All of these groups were in cahoots after all.

Initial cables note that the Taliban's "declared goals were to open up the roads and end the organized banditry of local commanders" and that "all visitors to Kandahar have told us they believe the Taliban must have access to considerable funding."[8] Sources told U.S. diplomats that the Taliban appeared to have built a fighting force of four thousand and was able to pay its troops three times what other Afghan commanders could. After taking control of Kandahar—just months after their initial emergence—the Taliban claimed to have eleven tanks, nine transport helicopters, several MiG fighter jets, and stacks of heavy weaponry and ammunition. They were setting up a police training school and seemed to be educating bureaucrats. When one U.S. contact asked the Taliban about their source of cash, "he was told that funds come from a combination of customs duties and taxes levied on local merchants," the embassy reported in January 2005. "Yet local *bazaaris* deny that the Taliban are taxing them at all."[9]

Two U.S. officials flew to Kandahar in February 1995 to try to pinpoint the Taliban's backers, meeting with the mayor of the provincial capital, Maulavi Abul Abbas, and six other midlevel Taliban. The meeting left the Americans with "more questions than answers," as they cabled back to Washington. The Afghans refused to name members of the Taliban's senior *shura*, or ruling council, or to be lured into discussion over who was supporting them financially. "This cannot be told," Abbas stated flatly. When asked about poppy cultivation, he promptly replied, "Narcotics is prohibited in Islam. This is very clear." The diplomats noted how this statement generated "considerable heated interjection" from other Taliban officials present. Abbas then rephrased his statement, calling poppy an "economic issue" for poor farmers with no alternatives. The Americans concluded that the Taliban had been "coached" but offered no suggestions in their cable to Washington as to who sponsored the group.[10]

Just four days later, the U.S. embassy in Islamabad would get the answer, although it's unclear from declassified cables if anyone in the mission appreciated its significance at the time. On February 17, a Kandahari close to Mullah Omar—probably the Taliban's future foreign minister, Mullah Ghaus—turned up at the embassy in Islamabad to explain the movement's origins.[11] He explained to a U.S. political officer how the Taliban emerged from a small madrassa in Maiwand owned by the "prominent trader" Haji Bashir Noorzai, a former commander who had fought under Yunis Khalis. Noorzai, the visitor revealed, was Mullah Omar's original sponsor as well as a key decision maker and leading member of the ruling council.

Today, Bashir Noorzai resides in a high-security Manhattan jail, having been sentenced to life in prison by a New York federal court on charges of conspiring to smuggle millions of dollars worth of heroin into the United States. Although there remains some dispute about whether Noorzai himself was a major drug trader at the outset of the Taliban movement, his clan was certainly well known to American counternarcotics agents. Their 1-million-strong tribe controlled tens of thousands of acres of poppy farmland, as well as the key roadway out of southern Afghanistan. Bashir's late father, Haji Mohammed Issa Noorzai, was a notorious dope smuggler who owned a string of heroin labs.[12] In the mid-1990s, Issa Noorzai was a leading member of the Quetta Alliance, a drug cartel identified in one declassified DEA document as a union of "three interrelated heroin and hashish smuggling groups" that routinely exported "multi-ton shipments of heroin and morphine base."[13] Ironically, the heavily redacted document indicates that the DEA office in Islamabad proposed to designate the Quetta cartel as a "targeted kingpin organization" in 1993, just one year before the Taliban emerged.[14] The designation would have focused U.S. law enforcement on the cartel and given DEA agents in Pakistan access to funds to track the group and build a federal case against it. The TKO designation never came, however.[15] In the years to come, Haji Bashir would actually meet DEA officials in an Islamabad safe house, boldly giving the American agents tips on the smuggling activities of Turkish smugglers who moved heroin through Iran and on to the West.[16]

The Kandahari man who visited the U.S. embassy that day in 1995 was there to cultivate the myth of the Taliban, concealing their real agenda under the cloak of Islam. He told the embassy's political officer: "Mullah Omar went to Haji Bashir and related a vision in which the Prophet Mohammed had appeared to him and told him of the need to bring peace to Afghanistan." Bashir believed Omar, the visitor claimed, and decided to back him. Using family and business connections, Bashir raised 8 million Pakistani rupees (about $250,000) for the effort and donated half a dozen pickup trucks and weapons he had left over from the jihad days. Bashir Noorzai sat alongside Mullah Omar on the eight-member senior *shura*, which made all policy decisions for the Taliban, he said.[17] Incidentally, another *shura* member the visitor listed was Haji Baz Mohammed, who today is also incarcerated in the United States, having pled guilty in 2006 to charges he smuggled heroin for the Taliban.[18]

According to relatives and business associates, Bashir Noorzai in 1993 was only a minor-league trader who could not have birthed the Taliban on his own. "He didn't have that kind of cash," another Noorzai clan member told me. "The original money came from his father." Sources close to Haji Bashir say the initial goal of his movement was to drive badly behaved warlords out of Kandahar, which was his control zone. "By the end, most *muj* had become very crude people," said an Afghan official who closely observed the Taliban's rise.[19] After Mullah Omar's stunning successes in his home district, the Noorzais convinced other partners in the Quetta Alliance, along with other businessmen in the Pashtun trucking mafia, to pitch in more funds.

As the Taliban conquered district after district in Kandahar, they attracted the attention of other warlords with ties to the opium trade. Abdur Ghaffar Akhundzada, the younger brother of Mullah Nasim, who controlled poppy cultivation in neighboring Helmand, was another early backer, reportedly declaring, "I am a Talib."[20] He later fell out with Mullah Omar when the Taliban chief signed on with a rival, and they battled for two months. In general, however, the Taliban army swept rapidly across Afghanistan. By September

1996, just two years after they emerged, they would roll victorious into Kabul.

As their reputation spread, so did their ability to capture towns without a shot. In areas "where the new movement's moral and religious standing failed to carry the day, generous disbursements of cash usually succeeded," wrote author Anthony Davis.[21] The Taliban's financial backers dished out bribes to regional strongmen as the turbaned fighters advanced on Kabul. Several key tribes agreed to join the cause after Mullah Omar pledged not to crack down on poppy, according to a November 1996 DEA document and western intelligence agents who tracked the movement.[22] Supporting the poppy trade not only garnered the Taliban financial backing. It also won them political support from tribes and the general public, especially in areas where years of warfare had left few viable alternatives for earning a living other than growing and trading narcotics. As a former U.S. counternarcotics official put it: "The Taliban rose to power by co-opting the drug trade."[23]

The Quetta-Kandahar trucking mafia—heavily tied up in both drug smuggling and the U-turn scheme—also poured money into Taliban coffers. Initially Mullah Omar received a monthly retainer from these groups, who came from the same tribes as leading Taliban. As his movement expanded westward, toward Iran, Omar demanded larger and larger payments. In March 1995, witnesses said the Taliban collected $150,000 on a single day at the Chaman border crossing, and $300,000 the following day in Quetta to prepare for an assault on the western Afghan city of Herat, which would open a trading gateway into Iran. For Pashtun smugglers involved in the U-turn scheme, business was suddenly booming, author Ahmed Rashid reported. Pakistan's Central Board of Revenue estimated it lost $275 million during fiscal 1993–94, and a staggering half-billion dollars the following year once the Taliban reopened the highways. In addition to the World Bank estimate that the smuggling of legal goods valued more than $2.5 billion, the UN calculated the narcotics trade to be worth another $1.25 billion annually. "The cross-border smuggling trade has a long history," Rashid wrote. "But never has it played such an important strategic role as under the Taliban."[24]

Pakistan is often described as the godfather of the Taliban. The truth is more complex. Although Islamabad tried to establish influence over the movement from soon after its inception, the Taliban's original benefactors—and the ones to whom they would remain unfailingly loyal—were smugglers. "Mullah Omar got the traders first and then the ISI behind him," says Mullah Roketi. There's evidence that Pakistan's spy chief at the time, General Javed Ashraf Qazi, initially warned Bhutto against getting in bed with the Taliban. "The general predicted that the Taliban could become a dangerous and uncontrollable force which could harm both Afghanistan—and potentially—Pakistan," reads a 1994 cable from the U.S. embassy in Islamabad.[25] Bhutto had just become prime minister for a second time. She and her interior minister, Naseerullah Babar, an ethnic Pashtun with a taste for intrigue, believed they could capitalize on the Taliban and gain control of regional trade into the former Soviet republics. They enlisted the help of the fundamentalist JUI leader Fazal-ur Rehman, at that time serving in Bhutto's government.

In mid-October 2004, Taliban soldiers attacked a garrison in the Afghan border town of Spin Boldak, taking control of a massive weapons dump. The assault was supported by an artillery barrage from a Pakistani Frontier Corps position and coordinated by

Pakistani officers, according to some accounts. Other reports say the Afghan commander in charge of the base handed over the keys to the arms cache after receiving a payoff from the trucking mafia.[26] As is often the case along the remote Pakistan-Afghanistan border, no disinterested parties were on hand to witness what happened. Observers and historians tend to agree this was the moment when Pakistan threw its chips in with the Taliban. Later that month, a thirty-truck convoy from Pakistan's National Logistics Cell—the same military-owned trucking firm that funneled arms to the mujahideen and reportedly transported heroin out—set off from Quetta for Turkmenistan carrying medical supplies. The ISI's most experienced Afghan hand, known by the nom de guerre Colonel Imam, led the operation.[27]

Just outside Kandahar, the convoy was stopped by mujahideen commanders each wanting a cut. The Taliban came to the convoy's rescue, buoyed by fighters flooding over the border from JUI madrassas. They wore new uniforms and carried weapons still wrapped in plastic, apparently from the Spin Boldak depot. The Taliban stormed on to Kandahar, triumphantly cutting chains blocking the highway. Most of Kandahar's corrupt warlords either fled or agreed to join the Taliban, reportedly after receiving large payoffs. Babar, Bhutto's interior minister, later took credit for the operation, privately describing the Taliban as "our boys" to Pakistani journalists.[28]

Western officials later characterized Babar's comments as more boastful than accurate. "I don't recall that anybody at the time had the notion the Taliban were Pakistan's creation or that the ISI had a lot of influence over them," says a U.S. official then posted to Islamabad. "I think they were just trying to exploit something they had no control over."[29] Throughout the Taliban's time in power, Islamabad would continue to try to establish influence. Short of funds in those post-Soviet resistance days, Pakistan provided logistical support: posting ISI agents to run the Pakistani consulates in Kandahar and Herat, training Taliban cadets, bussing young Pakistani madrassa students to the front, and allowing the Taliban to import wheat and jet fuel at subsidized rates.[30] "I became slowly, slowly sucked into it," Bhutto admitted later. It began with fuel and machine parts. "Then it became money," she said, direct from Pakistan's treasury.[31]

The Taliban played various factions within Pakistan's federal and provincial establishment against one another, as corrupt officials vied for profit from export permits to Afghanistan.[32] In November 1995, the "well-informed" political counselor from the Russian embassy in Pakistan, Zamir Kabulov, met U.S. officials, telling them that in Moscow's opinion "most Taliban funding still comes from Afghan traders," not Islamabad. Kabulov described Pakistan's military and financial assistance to the Taliban as "modest but pervasive," and said Islamabad's real boost to the Taliban came from "making no effort to stop the booming smuggling trade."[33] Individuals in Bhutto's government (then ranked the world's second most corrupt after Nigeria by the monitoring group Transparency International) profited enormously from continued chaos in Afghanistan. Bhutto would be thrown out of office a second and final time in 1996 amid charges that she and her husband, Asif Ali Zardari, bilked her country of $1.5 billion.

As it was, Islamabad never established much sway over the Taliban, who Pakistani officers complained were willful and stubborn. Pakistan's senior generals privately expressed worry to American officials that Islamabad's covert support for the Taliban had gathered a dangerous momentum no one could stop.[34] While the ISI urged Bhutto to support a push on Kabul, the army chief, General Jehangir Karamat, described the Taliban to a U.S. diplomat as "a millstone around our necks."[35]

In the spring of 1996, as Pakistan's generals fretted about how to extract themselves, the Afghan situation became yet more complex. A jet chartered from Afghanistan's state-run Ariana Airlines touched down on the dusty Jalalabad runway carrying a man who would become another key patron to the Taliban: Osama bin Laden. His return to Afghanistan heralded a new chapter in the Taliban chronicle, one that would have a dramatic impact on modern history.

The Saudi exile wasted no time in ingratiating himself with Afghanistan's new masters, helping to bankroll their takeover of Kabul. Bin Laden reportedly put up $3 million from his personal funds to pay off the remaining warlords who stood between the Taliban and the Afghan capital. The cash injection came at a crucial time, and Mullah Omar would not forget it.

In *The Ghost Wars*, author Steve Coll reports that the Taliban also received contributions from the trucking mafia, heroin traders, the ISI, and other Arab donors.[36] Once in control of the capital, the Taliban began issuing archaic decrees—banning girls from school and forcing men to pray five times a day—focusing the world's media on their exacting interpretation of Islam. Amid western outrage over their treatment of women and anxiety about their ties to Arab and Pakistani terrorist groups, the Taliban also came under international pressure to crack down on the poppy trade. On September 10, 1997, the Taliban's foreign ministry responded:

> The Islamic State of Afghanistan informs all compatriots that
> as [*sic*] the use of heroin and hashish is not permitted in Islam.
> They are reminded once again that they should strictly refrain
> from growing, using and trading in hashish and heroin. Any-
> one who violates this order shall be meted out a punishment in
> line with the lofty Mohammad and Sharia Law and thus shall
> not be entitled to launch a complaint.

The ruling was amended by a clarification ten days later outlawing cultivation and trafficking of opium as well.[37] No one paid it much attention. A year earlier, Afghanistan had produced 2,248 metric tons of opium, according to UNODC. That number climbed to 2,804 tons in 1997, dipping slightly the next year because of widespread drought, and then soaring to a whopping 4,581 metric tons in 1999 (see table).[38] By this time the Taliban controlled most of the country, and Afghanistan's poppy crop represented about 75 percent of global production; 97 percent of it was grown in Taliban-held areas.[39]

Afghan Opium Production (in metric tons)						
	2001	2000	1999	1998	1997	1996
U.S. government	74	3,656	2,861	2,340	2,184	2,099
UNODC	n/a	3,276	4,581	2,102	2,804	2,248

Courtesy of DEA website

Far from making efforts to stamp out poppy, the Taliban started taxing and regulating the trade. They collected a 10 percent tax (*ushr*) from farmers who grew poppy and other produce. *Ushr* was collected in kind at the farm level (as it still is today) and then spent locally, according to Bernard Frahi, a UNODC official.[40] In the south, the Taliban also began collecting a 20 percent *zakat*, an Islamic levy, on truckloads of opium leaving farm areas.[41] Following a law enforcement crackdown in neighboring Pakistan, heroin refineries based in the tribal areas shifted across the border.[42] The Taliban swiftly began taxing their output as well—charging between $50 and $70 a kilo depending on whether the final product was morphine base or crystal heroin. Zuber, a former lab worker interviewed in a Peshawar rehab center, reported that the Taliban collected as much as $5,500 a week during peak season from the lab where he bundled morphine base for export. He said there were about twenty-five labs with similar output capacity in the district where he worked.[43]

According to a top-secret 1998 CIA report, recently declassified, Haji Bashir Noorzai apparently forged a deal with the Taliban to pay $230 for each kilo of crystal heroin he exported by plane.[44] The Taliban also charged duties on road exports and handed out tax receipts for truckers driving their wares across the border into Pakistan or Iran. A scan of this receipt is posted on the DEA's website:

> *Gentlemen, the bearer of this letter, who possess 4 kilograms of white good, has paid the custom duty at the Shinwar Custom. It is hoped that the bearer will not be bothered.*

Signed: Incharge [*sic*] of Shinwar Custom Stamp, Nangarhar Province
Shinwar Loy Wolaswa Custom Section

How much the Taliban earned from taxing the drug trade each year was a matter of great debate. "It was very difficult to come by hard data," says Julie Sirrs, a former analyst with the Defense Intelligence Agency (DIA). "They seemed to have more money than what rich Arabs and the Pakistan government were providing them."[45] Estimates of their narcotics earnings ranged from $30 million to $200 million annually, and the real figure could have been higher.

Lower calculations of the Taliban's drug-related revenue generally accounted for just the 10 percent *ushr* collected at the farm level, extrapolating from the total amount of opium produced in their control zones. Higher estimates also took into account that the Taliban taxed trucks leaving southern farm areas and heroin refineries. There was also evidence that top traffickers and traders contributed directly to the regime, but no one knows how much or whether it was regulated. As well, the Taliban received millions of dollars' worth of commodities, including vehicles and weapons, from traffickers, traders, and visiting Arab sheiks. Since the Taliban kept virtually no computer or paper records, it is unlikely that the real figure of drug earnings will ever be accurately tallied. "They were controlling the industry completely," says a former ISI agent who worked in Afghanistan in those days. "Now there are so many people doing it, the profits are spread out. Back then, the Taliban made all the profit."[46]

Massive drug bazaars—with literally hundreds of stalls selling opium—operated in places like Ghani Khel in Nangahar Province, Sangin in Helmand, and Haji Bashir's hometown of Maiwand in Kandahar. In Ghani Khel, one could purchase up to ten tons of opium at a time, along with precursor chemicals like acetic anhydride and calcium carbonate, according to David Macdonald, a former adviser to the UN.[47] "Until the demise of the Taliban ... the larger factories mirrored the drug bazaars in scale," he wrote in his book *Drugs in Afghanistan.* "They were well-armed with rocket launchers, 5-50 caliber machine guns and AK-47s, had upwards of 30 employees, relied on UHF radio and satellite phone communications and had a daily production capacity of more than 100 kg of morphine base and 100 kg of brown heroin." Meanwhile, in the remote areas where it was grown, opium had literally become a form of currency. Local shopkeepers kept scales in their shops, as opposed to cash boxes or registers. One could purchase groceries with a golf ball–sized chunk of opium, according to Macdonald.[48]

Despite their generally brutal treatment of drug users, Macdonald came across evidence the Taliban had no compunction about making addicts of their enemies. He quotes a Northern Alliance fighter captured by the Taliban in the north. "After some time in jail he was taken to the front lines and promised unlimited hashish," Macdonald writes. But it was unlike anything the soldier had previously inhaled: "When I smoked this hashish, it felt different in my body. It made me feel powerful and fearless." Later on, the fighter discovered the hashish they gave him was laced with heroin. He became quite willing to go and fight against his former comrades in the Northern Alliance if the Taliban would just give him more heroin—which they did.[49]

Although they made public statements to the contrary, Mullah

Omar's ruling *shura* was deeply involved in planning and coordinating Afghanistan's drug output, according to declassified documents and ex-officials. "The Taliban liked to organize the traffickers," said the former ISI agent, who visited Afghanistan and the border region dozens of times during their regime. "Their manipulation of the trade was unquestionable." The 1998 CIA report said the Taliban instructed officials in several Afghan provinces to help increase opium poppy cultivation that year by training farmers:

> In addition, [word excised] Taliban officials authorized the establishment of six new heroin-processing laboratories in Taliban-controlled Helmand, Kandahar and Oruzgan provinces.[50]

There were almost sixty labs functioning in Helmand and Nangarhar provinces alone, the report said, adding that the Taliban instructed the labs to close down briefly during a visit by senior officials from UNODC. The top-secret report concluded:

> The Taliban continues to institutionalize its involvement in narcotics trafficking activities despite their public opposition to narcotics-related activities on religious grounds and pledge to work with the UN Drug Control Program to reduce opium cultivation.[51]

It's probably more accurate to say the drug traffickers who stood behind the Taliban—or who sat on the ruling *shura*, like Bashir Noorzai—were influencing the group's decisions about poppy production and lab permits. "The Taliban was right in the middle of things," said Bob Clark, a former DEA agent posted to Islamabad in the late 1990s. "But the Quetta Alliance was never going to give up control over the industry in the south."[52] As well, it was hard to imagine the ragtag Taliban leaders had enough understanding of market economics to be calling the shots anyway. "I always thought those guys had someone behind them," said Adan Adar, a former UN official then based in Kandahar.[53]

The Taliban's other major patron, who settled himself into a sprawling complex outside Kandahar city, also appears to have invested in Afghanistan's biggest export. Although U.S. counternarcotics officials say they never received direct confirmation of Osama bin Laden's personal role in the drug trade, there was overwhelming circumstantial evidence to suggest that the al Qaeda leader was deeply involved—not least since his terror camps were located in the same districts as heroin labs. "It was more or less just an assumption they were involved, but I don't recall any intelligence that we collected on the matter," says a former CIA official. "We didn't give a damn. The way the bureaucracy works, no one really wants to do narcotics."[54] The British government investigated the matter far more closely since the majority of heroin sold on their streets came from Afghanistan, and they had no doubt who was behind that fact. A spokesman for former prime minister Tony Blair said MI6 believed Mullah Omar and bin Laden each maintained personal opium stockpiles greater than three thousand tons.[55]

Blair told a 2001 gathering of Labour Party officials that bin Laden used drug money to finance Chechen and Uzbek rebels. A separate UN panel in December 2000 concluded: "Funds raised from the production and trade of opium and heroin are used by the Taliban to buy arms and war materials and to finance the training of terrorists and support the operation of extremists in neighboring countries and beyond."[56] Among pockets of the intelligence community, there was growing alarm that bin Laden wanted to strike in the United States or Europe. Concern mushroomed after the August 1998 attacks on the U.S. embassies in Kenya and Tanzania, and again after the USS *Cole* bombing in October 2000.

As the 1990s progressed, international sanctions against Afghanistan isolated the Taliban regime. There were signs bin Laden's influence over Mullah Omar was growing steadily. Western intelligence agents watched nervously from Pakistan as al Qaeda camps multiplied and drew more trainees. Arab "advisers" were spotted among the Taliban troops. "As the years went on, al Qaeda became their chaperones," the former ISI agent said. Meanwhile, Mullah Omar's pronouncements became ever more arbitrary and fanatic: he banned white socks, kite flying, even toothpaste. "Whether or not he had bought into all of bin Laden's beliefs from the first, Mullah Omar came to share his vision," wrote Daniel Benjamin and Steven Simon, two former officials at the National Security Council.[57]

Although bin Laden's public statements (like those of Mullah Omar) indicated he opposed drug use, the DEA received intelligence that bin Laden tried to recruit chemists to develop a "super heroin," which would have been more addictive, to export to the West. The plan apparently never came to fruition, and some U.S. officials later questioned the accuracy of the report itself.[58] There was stronger evidence that bin Laden served as a middleman between the Taliban and Arab drug smugglers from the United Arab Emirates, Qatar, and Saudi Arabia, using commissions from drug sales to fund his terror camps.[59] There were persistent reports that hunting trips he organized—and often attended—for rich Saudi and UAE sheiks were a mix of business and pleasure. The sheiks flew in on private jets and military transport planes, touching down at the Kandahar airfield and other smaller airstrips, some on the Pakistani side of the border in Balochistan. They allegedly came for the purpose of hunting the houbara bustard, an endangered species of migratory desert bird prized as an aphrodisiac in some Arab communities.[60] U.S. and British intelligence officials came to believe that at least some of those flights transported weapons and material to the Taliban and al Qaeda and flew heroin out.[61] In 2007, accused drug smuggler Haji Bashir Noorzai stated in testimony before a New York court that he brokered a deal for the UAE defense minister, Sheikh Mohammed bin Rashid al Maktoum, who later took over as ruler of Dubai, to lease lands outside Kandahar as a "hunting preserve."[62] British and U.S. intelligence and law enforcement officials suspected some Arab sheiks of traveling to southern Afghanistan for more than just its exotic birdlife.[63]

It was widely known these hunting teams brought lavish amounts of equipment including vehicles, rifles, and tents, which they left with the Taliban. A former senior UN official described a visit by Sheikh Mohammed in the 1990s when he imported one hundred vehicles—all of them four-by-four pickup trucks and Toyota Land Cruisers fitted with radios—which he left for his hosts. A 1992 *New Yorker* report detailed how he intermingled with alleged members of the Quetta Alliance on one such trip.[64] Counternarcotics officials were interested in the flight patterns of the bustard-hunting trips: they seemed to be heaviest in the spring planting season and just after the fall harvest.[65] Bin Laden himself was a regular visitor on these hunting trips, moving openly in the

Afghan desert. "He would be dead if the [U.S.] government had allowed us to kill him during one of these hunting trips," says a former U.S. official who helped track bin Laden. "But we weren't placed to know what went on in terms of conversations."

Private jets weren't the only planes on U.S. intelligence radar screens. With Mullah Omar's approval, bin Laden hijacked the state-run Ariana Airlines, turning it into a narco-terror charter service ferrying Islamic militants, timber, weapons, cash, and heroin to the Emirates and Pakistan, according to former U.S. and Afghan officials. "Al Qaeda moved drugs out, money in, and people around on Ariana," said Simon, the former NSC official.[66] Mohammad Fedawi, who was president of Ariana when the Taliban took over, said senior Taliban officials ordered him to hand out flight-crew passes to dozens of "foreigners," including members of al Qaeda, who were allowed to travel to whatever destinations the airline serviced—mainly in the Indian subcontinent and the Middle East.[67]

"Sometimes they would schedule special night flights to Kandahar and to the Emirates," mainly Sharjah and Dubai, Fedawi said. No one was allowed to see what they loaded on the planes. Another former Ariana employee, Hayat Zalmay, who worked out of Jalalabad, described packing crystal heroin into hollowed-out logs. "I remember going to the place where they packed it up and everyone had all the right equipment—special saws and drills," he said. "There was never any worry about getting caught because everyone at the top was involved."[68]

Under the Taliban, Ariana's passenger flight schedule disintegrated and the number of unscheduled cargo flights mushroomed. A frequent stop was Sharjah, the fundamentalist emirate neighboring Dubai where regulations are lax and inspections fleeting.

Abdul Shakur was a flight engineer with Ariana in the late 1990s. "In Dubai all the cargo would have to be taken off near the gates. No exceptions," he said. "But in Sharjah there was not too much tight security. When the planes came, they would park in isolated areas, and unload there." Arab passengers—"I guess bin Laden's people"—often came on the flights, recalled Shakur. "They would come off the planes with heavy bags and no one would dare ask them anything."[69] The Taliban appointed their own agent, a baby-faced cleric named Farid Ahmed, to run the Sharjah station, where depending on the season, Ariana flights sometimes landed as many as three times a day.[70] Ahmed badgered other cargo firms populating the white-domed airport with requests to buy millions of dollars' worth of weapons and long-distance cargo planes.[71] Mounting concern that Ariana was moving drugs and terrorists led to the UN sanctioning the Taliban in late 2000, barring Ariana from flying internationally.[72] The Taliban swiftly reacted in anger. On November 12, the day sanctions went into effect, rocket-propelled grenades were fired at the U.S. embassy and a UN office in Kabul.[73]

The Taliban turned to Viktor Bout, the notorious Russian spy-turned-smuggler whose Sharjah-based air cargo empire served as a sort of FedEx to criminals, rebel groups, and banana republics. Bout's initial contact with the Taliban was hardly auspicious, as documented in *Merchant of Death*, a book detailing Bout's smuggling empire from Africa to Asia. In 1995, a Taliban MiG-21 jet intercepted one of his Ilyushin-76 cargo planes ferrying ammunition to the Kabul government (which the Taliban would topple one year later). The Russian crew and plane remained hostages of the Taliban for more than twelve months as Bout, his brother Sergei, and the Russian foreign ministry tried to secure their release. Through-

out the negotiations, Bout delivered goods to the Taliban, sometimes as many as six flights a day—TV sets, clothes, Chinese
consumer goods—an apparent goodwill gesture that soon turned
into a profitable enterprise.[74] "Viktor is completely amoral," says a
U.S. official who tracks him. "He'll work with anybody."[75] After a
year of negotiations, the Russian crew would fire up the jet and hur-
tle down the runway on a blistering afternoon while their guards
dozed.

It was a daring "escape" Bout himself discounted in a subsequent
interview. "Do you really think you can jump in a plane that's been
sitting unmaintained on the tarmac for over a year, start up the en-
gines, and just take off?" he asked a 2003 interviewer in Moscow.
"They didn't escape. They were extracted." Asked to explain, Bout
fell silent. "There are huge forces," was all he would say.[76] A subsequent news report would suggest Afghan traders in the Emirates
intercepted on Bout's behalf.[77] And a former Bout associate said
Bout's Afghan traffic serviced shadowy clients behind the Taliban.
Despite the international embargoes on Afghanistan, Bout always
received payments for his Afghan work from Swiss bank accounts,
according to his associate, who said: "He flew to the Taliban, not
for the Taliban."[78]

Between 1998 and 2001, Bout sold the Taliban twelve air
freighters and continued to fly weapons, spare aircraft parts, and
other supplies into Afghanistan. U.S. and British officials became
highly concerned about the pace of flights into Kandahar, where bin
Laden had resettled and built several training camps. Arabs were a
constant presence at the Kandahar Airport, and western officials
worried flights were ferrying Islamic militants, guns, maybe even
WMD.[79] Heroin smuggling was another concern; U.S. and British

counternarcotics agents wanted to send an undercover team to Sharjah to swab down the planes, according to several former U.S. officials, who said the plan never passed the proposal phase.[80]

After UN sanctions went into effect, an Emirati charter agency named Flying Dolphin won permission to fly humanitarian supplies and aid workers to Afghanistan. The airline was owned by Sheikh Abdullah bin Zayed bin Saqr al Nahyan, a former UAE ambassador to the United States and member of Abu Dhabi's ruling family.[81] Incredibly, Viktor Bout was Zayed's silent partner.[82] An April 2004 intelligence document shown to the author spelled out the conclusion among western intelligence agents: "Under the Taliban government everyone, including Arabs, was active in the narco-trade. As part of this, flights with narcotics went direct from Helmand to the United Arab Emirates." This continued after the UN sanctions went into effect. "The U.S. government was aware there were Taliban flights breaking the embargo," Julie Sirrs, the former Defense Intelligence Agency analyst, told me. "It was widely believed they were moving drugs on those planes."[83]

Far from being hurt by the sanctions, the Taliban seemed to have a steady supply of weapons and money. There was a lot going on in Afghanistan in those days that was alarming to Washington. As in the 1980s, narcotics were not the priority. "The drug issue was one thing on a long list that we were trying to get the Taliban to move on," says Karl Indurfurth, then the assistant secretary of state for South and Central Asian affairs. "Girls' schools, terrorist camps, women's rights. After the embassy bombings in Africa, Osama went to the top of that list."[84] Between 1996 and 2001, the U.S. government pressed the Taliban on thirty different occasions to expel bin Laden from Afghanistan, according to a State Department document.[85] "The message to the Taliban pre-9/11 was, 'We don't like you, but we are willing to live with you if you give us al Qaeda,'" said Teresita Schaffer, another former assistant secretary of state for South Asia.

U.S. officials raised the counternarcotics issue during infrequent exchanges with the Taliban, but after the 1998 terrorist attacks, no one in Washington thought raising the poppy issue would encourage the Taliban to cough up bin Laden. The UN kept up the pressure over drugs, bringing Taliban officials to Pakistan to consult Islamic legal experts on growing and trading narcotics.[86] The Taliban appeared desperate for international recognition of their regime, and wanted UN sanctions lifted. The executive director of the UN's drug control program, Pino Arlacchi, offered the Taliban $250 million in alternative livelihood aid if they could eliminate poppy—a promise he would fail spectacularly to keep.[87]

UN efforts appeared to pay off in July 2000. Just before the autumn planting season was to begin, Mullah Omar announced a total ban on poppy cultivation. To everyone's amazement (and despite some protests in Nangarhar, where farmers shaved their beards and played music) the ban held. American satellite photos and UN ground surveys indicated just 8,000 hectares were planted the following spring across Afghanistan—down from more than 82,000 hectares a year earlier. Most of it was growing in areas not controlled by the Taliban. It represented the largest single cutback in illicit drug production ever. Bernard Frahi, who brokered the deal for UNODC, called it "one of the most remarkable successes ever" in the fight against narcotics.[88] But as with so many things in Afghanistan, the truth was murkier.

Almost overnight, the price of opium at Afghanistan's border shot up from an all-time low of about $28 per kilo to between $350 and $400, according to UNODC and DEA accounts. And despite the ban on growing poppy, western authorities noticed that the Taliban made no effort to seize drug stocks or arrest traffickers. On the contrary, opium bazaars continued to do a brisk business, and the Taliban still collected tax—now earning much higher revenues from a product that had increased tenfold in value. Levels of heroin purity dipped slightly in western markets over the coming year, but the street price of heroin remained stable, indicating there was virtually no supply shortage.[89]

The poppy ban may have been the ultimate insider trading con. The Taliban gambled they could win millions of dollars in international aid—and perhaps even recognition of their government—while top leaders sold off their opium hoards at far higher prices. Just before the ban, top Taliban leaders purchased huge amounts of opium—especially Haji Bashir Noorzai, according to sources close to the movement. "That was when Haji Bashir really broke into the market on his own," says a relative. "It wasn't religion," a smuggler told me in 2003. "It was good business. They bought low, they sold high."

Mullah Omar shifted himself into an enormous and garish new estate on the outskirts of Kandahar. The ornate main palace featured crystal chandeliers and kitschy murals. The compound also boasted a mosque, servant's quarters, and an ample guesthouse.[90] The UN-affiliated Narcotics Control Board concluded that, after four years of bumper crops, stocks of Afghan heroin were high enough to supply the European market for up to four more years.[91] "Everyone close to Mullah Omar benefited," said the former ISI agent. Ahmadullah Alizai, who was the counternarcotics chief in Kandahar after 2001, put it more simply: "They all made millions."

The poppy ban also sparked a humanitarian disaster, from which some Afghan farmers have never recovered. Hundreds of thousands defaulted on loans or were unable to make it through the winter months without credit and fled to the Iranian and Pakistani border areas. Many sold off land and livestock, even trading their unmarried daughters to poppy merchants to settle their arrears.[92] A farmer from Khogiani, in eastern Afghanistan, who took a $400 advance on four kilograms of opium in 2000, did not have the harvested crop to repay his debt. Interviewed in early 2004, the farmer remained heavily indebted to the lender, owing twenty kilograms of opium, then worth $7,200. By giving the trader his daughter, he deducted $3,200 of the loan, and then mortgaged part of his land against the remaining $4,000 owed. He hoped to repay the remainder by growing more opium.[93]

During the 1990s, western aid poured money into anti-narcotics efforts in Pakistan, mainly crop substitution efforts, which succeeded in reducing poppy output from a high of eight hundred tons per year to about two. Pakistan was no longer a heroin producer. Instead it became a major transport route for opiates produced in Taliban-held regions, which utilized the same network built up a decade earlier. As Ahmed Rashid wrote, "The same dealers, truck drivers, madrassa and government contacts and the arms, fuel, and food supply chain that provided the Taliban with its supplies also funneled drugs—just as the same arms pipeline for the mujahideen had done in the 1980s."[94] Although the poppy fields and the processing labs had shifted into Afghanistan, the command and control

of the drug trade remained in Pakistan. "Most of the labs in southern Afghanistan are controlled by or associated with a powerful
consortium of traffickers known as the Quetta Alliance," read a
joint U.S. intelligence report issued in the year 2000. It described
the cartel as the "dominant trafficking organization in Southwest
Asia."[95]

Amid rising alarm over exploding addiction rates in Pakistan,
counternarcotics police worked to crack down on growing traffic.[96]
Powerful smugglers grew more sophisticated. They welded secret
compartments inside cargo tanks of fuel trucks and under seats in
passenger buses and filled them with morphine base. One former
director of Pakistan's Anti Narcotics Force recalled intercepting a
shipment of cabbage with an ingenious concealment method. A bag
of heroin had been placed inside each bud as it sprouted, he said,
and the mature cabbage heads had grown around the drug packets.[97] Heroin shipments became smaller but increased in frequency,
making them harder to trace. There were growing signs that international organized crime rings were getting in on the action. The
mid-1990s brought a sudden influx of Nigerian visitors to Pakistan,
who routinely got caught carrying heroin—usually no more than a
few kilos—inside rubber pellets they had ingested, according to
former British, U.S., and Pakistani counternarcotics officials. "We'd
take them to the hospital, pump them full of laxatives, and watch
them lay eggs for days," said the former ANF director. Still today,
Nigerians account for almost three-quarters of the heroin carriers
arrested in Pakistan.[98]

Islamabad came under pressure to do something about the massive quantities of opiates moving through its territory. However,
there remained worrisome signs of collusion between the traffick-

ers and elements of the military and intelligence services. In 1996, Islamabad announced that its anti-drug agents had intercepted two tons of brown sugar, or morphine base, in southwestern Baluchistan. Foreign diplomats were invited to an elaborate ceremony to watch Pakistanis set the drugs ablaze. Before they did, U.S. agents took a sample. It turned out that the huge pile of dirt contained just traces of opium. The Clinton administration angrily denounced the seizure as a "hoax."[99] A year later DEA agents arrested a senior Pakistani air force officer trying to sell two kilograms of heroin in a New York City McDonald's. Islamabad was furious about the bust, believing the officer had been set up by the DEA. But after an investigation, Pakistani authorities arrested another air force officer in a Karachi hotel, claiming the pair were part of a "small drug ring" within the military.[100]

Many believed there to be far wider involvement. Rumors swirled in Islamabad diplomatic circles that the same ISI trucks bringing covert military aid to the Taliban carried heroin out. As the 1990s wore on, the U.S. embassy reported that ISI support for the Taliban appeared to have grown.[101] A pair of raw intelligence reports detail a widening flow of supplies, including "munitions, fuel and food," with one noting that the spy agency used a private trucking company to cover its tracks.[102] By this time it was widely accepted that Pakistan's Pashtun trucking mafia was closely tied to the drug trade. British authorities tracked private jets making frequent night flights between the Persian Gulf and Quetta, according to a former western police official. A Thai diplomat got nabbed trying to enter the UK with two suitcases full of heroin. He told British investigators he picked up the bags at an ISI safe house.[103]

At a time when the West had isolated Pakistan, first over its nuclear efforts and again after General Pervez Musharraf's 1999 coup, there was less and less engagement with Pakistani authorities. It was never clear if the accumulating events were just another sign of Pakistan's massive corruption problem or a covert policy to raise funds through drug trafficking. "We heard about things all the time, and if you hear it enough, it starts to sound credible," said William Milam, who was U.S. ambassador from 1998 to 2001. "But we never had any real proof."[104] Milam's successor, Wendy Chamberlain, would later characterize the ISI's role in the drug trade in the 1990s as "substantial" during testimony before the House of Representatives.[105] Another western official put it this way: "At the end of the day the ISI is no different from any other intelligence agency. They have to get funding for covert operations one way or another."[106]

Another murky web of concern was Islamabad's covert aid to the Taliban and to Pakistani extremist groups operating in Indian-held Kashmir and training in al Qaeda camps. Washington became alarmed in the year 2000, after Musharraf came to power, that "while Pakistani support for the Taliban has been long-standing, the magnitude of recent support is unprecedented." The State Department issued a bulletin to the Islamabad embassy describing large numbers of Pakistani troops crossing into Afghanistan to support the Taliban's campaign against the dwindling opposition coalition commonly known as the Northern Alliance. The U.S. ambassador was ordered to convey Washington's displeasure over the situation to senior Pakistani officials.[107]

Was support for extremists the state policy in Pakistan or a worrisome sign that the military ruler actually had little control over his own security agencies? For years, there have been numerous reports describing the ISI as a "state within a state," beholden only to its own grand designs. Some historians and diplomats suggest there's a small clique within Pakistan's intelligence community handling black operations like supporting Islamic extremists and developing (and proliferating) nuclear technology. For longtime Pakistan watchers, questions over the existence of this rogue element have been central to western policy toward the country— driving debate over whether to isolate or engage Islamabad.

In his 2006 autobiography, then President Musharraf claimed his government actually had little sway with Mullah Omar. Contrary to popular belief, he wrote, "our relations with the Taliban were never smooth; in fact they were quite uncomfortable."[108] A U.S. official then on his second posting to Pakistan agreed with the president's assessment, saying that when he returned to Islamabad in the late 1990s, his contacts told him, "al Qaeda replaced us out there. They have the checkbooks." When the Taliban blew up the ancient Buddhas of Bāmiān, even after Islamabad had dispatched its foreign minister to beg them not to, the Americans concluded Islamabad had created a monster it could no longer control. "I can only say I was underwhelmed by their level of influence in Afghanistan," said the U.S. official.[109] The persistent and contradictory indications that elements of the ISI were deeply involved with the Taliban, while other Pakistani officials tried and failed to rein them in, would continue to muddle U.S. policy toward the increasingly complex region.

By spring of 2001, threat reporting related to al Qaeda had surged to a level the U.S. intelligence community had never before seen. Between May and July, the National Security Agency reported at least 33 intercepts indicating a terrorist attack was imminent. The FBI tracked 216 secret threat warnings between January 1 and September 10, 2001. And the Federal Aviation Administration issued 15 separate warnings about possible attacks on American airlines.[110] CIA director George Tenet would later tell the 9/11 Commission: "The system was blinking red."[111] The Bush administration would consider backing the Taliban's opposition—then led by the Tajik commander Ahmed Shah Massood—and arming a Predator drone to assassinate bin Laden. Tenet even traveled secretly to Islamabad to meet with his Pakistani counterpart, ISI director general Mahmoud Ahmed. Among other things, they discussed the possibility of getting to bin Laden through counternarcotics channels.[112] By summer, U.S. spies were scrambling to get a handle on what was coming down the pipeline. Their failure to do so would cost the lives of more than three thousand people on 9/11, and send the United States to war.

On September 11, 2001, the regional price of a kilogram of opium had reached an all-time high of $746. Within weeks, it had dropped to $95 a kilo, according to the DEA, indicating its owners were dumping their stocks in anticipation of the U.S.-led invasion, possibly for hard currency, possibly to trade for weapons.[113] UN officials believed the Taliban, al Qaeda, and allied drug lords possessed more than 2,800 metric tons of opium. Sold on the wholesale market in Pakistan, the opium would fetch more than $1 billion, UN officials worried. If processed into crystal heroin and smuggled to the West, the deadly harvest could keep every addict there high for more than three years.[114]

As the United States ramped up for war, the Joint Chiefs of Staff and top Bush administration officials complained that there were few targets in Afghanistan of military consequence. "We're bombing sand," President Bush said in an interview. "We're pounding sand."[115] CIA sources say the agency prepared a comprehensive list of potential targets, which included twenty-five major drug labs, storage warehouses, and other opium-related facilities.[116] The British government also provided Washington with the locations of about two dozen drugs labs and storage areas, according to former INL chief Bobby Charles.[117]

The California congressman Dana Rohrabacher also put together a team "who knew all the players in Afghanistan." The outspoken Republican lawmaker harbors an obsession with the global drug trade, had a long history with Afghanistan, and openly supported the mujahideen during the Soviet resistance. "I had six guys working for me around the clock," he said later. "We identified four storage areas where we believed the Taliban had a billion dollars' worth of drugs hidden."[118]

However, from the start of military operations in Afghanistan, the Bush administration and the Pentagon would conspicuously avoid taking on opium traders. On October 11, four days after Operation Enduring Freedom began, Bush sat down with his National Security Council, discussing, among other things, the continued search for installations U.S. warplanes could target. Then Defense Secretary Donald Rumsfeld said the Pentagon considered hitting drug labs and heroin storage areas, but didn't because of concerns there would be "collateral damage."[119]

The CIA later concluded that bombing those targets would have slowed down opium production in Afghanistan for more than a year. "The drug targets were big places, like small towns that did nothing but produce heroin," a CIA official said. "The British were screaming for us to bomb those targets because most of the heroin in Britain comes from Afghanistan, but they refused."[120]

When he learned of the decision later, Rohrabacher was infuriated. "I kept telling them, this is going to be used to kill Americans," he said. "At a time when I think they could have disappeared, I think this opium kept the Taliban alive."

4. THE NEW TALIBAN

WHEN THE END CAME FOR THE TALIBAN'S TREASURER, HE was hurtling along an isolated smugglers' trail in a rocky wasteland known as Dasht-e Margo—the "desert of death."

Mullah Akhtar Mohammed Osmani traveled in a four-by-four with a regional Taliban subcommander named Mullah Abdul Zahir. A third passenger was Haji Masooq, one of the biggest heroin smugglers in Helmand province.[1] It was December 19, 2006. Unbeknownst to Osmani, a British Royal Air Force R1 monitoring plane had picked up his trail when he spoke earlier on his satellite telephone. According to British officials, the spy plane made contact with a U.S. Special Operations Team hunting high-value targets. The RAF also reached out to Task Force Orange, a military intelligence unit tracking terrorists electronically.[2] Once they confirmed they had Osmani on the phone, a U.S. warplane took off from Bagram Air Base and sped to Helmand, launching a precision air strike the moment Osmani's vehicle moved out of a populated area. The four-by-four was obliterated in a flash. Osmani and the others never knew what hit them.

As Mullah Omar's treasurer and the military commander for six key provinces in the south, Osmani was at the time the highest-ranking Taliban official to be eliminated since the U.S.-led coalition invaded Afghanistan in October 2001. Although NATO officials and the western media hailed his killing, a key circumstance of Osmani's death got little attention: the man in charge of the Taliban's finances got taken out while he was doing a dope deal.

The circumstances surrounding Osmani's death came as no surprise to U.S. and Afghan officials tracking the Taliban's links to the opium trade. By late 2006, the Taliban was deeply dependent on the drug trade for its operational funding. Although the Taliban leadership maintained close links to drug smugglers from its inception and relied on taxing the trade while in power, that level of dependence rose even further after the regime fell from power. Opium played a critical role in supporting the Taliban's resurgence from the brink of extinction.

When U.S.-backed Afghan forces retook Kabul in 2001, they caused the Taliban and al Qaeda to scatter, but failed to put down the enemy once and for all. Rather than mounting a nationwide invasion with large numbers of foreign troops, the United States and its allies opted for a "light-footprint" approach, relying on local proxies with predictably unfortunate results. Many al Qaeda and Taliban leaders fled over the border into Pakistan. Most famously, Osama bin Laden escaped the Tora Bora siege down a smugglers' trail, reportedly on the back of a donkey.[3] Other Taliban commanders lay low in Pashtun regions of southwest Afghanistan. Quite a few ended up in the fertile plains of west Kandahar and Helmand that also cultivate poppy. "There was no coordinated effort—they just escaped to places where they knew they'd find safe haven," said journalist Rahimullah Yusufzai.[4] It wasn't hard to melt away and hide. Throughout 2002, there were just 4,500 troops dedicated to the International Security Assistance Force in Afghanistan, all of them based in the capital, Kabul.

Limited numbers of U.S. forces fanned out around the south and southeast, focusing on hunting down "high-value targets" in al Qaeda, not Taliban. CIA agents and U.S. military officials dished out millions of dollars to anti-Taliban warlords whose questionable records on narcotics and human rights have been documented by historians, journalists, and human rights groups. Gary Schroen, the CIA agent sent to coordinate with the Northern Alliance, wrote about handing $500,000 to its leader, Marshal Fahim, during their first meeting.[5] Gul Agha Sherzai, a corrupt former governor of Kandahar, received Land Cruisers full of cash to help him reconquer that southern province. "During the march on Kandahar," wrote author Peter Maass, "Gul Agha's wallet was a Toyota."[6]

Behind a barrage of U.S. firepower, Northern Alliance troops took over Kabul, installing ethnic Tajiks in security posts around the city. The December 2001 Bonn Agreement named Hamid Karzai as interim leader, appointing Fahim as defense minister. Eastern warlord Hazrat Ali took control of Nangarhar, a province rich in poppy. Western strongman Ismael Khan reinstalled himself in Herat, where he could tax lucrative cross-border traffic with Iran. The Uzbek warlord Rashid Dostum muscled his way into Mazar-e Sharif, and control of trade to the north. He battled over the spoils with a rival warlord, Mohammed Atta. Sher Mohammed, the young nephew of Nasim Akhundzada, earned the governorship of Helmand.

Western officials privately acknowledged the unsavory behavior of certain members within the new power structure, in particular the allegations that some were tied to drug trafficking. They claimed, however, that such individuals were providing critical support in the hunt for al Qaeda fugitives, despite the fact that relatively few terror leaders were ever captured on Afghan territory. Looking back, it was another case when Washington's priority concern—capturing terrorists—took precedent. It absolved other problems at hand. As the International Crisis Group put it, "a culture of impunity was allowed to take root in the name of 'stability.'"[7] In 2001, with the Taliban ban on poppy cultivation in place, Afghan farmers had harvested just 8,000 hectares of opium poppy—mostly in areas that had been outside the Taliban's control. A year later, after the international community made no concerted effort to help Afghan farmers shift to other crops, poppy fields carpeted 74,000 hectares across the country. In one season, Afghanistan had leapt back into the dubious position as the world's leading producer of opium.

Drug bazaars quickly reopened, selling vast reserves traders and farmers alike had squirreled away. Within days of Kandahar falling to American forces, hundreds of shopkeepers were doing a brisk trade at the Hazrat Gi Baba market, just a few miles from where the U.S. military was setting up a new base. Bob Woodruff, a correspondent for *ABC News*, visited a separate opium bazaar in nearby Maiwand in December 2001 where traders were scooping the sticky resin onto metal scales. "It was incredible," he said. "They were selling it openly in big plastic sacks."[8]

Across the border, agents from Pakistan's Anti Narcotics Force got a taste of the amount of contraband leaving the region when an ANF team ambushed a camel convoy in the windswept outreaches of the Baluchistan Desert. The camels carried nearly a ton of heroin and morphine base on their backs. Worth millions of dollars on the wholesale opium market in Pakistan, and more than

$1 billion if it had been smuggled to the West, it was one of the biggest drug hauls in history.[9]

If smugglers were quick to get back on their feet, the international community was painfully inefficient. After twenty-five years of war, virtually everything had to be rebuilt from scratch, from the roads to the power grid to the justice system to the police force. "Like so many of its people," wrote Barry Bearak in *The New York Times Magazine*, "the nation is missing limbs."[10] The Bonn Agreement divided the mammoth task of regrowing them between the various donor nations: the British took on drugs; the Italians, the justice system. The United States would build an army; the Germans would craft a police force. Funding was scarce, however, and no mechanism existed to coordinate between donor nations. Disputes arose immediately. "There was always the question of where to start," said General David Barno, who commanded the Afghan coalition from 2003 until 2005. "It was the tyranny of the urgent over the important." As in the mujahideen era, when counternarcotics was considered secondary to fighting the Soviets, in post-9/11 Afghanistan, the fight against drugs was deprioritized to the hunt for terrorists. "Right now, we realize our work has to take a backseat to the War on Terror," a DEA agent told me in 2003.[11] The first counternarcotics policy—implemented by the British—offered cash handouts to poppy farmers if they agreed to pull up the poppy plants and grow something else. Not surprisingly, thousands more enterprising farmers planted poppy, just to get their hands on the easy money. The program was hastily dropped the following year.[12]

Widespread corruption took root in Kabul, along with a dangerous security vacuum in the Pashtun south. Few foreign troops were posted outside Kandahar city, and promised reconstruction projects got underway slowly. The Taliban quietly began to re-group. Cautiously, Taliban commanders began reaching out to each other, according to sources close to the movement. One by one, Mullah Omar contacted his deputies and appointed them to organize his fighters, pick up fresh recruits from Pakistani madrassas, locate weapons stashes, and raise funds.[13] Drug smugglers close to the Taliban were some of the first investors, putting up small amounts of cash to help the movement start to rebuild, according to local sources along the border and intelligence reports seen by the author.[14]

It appears that Taliban commanders raised money by selling off opium stores. There were reports Taliban fugitives tapped into Mullah Omar's legendary 3,800 metric ton opium stockpile, which DEA informants believed was buried outside Kandahar. "After the invasion, we think they parceled it out in small chunks and sold it to raise money," one U.S. official told me.[15] Omar's opium stash was like Blackbeard's treasure; there was some question as to whether it actually existed. Regardless, it's now clear that Taliban officials do maintain multi-ton drug stockpiles, which function in effect as their federal reserve.

The Taliban built their resources methodically, displaying a steady patience that gave rise to a popular adage: "The Americans have the watches, but the Taliban have the time." The insurgents started out with low-intensity attacks in 2003, using fighters on motorcycles to ambush foreign troops and aid workers. Off and on, they set off small bombs.[16] Over time, cross-border attacks from Pakistan became more frequent. When Washington shifted focus, the Taliban surmised the moment was right. In March 2003, just as the United States was invading Iraq, Yusufzai got a call from Mullah Dadullah, the vicious, one-legged military commander. The Taliban had "regrouped," he announced, and would soon launch a jihad to retake Afghanistan.[17]

Three months later, Mullah Omar appointed a new ten-man *shura*, or ruling council, to lead the resistance.[18] He named the legendary mujahideen commander Jalaluddin Haqqani, whose rear base of operations was North Waziristan in Pakistan's tribal areas, as his ally in Afghanistan's southeastern region. Mullah Dadullah Lang would command the south. The Taliban even mended ways with their former rival Gulbuddin Hekmatyar, who would lead the eastern flank from the mountainous provinces of Kunar and Nuristan. It was a loosely grouped alliance, with each region more or less responsible to raise its own funds, according to U.S. and Afghan officials. As the mujahideen had done during the Soviet resistance, commanders immediately began taxing farmers in their control zones and charging protection fees to smugglers moving all sorts of contraband, not just opium. It wasn't long before the money started flowing.

Mirwais Yasini, who then headed Afghanistan's Counter Narcotics Directorate, estimates the Taliban took in as much as $100 million in revenue from poppy farmers, truckers, and drug traffickers in 2003 alone.[19] There were reports that al Qaeda operatives in Peshawar were taking delivery of 2,200 kilos of processed heroin every two months, which they could have sold on the wholesale market for between $38 and $59 million annually without even exporting it from Pakistan.[20] A 2004 Congressional fact-finding mission to the border region reported that bin Laden was earning up to $24 million annually off of a separate Kandahar heroin network.[21]

In late 2003, a separate pair of incidents gave rise to concerns that al Qaeda was closely tied into moving drugs out of the region—the very point in the trade where the profit margins are greatest.[22] First a British intelligence report in early December mapped out how Pakistani smugglers would hook up with Middle Eastern syndicates on the high seas. Seen by the author, the report said powerful motorboats packed with heroin and hashish set off from Pakistan's southern Gwadar Port, pursuing a course for "210 degrees on a southwesterly heading, and sailing for seven hours at a speed of 12 knots." Using satellite phones, the speedboats would rendezvous with larger dhows in the Arabian Sea, transfer their cargo, and then return to Pakistan. Money would change hands separately using the informal money transfer network known as *hawala*, the intelligence report said. Speedboats carrying drugs also took off from Qasm in southern Iran, the report said, landing in Port Sha'am in UAE, where Turkish smugglers took the shipments onward.

According to a western official, information gleaned from this intelligence briefing led directly to three seizures by the coalition in the Arabian Sea at the close of 2003. They would provide key evidence of al Qaeda's role in the drug trade. In the first seizure on December 15, a U.S. Navy team from the guided-missile destroyer USS *Decatur* boarded a dhow carrying two tons of hashish worth an estimated $8 to 10 million. Three of the twelve crew members were found to have links to al Qaeda, according to a U.S. Navy statement.

Three days later, a P-3K maritime patrol aircraft from the Royal New Zealand Air Force picked up the two other suspect dhows on the Arabian Sea. Spy planes from Australia, the UK, and the United States tracked the vessels for forty-eight hours. With a British Royal Air Force Nimrod patrolling overhead, the USS *Philippine Sea* intercepted the two boats late on December 19. A Navy boarding team found millions of dollars worth of heroin and amphetamines on board, and more low-ranking al Qaeda operatives.[23] U.S. officials worried they were being moved into position in the West, fund-raising for the terror network, or maybe both.[24]

When the 2003 seizures took place, western intelligence was already concerned that al Qaeda was using the high seas to move terror cells and material. According to *The Washington Post*, American spies identified approximately fifteen cargo freighters around the globe that they believed were controlled by the terror network or simply used by it to ferry operatives, bombs, or money. Osama bin Laden owned boats for years, the report said, some of which transported legal commodities like cement and seeds for his web of companies. At least one vessel had been tied to terrorism: it delivered the explosives used to bomb the U.S. embassies in Kenya and Tanzania in 1998. In the murky world of ocean transport, where records are few and easily faked, American officials never figured out precisely how most of the terrorist freighters were being used, "except that some are generating profits for al Qaeda," the report said.[25]

To this day, some senior U.S. officials continue to argue that al Qaeda is not systematically involved in drug smuggling, although many acknowledge that low-rank operatives get involved now and then to earn money. Afghans, especially those who had fought in the anti-Soviet resistance themselves, were clear on the issue from the start. "Everyone is involved," a former commander from Nangarhar told me. "The top guys won't touch the trade themselves—they consider it dirty. But if it's happening in their region, you can be guaranteed top leaders are making a cut."[26] Using drugs themselves might be *haram*, or forbidden, but selling it to the enemy was a considered an act of war. "It is an unholy alliance," said Abdul Ghaus Rasoolzai, who headed the anti-narcotics department in eastern Afghanistan. "Al Qaeda is using drugs as a weapon against America and other Western countries. The weapon of drugs does not make a noise. The victim does not bleed and leaves no trace of the killer."[27]

Meanwhile, authorities in the remote tri-border region where Pakistan, Afghanistan, and Iran converge were observing another blurring of commerce and terrorism. In this case it was growing cooperation between people traffickers, drug traders, and terrorists. Coalition spy planes and an increased Iranian troop presence along the border made it difficult for drug traffickers to move their product in massive camel convoys, so they got creative. Iranian police found heroin hidden in the bellies of nine sheep and goats being led across the desert in 2004. In another case, smugglers in Afghanistan painted their vehicle to look like it belonged to a local demining group.[28]

Top authorities from all three countries said drug smugglers were increasingly hiring migrant workers trying to get to the West to use as drug mules. Pakistani and Afghan counternarcotics teams found individuals carrying heroin that had been sewn into the cuffs and seams of women's dresses, stuffed into hollowed-out high heels, and even glued into walnuts that were carefully split and then resealed.[29] "We even found heroin sewn into badges honoring Queen Elizabeth," said Major General Khalid Jaffery, the director general of Pakistan's Anti Narcotics Force. "Thank God she doesn't know."[30]

A July 2004 CIA report, seen by the author, described a human and narcotics smuggling operation run by an ethnic Uzbek who ran a network of buses and hotels to illegally shuttle people to the West.[31] By paying large bribes to police in Afghanistan and Iran, the report said, the trafficker was able to move large amounts of heroin into Turkey. "Many [carriers] were illegal immigrants trying to get work in [the] Persian Gulf," the report said. The trafficker also employed terrorist operatives from the Islamic Movement of Uzbekistan (IMU), an al Qaeda–linked group, to ferry heroin. Key to his operation's success, the report said, was the trafficker's ability to "provide photo substituted passports from Pakistan, Afghanistan, Iran, and Turkey."

Local officials and western diplomats said there was a sudden flood of reports of this type in 2003 and 2004 indicating that people smugglers, drug traffickers, and terrorists were at least using the same routes and modes of transport, if not always working together actively. "Investigators believe if we could wrap up the people smugglers, we would go a long way toward solving this whole thing," said one western envoy.[32] But U.S. military intelligence and CIA agents focused on hunting down terrorists still tried to maintain a separation between the insurgents and the criminals. "I always told them, 'If we pursue these avenues together, you will turn up some of the guys you are looking for,'" a U.S. counternarcotics official posted to Kabul told me. "I used to have shouting matches about this with the agency guys."[33]

Although the U.S. military resisted getting involved in interdiction, the United Kingdom, which took the lead on counternarcotics in the Bonn Agreement, developed Task Force 333, the top-secret paramilitary strike team that raided laboratories processing opium into crystal heroin, the high-end product smuggled to the West.[34] Commandos from Britain's Special Air Service regiment trained and mentored the elite Afghan unit which began launching strikes in 2004.[35] "It was basically a drop 'em in and shoot it up operation," said a western official who assisted their operations.[36] Whenever the group hit a lab in the south, it was almost guaranteed that Taliban soldiers would swarm in to protect the compound. Force 333 planners had to keep their operations top secret, or corrupt officials would tip off traffickers. "The Taliban protect drug traffickers like a mother protects her babies," said a Force 333 commander. "And it is almost impossible for us to snatch these babies, not just because they are better equipped and better armed, but also since they have people within the government."[37]

For years after the 2001 invasion, U.S. officials often acknowledged that the Taliban was collecting revenue from taxing opium and other commodities moving through their region. However, it was generally defined as a passive type of involvement typical to Afghanistan, where every local power broker takes a cut of what passes through his control zone, and not critical to their overall funding. The fact that Taliban forces had begun protecting drug labs provided confirmation for counternarcotics agents that the insurgents were becoming more deeply involved in the opium trade than previously acknowledged. "There's a big difference between getting a cut of the action and getting payment for services performed," said a western official.

The Taliban also began using its armed fighters to guard opium convoys, earning millions of dollars a year in protection fees—often as much as 20 percent a consignment. Taliban fighting units attacked government security checkpoints so drug convoys could get past, or in some cases launched diversionary strikes to draw NATO forces away from a major consignment passing through. Campaigns for territorial gain, such as a 2007 Taliban push into Deh Rawood district in Uruzgan, now support smuggling activities.[38] Deh Rawood is perched along the most important drugs and arms trafficking route that connects to Iran in the west and Pakistan to the south. The transformation in battlefield tactics mirrored similar patterns set by the FARC in Colombia. Their military strategy was increasingly geared to supporting drug trafficking activities. In the summer of 2006, DEA agents in Kabul set up a sting operation that contracted a Taliban commander to buy morphine base, locally known as "brown sugar," and sell it down the line to DEA informants. "When that worked, we could prove that they were tied into the transport and delivery end of things," said an official close to the case.[39]

Insurgents collaborated with traffickers about farm output as well, distributing "night letters" in some districts of the south that offered protection to farmers who grew poppy and which threatened dire consequences for anyone who didn't. "The one who is not cultivating poppy in their lands and accepting the governor order for destroying their poppy cultivations will be killed by Taliban," said one message with typically poor syntax pinned to a mosque door.[40] Locals said the Taliban did not manage the opium trade themselves, but supported poppy cultivation on behalf of poppy merchants and drug smugglers, who often paid them in the form of vehicles and weapons.[41] Major traffickers have launched even more grandiose schemes, with the Taliban's protection. Spy satellites in 2008 captured images of massive irrigation projects underway in the windswept deserts of southern Helmand. "They are trying to create more farmland so they can grow more poppy," said a senior western envoy.[42]

Village-level Taliban field commanders used personal contacts to develop information about people in their area, paying as much as $10 a tip to informants, according to local sources. They work over the local community like mafia henchmen, even using the old "good cop, bad cop" routine. In one typical exchange, Haji Bado Khan, a landowner in Kajaki district in northern Helmand, described how a local Taliban field commander, Haji Khan Gul, wanted to start billing him $3,000 a season. Gul showed up late one night at Khan's house with a clutch of armed men. "We know you have been earning a lot of money these days. We hear you're growing your own poppy and buying it from others to trade," Gul said. "You will have to start sharing some regular money with the mujahideen." Being from the same district, the two men had known each other most of their lives. Gul told him, "I am here as your friend, but if you fail to pay this, I'll have to report you to my commander. No matter what I say, I know he will get someone to come after you." Khan bargained the rate down to $1,500, and paid it in the form of two motorcycles.[43]

Gul charged a 5 percent tax on commodities moving through his control zone and skirmished over taxing rights with commanders in neighboring districts, according to locals. Insurgents like Gul routinely sought room and board as they moved through the region. One farmer in Sangin district reported having to feed a group of thirty Taliban fighters twice a week. "They came with guns one night and told me to be ready for them," Haji Khan said. "Sometimes a government official comes by in the daytime and asks me, 'Why are you doing this?'" he said. "Once, I said to the guy, 'You think I want this? If you would just come out here and stay for two hours a day, I won't have to feed them anymore.'"[44]

Under Taliban protection, traffickers sent out armies of poppy merchants, who prepurchase crops at planting time for prices below what farmers could fetch at harvest. The salaam system provided the cash needed by poor farmers and sharecroppers to get through the winter, but it was geared to trap them in debt come harvest time. Many get caught in a vicious cycle of owing more every year, and there are appalling tales of farmers selling off their daughters to settle their arrears.[45] In some districts, the Taliban have provided security for farmers, building defensive positions around poppy fields, or planting mines and IEDs ahead of visits by eradication teams.[46]

When not coerced to support the Taliban, a complex blend of motives appears to inform decisions by Afghan villagers to engage their protection or even take up arms and join them. Canada's *Globe and Mail* newspaper conducted a video survey of forty-two Taliban foot soldiers in Kandahar in 2007, finding the overwhelming majority were poppy farmers. The sample group was small; however, the uncanny similarity of their responses also supports the theory that Taliban leaders—perhaps with the support of traffickers—conduct a campaign of indoctrination on the poppy issue. One-fifth of the respondents said they grew poppy because their mullahs ordered them to, and sixteen said they hoped to make addicts of non-Muslims. "It is obvious to everyone that the

Americans hate poppies," said soldier 18. "And if we grow it in this era, it will be better for us and worse for the Americans." The soldier added: "Islam says not to grow it and we are not opposed to Islam, but our *ulema* [Islamic clerics] say to grow it as it is harmful for non-Muslims." When the interviewer asked how it got transported to the West, the soldier replied: "They have their own businessmen who take it to their own countries."

About half the Taliban fighters said their poppy fields had been targeted by government-led anti-drug teams, a striking statistic in a province where just 8 percent of the entire poppy crop was eradicated in 2007.[47] "It's a bit of a chicken and egg thing," said *Globe* correspondent Graeme Smith in the multimedia report. "Do they join the Taliban because their fields get targeted or do their fields get targeted because they are Taliban?" This is a crucial question. Some analysts studying Afghanistan's poppy trade believe iniquitous eradication policies, particularly in Kandahar and Helmand, have tended to benefit rich landowners and tribal federations close to the provincial and federal power structures, dividing communities across the southern poppy belt and driving many poor farmers to join the Taliban.[48] Put simply, tribes that hail from the same federation as Karzai's Popalzai tribe tend to suffer less eradication; rivals more frequently get pushed into the arms of the insurgents.

Poppy may fetch a higher price than most other licit crops, but other factors like poor security and infrastructure, the predatory nature of the farm loans, and Taliban taxes erase any real profit. "The farmers have never benefited from poppy cultivation," said Haji Mahuddin Khan, a tribal leader in Helmand. "The profits are taken by those [officials] who tell farmers to engage in cultivation but then threaten their crops with eradication. The international mafia is the main benefactor, while we are being held responsible for it and portrayed as criminals."[49] Although farmer and fighter may forge alliances out of economic desperation, poppy growers interviewed for this project, even in the poppy heartland of Helmand, expressed an urgent desire to get rid of the Taliban and grow something legal instead. Some appeared to side with the Taliban only since they perceived the local government to be more inefficient, corrupt, and violent. And many described themselves as caught in the middle of a never-ending storm. "I voted in the elections because we were told we'd get roads and clinics," said Dastagir Khan, a farmer in Sangin, the scene of bitter warfare between the British NATO troops and the Taliban. "Instead, there's been nothing but bombs."[50] Like other farmers, Khan acknowledged that growing opium was "unholy," but said he couldn't find buyers for anything else he grew. "The only people who ever visit this village are opium agents who come to buy the crops," he said. "And they come with the Taliban."

When thousands more U.S. Marines poured into Helmand in 2009 and 2010 as part of General McChrystal's counterinsurgency campaign, the most common question they heard from locals was "How long are you going to stay?" The Taliban launched a whisper campaign suggesting the American would pull out within months and warned that anyone who cooperated with the Marines would be marked for death.[51] "[Villagers] are very hesitant to trust us, and I don't blame them," Captain Frank Biggio, a Marine reservist who headed a civil-affairs team, told the *Los Angeles Times*. "For centuries, they've seen foreigners come and go, promises made and broken."[52]

That could be changing, although it will likely depend on the level of international commitment remaining consistent. An intensive, multipronged effort to reduce poppy output appeared to have at least initial success in Helmand in 2009, where the rate of cultivation in a six-district focus zone declined by 37 percent. The focused aid program, cofunded and implemented by the United States and the U.K., blended improved security, an intensive public awareness campaign, the distribution of high-grade wheat seed and fertilizers to farmers, and law enforcement activities, including an eradication program run by Gulab Mangal, the effective provincial governor there. There's a historic factor that may help American forces in that particular province: many older residents in Helmand have positive memories about a U.S. aid project implemented in the valley in the 1960s, a time when the provincial capital Lashkar Gah was dubbed "Little America." The multimillion-dollar program built a network of irrigation canals and constructed a large hydroelectric dam. The program was abandoned when the communists seized power in 1978.[53]

Whereas poppy output dropped by a third in Helmand's focus zone in 2009, poppy cultivation in insurgent-held zones in the province climbed 8 percent the same year, partially offsetting any gains.[54] Reports emerged that the number of heroin refineries had increased in the districts of Helmand that border Pakistan, and were becoming mobile as a result of a dramatic increase in coalition operations to destroy them.[55] The number of sites turning opium into heroin climbed past fifty, many of them operating off the back of souped-up pickups hurtling across the barren terrain near the Pakistan border.[56]

The district of Musa Qala, which has shifted between Taliban and coalition control in recent years, is emblematic of the type of unending violence ordinary villagers have endured. It also provided a rare window into life under the Taliban. NATO troops, mainly from Britain, fought a bloody campaign there in 2006, withdrawing in October after reaching a peace deal with tribal elders who pledged to keep the Taliban away on their own. The deal fell apart in February 2007, and Taliban swarmed back into the district, establishing a district government with a governor, police chief, and sharia courts.

Local journalists from the Institute of War and Peace Reporting were invited into Musa Qala to report on life under the Taliban in November 2007.[57] They found schools and hospitals shuttered. Taliban fighters patrolled the streets by the hundreds, driving through town on stolen police trucks, extorting money for the insurgency. One report described a bustling drugs bazaar where buyers piled sacks of opium into trucks.[58] Little of the drug money seemed to benefit ordinary villagers, for whom basic necessities were scarce. One IWPR reporter found as many as 75 percent of the town's residents had fled and the only shopkeeper still operating reported business down by 80 percent.

"The only people left are those who couldn't afford to go. We are in a very bad economic situation," said Haji Nazar Mohammad, a town elder.[59] The reporter, Aziz Ahmad Shafe, said he was followed by an armed guard, and believed many people he interviewed were fearful of speaking against the Taliban. Some residents praised them for bringing security, saying corrupt officials from the Kabul administration had performed no better. "If the government wanted to help, why didn't they do anything before the Taliban came?" said Amruddin Kaka, an elderly resident.[60]

When Afghan and international troops retook Musa Qala in December 2007, they found the Taliban had hung alleged spies in the town square and oversaw heroin production at more than fifty heroin labs. The number of labs in operation had expanded while the insurgents were in control, with some employing as many as sixty men. Fariq Khan, a Musa Qala resident who owns a telephone shop, said Taliban collected about $8 from each family every month at the mosque. Trucks passing through paid $50 each and poppy farmers had to turn over 10 percent of their profits, Khan said.[61]

Though life under the Taliban was brutal, repeated, heavy bombardments flattened homes and businesses in Musa Qala and elsewhere, killed scores of civilians and hardened people against the NATO coalition as well. "I swear I will never forget my little daughter's screams," said Zmarai, from the Chenai village. "She was scared to death of the bombs. There was blood coming out of my son's ears."[62] The high number of civilian casualties caused by the coalition since 2001—and the deep resentment that has caused—will present American forces with one of the hardest obstacles to overcome as the surge of troops enters Helmand. General McChrystal made reducing civilian deaths one of his key strategic priorities, and by the end of 2009, the United Nations reported that insurgents had caused 70 percent of the civilian deaths in Afghanistan in 2009, up from about 46 percent in 2007.[63] Gaining trust will take time and patience, especially among civilians who have endured years of violence and repeated failed promises to deliver development. "I heard the government on the radio saying they'd help us," villager Gul Mohammed told IWPR. "But we don't want their help. We are not going to forget our dead just because they give us a plate of food."[64]

Ironically, just as General McChrystal sought to implement a "population-centric" strategy focused on protecting ordinary civilians, a parallel effort was underway by the Taliban leadership that appeared to be aimed both at implementing better governance and shoring up control over money flows. Mullah Omar revamped his command structure, pushing out unruly commanders with a history of extreme violence and not following orders.[65] He created a shadow network of sharia courts to settle local disputes that was widely seen as fair and more efficient than the official Afghan court system. In addition, the Taliban established provincial-level commissions where Afghans could present their requests or complaints to a local council of religious scholars, who answer back to the ten-man executive council, known as the Shura Majlis or Quetta Shura.[66] In at least one reported case the Taliban commission in Helmand castigated a judge in Musa Qala whom the Taliban themselves had appointed. "One judge was found taking a bribe and the Taliban put black all over his face and tied him to a tree," said businessman Eitadullah Khan. "When he was released, he was fired."[67]

Perhaps most significantly, Omar issued a thirteen-chapter code of conduct for Taliban subcommanders in May 2009 that was accompanied by an intensive propaganda campaign on militant radio and Web sites suggesting the Taliban leader wanted to limit the way his fighters victimized ordinary Afghans. "The mujahideen should strive to win the hearts and minds of Muslims by treating them with justice and good faith," it said. The Quetta

Shura ordered Taliban forces not to attack schools, clinics, bridges, or roads, and prohibited commanders from harassing people on the highways for money. The new code, partially authored by Mullah Agha Jan Mutassim, head of the Taliban's powerful finance committee, also seemed geared at limiting low-ranking commanders from taking independent action both in terms of fund-raising and strategy, instead ceding most decision-making power to the provincial commissions. It moved to streamline flows of money into the Taliban's central coffers, institutionalizing among other things a system whereby commanders could hold onto 80 percent of whatever booty they collected, but decreeing that 20 percent had to be sent to the Shura Majlis.[68]

In a war zone where there's little to buy with hard currency, Taliban field commanders often collect commodities like food, fuel, weapons, or motorcycles that are useful to their war effort. Insurgents also demand mobile phone handsets, as well as "top-up" cards providing airtime credit on the Afghan mobile phone and Thuraya satellite networks. In some districts, farmers and shopkeepers receive receipts for the taxes paid to the local Taliban subcommander, which come stamped with the official seal of the Islamic Emirate of Afghanistan, the official title of the Quetta Shura's shadow regime. The Taliban hierarchy is strict when it comes to assigning regions of influence, meaning there is little risk for farmers and shopkeepers to be charged twice. In cases when farmers complained to the Taliban commissions that they had been charged twice by rival commanders, the Taliban leadership responded by punishing the commanders.

U.N. officials and western counternarcotics agents believe funds earned at the village level are put directly toward the operational cost of running the insurgency, often quite directly. In the poppy belt, for example, the agricultural tithe is routinely paid in opium. Taliban commanders will literally cart off 10 percent of a farmer's gross output. One Afghan intelligence officer based near Musa Qula described opium storehouses where Taliban commanders could deposit and later withdraw quantities of poppy as if using an ATM machine.

From the fields of Helmand to the hawala stands of Pakistan, elaborate mechanisms filter drug money through the Taliban hierarchy, according to dozens of interviews with smugglers, fighters, and Afghan officials. Each district commander had to kick a percentage of the taxes he collected up to his regional commander; then it went to the provincial commander, and so on up the command chain. "The Taliban are very organized," said an Afghan intelligence official tracking the drugs trade in the south. "Each commander has his own financial representative—the guy who looks after the money side of things. He will have to come to Quetta and deal with the Taliban's finance committee."[69] Money can travel in both directions. Subcommanders from districts with good earning potential might have to pay into the central coffers, while others in strategic regions with less earning potential might collect a monthly stipend for operational expenses.

The Quetta leadership contracts major traffickers to provide a certain number of four-by-fours and Toyota Hilux pickup trucks every year. A number of smugglers have built Islamic madrassas in Pakistan where recruits can be trained. Several own hotels where Taliban fighters can escape for R&R. Smugglers also pay medical expenses for Taliban injured on the battlefield, and at least one ran a four-story hospital in Quetta, which was reportedly filled at any given time with wounded Taliban fighters.[70] Major drug dealers—those who own refineries and who traffic in tons of narcotics—also pay directly to the senior Taliban leaders, often to the tune of millions of dollars annually, according to contacts on both sides of the border.

Insurgents across Afghanistan also earn from a wide variety of criminal activities beyond just the poppy trade. The Taliban protect and tax the brisk marijuana trade, and engage in widespread extortion, shaking down small and large businesses alike. Shopkeepers, like farmers, could expect to hand over about 10 percent of their monthly take, either in the form of cash or commodities. One grocer in Ghazni described having to supply local insurgents with cooking oil and rice in lieu of a monthly payment, and said he received a receipt.[71] There were similar reports from Kunduz, after Taliban forces swarmed into the northern province in 2009. There, they handed out receipts to shopkeepers, farmers, and truck drivers alike.

In the southern part of the country, the Shura Majlis streamlined the collection of protection fees charged to larger businesses and aid groups, as well as the trucking firms that ply the congested Kandahar-Quetta corridor and other southern roadways. The Taliban leadership apparently feared a replay of the anarchy that existed on southern Afghanistan's road network in the early 1990s, and wanted to ensure that a larger percentage of this key source of money was flowing directly into the central coffers. Armed Taliban fighters used to hit up trucks at designated checkpoints along the road in Taliban control zones, meaning they had considerable wiggle room on reporting their earnings to their superiors.

Under the new system, trucking firms had to deposit protection payments with specified moneychangers in Quetta and Kandahar, who would transfer those funds direct to Quetta. Drivers reported receiving a code—"the tiger is wounded but alive" was one example—that they could give if armed men stopped them on the road. Trucks carrying goods for the local market, or transiting across Afghanistan, were levied about 10 percent of the value of their shipment. Convoys carrying goods for the coalition paid a higher rate, ranging from 25 to 40 percent of the total value being carried, according to truckers and officials at trucking firms.[72] Insurgents aren't the only actors charging protection fees; trucking firms reported that corrupt provincial governors and warlords also demanded a cut in many areas, all of which contributed to soaring costs for development work and supplying the coalition.

The Quetta Shura also demanded money collected from larger businesses, notably the telecom sector and construction projects funded by international aid organizations and NATO. Sargon Heinrich, a Kabul-based U.S. businessman in construction and service industries, was quoted in a September 2009 *Time* magazine report as saying that 16 percent of his gross revenue went to "facilitation fees," mainly protecting shipments of valuable equipment coming from the border.[73] The report aptly described the circular nature of the problem: the U.S. government provides money to local contractors to build roads, schools, and bridges as part of the counterinsurgency campaign, and the contractors pay off insurgents to avoid having those projects attacked. The insurgents then spend the money they raise to purchase weapons and explosives, which in turn get used to kill NATO troops. "It becomes a self-sustaining war," the article quoted an adviser to the Afghan Ministry of Interior as saying. "A self-licking ice cream."[74] Extortion is believed to be the largest source of income for insurgents in parts of the country where there is little or no poppy grown, especially in districts where there is major construction work or busy roadways.

The Taliban also targets Afghanistan's mobile phone network, which in annual dollar terms represents the country's second largest industry after narcotics. Three of the four main Afghan telecom firms, which service about two million subscribers between them, pay monthly protection fees in each province, or face having their transmission towers attacked.[75] One local businessman, whose firm builds transmission towers, estimated that about one quarter of his company's budget went to protection fees on the roads and at building sites. "Most Taliban, they act just like businessmen in a way," he said. "They tell you: 'We will make sure your people are not kidnapped and your sights are not burned.' But they expect regular payments." In Helmand and Kandahar, the Taliban established a new system in 2009 in which payments had to be paid direct to Quetta, forcing businesses to send representatives to Pakistan to deposit the fees.[76]

The Taliban appeared to be extremely well funded by 2009, using offers of high wages to attract recruits and to fund a strategic push into new districts of operation close to the capital Kabul and in the north and west of the country. NATO officials in 2009 reported that the Taliban were paying contract soldiers between $250 and $300 a month—a hefty wage in a country where the average annual income is less than $500. In December 2009, the coalition boosted salaries for Afghan National Army and police to

$240 monthly to stay competitive, a rate that critics view as unsustainable.[77]

There was also evidence that the insurgents oversaw a mega-supply chain of drugs, explosives, and weapons. Afghan forces in the Kandahari border district of Spin Boldak in 2008 uncovered a network of Taliban trenches holding 237 metric tons of hashish, making it the largest drug seizure in global history. A year later, NATO and Afghan forces made a 91 metric ton seizure in Marjah, in neighboring Helmand Province, which included opium, morphine, heroin, poppy seeds, and precursor chemicals. That was the world's second largest drug seizure. Troops found the stash in an opium market that shared space with a sophisticated Taliban command and communications center, which was stacked with suicide vests, weapons, and components for making improvised explosive devises (IEDs).[78]

The poppy may be grown in Afghanistan and processed along the border into opium base or heroin, but the command and control center of Afghanistan's drug trade, like the insurgency itself, is based in Pakistan, which is off-limits to NATO troops and western law enforcement. "The problem is that even if we work hard to stop this in Afghanistan, the money will still move though Quetta, and we can't get to it," an exacerbated U.S. official told me in 2007.

In addition to receiving payments for extortion fees in Quetta, small, nondescript guesthouses in the Pakistan frontier are routinely used as temporary centers for massive, drug-related financial transactions, which take place roughly once a month to six weeks, according to multiple sources on both sides of the border. In some cases, fighters will come for R&R, and during that time will collect funding and instructions for the next battle. Commanders will also send their financial emissaries to meet the powerful financial committee, which decides how funds are spent. The committee has tremendous influence over which subcommanders rise or drop in the rankings since fighters will win appointments to more lucrative postings according to their fund-raising ability.

"There has always been a healthy competition between the commanders in this regard," said Yusufzai, the veteran Peshawar-based journalist. As happened during the internecine battles of the Soviet resistance, that "healthy competition" sometimes erupts into violence. In one incident in September 2007, state-run Afghan Television reported that eight people died in Kapisa province when fighting broke out between two Taliban commanders over who had the right to collect tax in a given district.

There are tantalizing reports indicating rivalries over money pervade even the highest echelons of the Taliban movement. The former Defense Minister Mullah Obaidullah, who held responsibility for coordinating Taliban military and financial supplies, clashed with the late Mullah Dadullah, the commander of the southern region, according to sources close to the Taliban. Obaidullah worked closely with senior smugglers to export drugs and import weapons. Coordinating with commanders along smuggling routes, he organized protection of drug shipments and negotiated payments in money, weapons and vehicles. Obaidullah clashed with Dadullah after he tried to muscle in on profits and resources in the poppy-rich south.[79]

Dadullah, a fiercely independent commander who ran afoul of Mullah Omar from time to time, also struggled for power with the late Mullah Ahktar Osmani. Osmani's patch included the smuggling hub at Baramcha. After Osmani's death in the December 2006 air strike, there were persistent rumors among insurgent ranks that Mullah Dadullah had passed information about Osmani's whereabouts to NATO authorities in order to wrest control of the lucrative Baramcha market.[80] When Dadullah was killed in a firefight in Baramcha the following year, there were reports Obaidullah had tipped off NATO troops to Dadullah's whereabouts. Mistrust among high-level Taliban officials, and indications that they compete over criminal spoils, could provide opportunities for intelligence and law enforcement agents to play Taliban rivals off each other and weaken the core movement. Sources close to the Taliban suggested Mullah Omar's move in 2009 to exert more control over money streams was in part an effort to settle growing numbers of disputes between greedy commanders.[81]

Representatives of the Quetta Shura sit down with their counterparts from the Haqqani Group and HiG, and also collaborate with members of the Pakistani Taliban and foreign *jihadi* groups including al Qaeda. In these meetings, which occur routinely in Pakistan's tribal areas and the Baluchistan frontier, leaders of the various insurgent factions decide how to divide up control zones and split criminal earnings from district to district.[82] Although the Haqqani group and the HiG had not streamlined the way they collect criminal funds, as have the Taliban, there is a similar upward flow of cash through their command chains. In these zones there are indications that the top commanders—Jalaluddin Haqqani and Gulbuddin Hecmatyar respectively—work closely with foreign *jihadis* linked to al Qaeda to move heroin and other commodities out of the region.

HiG commanders in the mountainous eastern provinces of Kunar and Nuristan have long been tied to protecting shipments of semiprecious gemstones, mainly tourmaline and lapis that are smuggled out of the region, as well as the opium poppy grown in the Pesh and Korengal Valleys. A 2004 U.S. intelligence document seen by the author concluded that HiG commanders would "cooperate or assist any group that paid them." The HiG also protects a bustling illicit timber trade in Korengal, an enterprise that received a boost after the Karzai government tried to regulate and tax timber exports. The insurgents and the timber mafia use long-established smuggling routes to move timber to the Pakistan border, and appear to work in collaboration with the local al Qaeda commander, Abu Ikhlas al Masri, an Egyptian-born militant based in Korengal who married locally during the Soviet resistance and who is considered a key target by American troops operating there.[83] Western counternarcotics and military officials say the HiG keeps about 50 percent of the funds it earns off smuggling, and funnels the other half to allies in Chechnya and Central Asia. "The HIG is a full-fledged narco-terror organization," one western official told me.[84]

The Haqqani network, meanwhile, has demonstrated a much closer relationship in recent years to foreign jihadist elements, staging sophisticated joint attacks including the January 2009 assault on the Serena Hotel in Kabul that left eight dead, a July 2009 car bomb outside the Indian Embassy in Kabul, and a multistage suicide attack at a U.S. military base in Khowst in August of 2008. The group's close links to al Qaeda have raised concern that the group might offer the terror group a sanctuary if it ever regained control of the southeastern zone of Afghanistan where it operates.

The Haqqani group operates a series of camps in the border districts of Paktia province—including Jaji and neighboring Dand Wa Patan, which locals describe as a central station for moving contraband. Local sources and Afghan officials say heroin gets smuggled down from HIG-controlled areas in the east and from labs in Nangarhar, using centuries-old mountain trails long-traveled by traffickers and mujahideen. Haqqani's network protects local smugglers—many of whom are from Haqqani's own Zadran tribe—who move the drugs across the porous border into the Waziristan agencies. From there, Pakistani smugglers pick up the consignments for the onward journey. Smaller loads tend to travel out of Pakistan on flights to the Gulf from the nearby Peshawar Airport. Larger consignments snake west through the tribal areas to Baluchistan province, where they are picked up by new couriers and ferried onward to Iran.

The Haqqani network also extorts commodities moving through its control zones, with a particular focus on timber operations, stone and marble quarries, and weapons smuggling, according to locals in the southeast and Afghan officials. Like the Taliban, insurgents from the Haqqani group also shake down farmers, local businesses, and the telecoms network, and also pillage convoys bringing supplies to the coalition.[85] Perhaps the largest source of income for the Haqqani network is the elaborate cross-border kidnapping it operates in collaboration with the Pakistani Taliban. The most well-publicized case was the abduction of *New York Times* reporter David Rohde, who was kidnapped in Logar province with his driver and translator and driven by his captors across the border into North Waziristan, where he was held for more than seven months.

In a six-part series published in *The New York Times* in October 2009, following Rohde's escape from captivity, he wrote that the Haqqanis "oversaw a sprawling Taliban ministate in the tribal areas with the de facto acquiescence of the Pakistani military." Rohde was held in relative comfort in a compound with electricity and plumbing. The militants, who provided him bottled water and English-language newspapers, took the trouble of driving him several hours to a snowy mountain area in order to film a propaganda video of him that would make it appear as if he was being held in crude conditions. In fact the opposite was true; Rohde wrote later that he observed a state within a state in North Waziristan, where Taliban policemen patrolled the streets and road crews carried out construction projects. "The Haqqani network's commanders and foreign militants freely strolled the bazaars of Miram Shah and other towns," he wrote. "Young Afghan and Pakistani Taliban members revered the foreign fighters, who taught them how to make bombs."[86]

Rohde's case also illuminated a key manner in which the militant mind-set has changed since the last high-profile capture of a Western journalist. *The Wall Street Journal*'s Daniel Pearl, who was beheaded on camera by al Qaeda–linked militants in Karachi, became a grisly political statement for the militants. Rohde was, as his captors put it, "the golden hen," through whom they expected to earn millions in ransom payments.[87] Although his case received considerable media attention, the vast majority of victims of the widening kidnapping industry in Afghanistan and Pakistan are locals, usually from middle-class and wealthy families. Relatives who have negotiated with the captors say militants on both sides of the border somehow obtain detailed financial information about their victims, and use their knowledge about the family's property ownership and income to determine how much they can charge in ransom.[88]

In Pakistan, the involvement of local militants in abductions, extortion, looting, and theft across the tribal areas and the Northwest Frontier Province fueled a widening perception that the Taliban Movement of Pakistan, a loose alliance of five local militant factions known by its Urdu acronym TTP, was little more than a broad gang of thugs. Soaring terrorist violence, as well as fighting between the Pakistani Taliban and the army, which sent 2.5 million people fleeing the tribal belt and the Swat Valley, turned many ordinary Pakistanis firmly against the Taliban, particularly in the country's northwest where they had previously enjoyed a degree of popular support.[89] "They are not friends. They are not our allies," a refugee from Swat told the BBC. "They're our enemies. They are criminals. They are gangsters."[90]

When the Pakistan army inked a February 2009 peace accord with the militants, allowing them to establish sharia law in Swat and neighboring Malakand, the Taliban swept through the area unleashing a wave of senseless violence: Militants blew up barbershops and girls schools and targeted feudal landowners and local police for assassination, hanging the mutilated bodies of their enemies in busy squares.[91] Pakistanis were particularly horrified when a grainy video emerged of Taliban militants flogging a young girl in a pubic square, allegedly for having sex outside marriage.[92]

As the Taliban's shock troops stormed across the scenic valley, long a popular tourist destination for Pakistanis, they looted hotels and resorts, auctioning off thousands of dollars' worth of computers, cutlery, carpets, and furniture from hotels, restaurants, and other tourist venues.[93] In June 2008, militants emptied the Malam Jabba Ski Resort, the country's only alpine destination, burning down half of its stately white hotel and torching the ski lifts.[94] Targeting the tourism industry, which employed more people than any other industry in Swat, enraged locals. In addition, TTP militants went on a thieving rampage, tearing through abandoned homes and shops, along with food storage depots, including a World Food Program warehouse. They commandeered vehicles by the dozen, particularly 4x4 trucks and jeeps from aid groups and the government.[95]

The peace agreement, which ended in April when the Pakistan army launched an offensive that drove out the Taliban, provided the militants a brief and unprecedented opportunity to exploit the rich natural resources and local industry in the verdant valley and beyond. The TTP muscled in on the region's timber trade, collaborating with smugglers to export rare hardwoods and sell them cheaply. By one official count smugglers and Taliban deforested more land in northwest Pakistan in 2008 than in the past two decades put together, an environmental tragedy.[96] In Swat, the Pakistani Taliban reopened three emerald mines that had shut down when fighting began a year earlier, and dumped hundreds of thousands of dollars' worth of gemstones at below-market rates, according to businessmen in the gem business and local media reports.[97] Seizing another opportunity to take over the dominant local industry, the TTP commandeered thirty-five marble factories during their brief takeover of the Buner district, unloading roughly 300 truckloads of marble on the black market and raising by some estimates as much as $719,000 in just one week.[98]

In other parts of Pakistan's northwest, TTP militants hijacked vehicles plying the roads, in particular targeting Pakistani security forces, but also robbing vehicles from ordinary civilians. They were blamed in robberies around the country, including one case where militants robbed a moneychanger in the southern port city Karachi and brought the cash all the way to South Waziristan.[99] By the end of 2009, Pakistanis in several districts had decided they'd had enough, and formed local posses known as "lashkars" to drive back the Taliban, in some cases with support of the Pakistan military.[100]

After a U.S. Predator strike in South Waziristan killed the Pakistani Taliban leader Baitullah Mehsud in August 2009, there were weeks of infighting between rival contenders to take over the group. The position was highly sought after, because it brought both money and power. Not only would the new "emir" nominally control all the Pakistani Taliban factions, he would receive a cut of all their criminal earnings, militants said.[101] By the end of August, there appeared to be consensus that Hakimullah Mehsud, a vicious thirty-one-year-old sidekick of Baitullah, would take over. Some credit Hakimullah's rise through the Pakistani Taliban ranks to his brazen attacks on truck convoys carrying NATO supplies into Afghanistan, a campaign said to raise hundreds of thousands of dollars for the militants. He made a splash at his first press conference with local journalists when he arrived in a U.S. Humvee that he reportedly commandeered in the Khyber Pass, with his bodyguards trailing in a United Nations vehicle he had also stolen.[102]

According to his own handwritten autobiographical sketch, Hakimullah started his career as a young militant fighting amongst the Afghan Taliban in Khowst and Helmand, and was later sheltered by Arab and Uzbek fighters.[103] Ties to foreign militants may have helped him secure the TTP helm, as there were reports that Mullah Omar and the Haqqani network both dispatched emissaries to Waziristan to help negotiate the transition of power following Baitullah's death.[104] Hakimullah's takeover may have brought the TTP even closer to al Qaeda. Under his command, the alliance launched a rash of sophisticated attacks, including a brazen ambush at the Pakistan Army's Rawalpindi headquarters. And in January 2010, Hakimullah Mehsud himself appeared in the suicide video of Humam Khalil Mohammed, the Jordanian doctor and apparent double agent who blew himself up inside an American base in southern Afghanistan, killing seven CIA agents and a Jordanian spy.[105]

The Pakistan military launched a major offensive at the end of 2009 to drive the Pakistani Taliban out of South Waziristan that was described as successful in capturing most of its bases in the difficult terrain along the Afghanistan border.[106] That said, the push may have simply swept the militants into smaller cells scattered around central Pakistan and into Afghanistan.[107] Pakistani intelligence officials and police have privately raised concerns that militants throughout the country may be increasingly supporting smuggling activities, including narcotics. The August 2009 capture of seven militants in Karachi who had both heroin and suicide belts in their possession confirmed their fears. "They provide safe passage to the transporters and smugglers, who smuggle goods from Iran and Afghanistan to Pakistan. In return, they pay them hefty amounts as taxes," said a Pakistani intelligence official, adding that the problem remained especially acute in the border areas.[108]

The militant group that appears to have the deepest reach in the regional drug trade is the Islamic Movement of Uzbekistan (IMU). Founded in the late 1990s by a group of radicals calling for Islamic revolution in Uzbekistan, the group now has fighters scattered across Pakistan's tribal areas and in shifting pockets of Afghanistan. The IMU was cultivated by bin Laden in the 1990s to develop roots in Central Asia. He may have recognized the group's earning potential: Interpol and the DEA have estimated that the IMU controls as much as 70 percent of the heroin trade through Central Asia.[109] "The IMU was deeply involved in drug smuggling from its inception in the Tajik mountains," says Ahmed Rashid, who authored *Jihad*, a book probing extremism in Central Asia. "Since then they have helped expand al Qaeda and Taliban drug smuggling to Central Asia and onto Russia."

While the Taliban was in power, IMU fighters protected heroin shipments leaving Afghanistan through northern routes into Central Asia. As opium output soared under the Taliban, IMU leaders visited Kandahar to brainstorm with bin Laden and Mullah Omar, Rashid reports in *Jihad*. By the time the Taliban banned poppy cultivation in 2000, the UNODC estimated the IMU held a stockpile in northern Afghanistan of more than 240 metric tons.[110] That same year, the U.S. government put the IMU on its list of designated terrorist groups, after receiving intelligence that its operatives were providing information to al Qaeda about the movements of U.S. diplomats stationed in Central Asia.[111]

After the U.S.-led invasion of Afghanistan, IMU fighters fled over the border and reassembled in South Waziristan, in Pakistan's tribal belt. Counterterrorist officials believe Uzbeks served as bin Laden's outer security perimeter while he was hiding out in the Shaghai district of South Waziristan, where he was believed to have fled after escaping the siege at Tora Bora.[112] They also reportedly continued to support smuggling operations through northern and western Afghanistan. One U.S. intelligence report seen by the author described a smuggling route snaking up through Afghanistan's northwest provinces of Baghdis, Faryab, and Jozjan and into Turkmenistan. It was being used as of mid-2004 by "extremists associated with the Taliban, the Islamic Movement of Uzbekistan, and al Qaeda," the report said. Traffickers would move "both heroin and extremists" along the route and "then onwards into other countries in Central Asia," the document said.

IMU fighters are known for being well supplied with weapons, uniforms, and food, for never being short on funds, and for carefully paying local villagers for any supplies they use—often in U.S. dollars, according to tribal contacts. In 2008 and 2009, IMU fighters began working as mentors and militant experts inside local Taliban fighting columns on both sides of the Afghanistan-Pakistan border. A number of Uzbek fighters turned up to support the Pakistani Taliban when they moved in Swat in 2008, according to Pakistani officers and witnesses who conversed with them. In a country where day laborers take home as little as 40 rupees (60 cents), the militants in Swat were hiring soldiers for 200 rupees ($3.35) a day, according to Major General Nasser Janjua, who commanded the Pakistani troops there. As in other areas where the IMU appeared, they were unusually well funded. There are widespread reports that Uzbek and Chechen trainers are now operating inside insurgent fighting columns across the three factions of the Afghan insurgency. Uzbek fighters turned up in Kunduz when Taliban forces swept back into the strategic northern province in 2009, equipped with laptops and satellite transmission devices.[113] The shift into the north may support smuggling activities: One of the main northern routes out of Afghanistan snakes through the province into Tajikistan.

In both Pakistan and Afghanistan the cancer of state corruption greases the wheels for drugs and other smuggled commodities to move smoothly. The fact that instability is vital for the drug trade and other illicit activities creates a powerful disincentive for corrupt Afghan and Pakistani government officials to stabilize their troubled nations.

One report on drug-related corruption within the Karzai administration, compiled by the U.N. and described to the author by one of its authors and numerous officials who read it, mapped out a complex system of kickbacks—very similar to the one existing inside the Taliban. U.N. researchers identified thirty-six districts across Afghanistan—either located in poppy-producing areas or along smuggling routes—where governorships, customs, and police postings were the most sought after. The report estimated officials who won plum assignments stood to earn hundreds of thousands of dollars a month in dirty money. One indicator: the huge sums they would have to kick upstairs just to hold onto their jobs. According to one researcher who contributed to the report, top police officials in lucrative districts might have to pay as much as $40,000 a month for job security.[114]

The U.N. researchers who conducted this study concluded the man at the top of the organizational chain was Ahmed Wali Karzai, the half-brother of the president. He's been implicated in multiple U.S. intelligence reports seen by the author as having ties to the drug trade, and western diplomats say NATO has intercepted him making apparent drug deals on the telephone. As with other senior officials and insurgent commanders who profit from drugs, "you won't see Ahmed Wali actually touching the trade," says a U.N. official who worked on the report. "He has influence over who gets what position—and that gives him extraordinary power." The president's sibling has stoutly denied his ties to the opium trade in the media.

Corrupt officials and Taliban don't negotiate face-to-face over drug smuggling. Rather, smugglers act as go-betweens, working out how to move illicit consignments through specific areas. Sadoo Agha, a poppy farmer in Gereshk, said the local Taliban commander there—who has a force of about twenty full-time fighters—works in partnership with a local smuggler to buy all the opium farmers there grow. "The Taliban commander has the firepower, and the drug dealer has the money," Agha says. They pay off local officials in the district to move the consignments out. "The opium gets transported in police vehicles, or other times I have seen them take opium away in convoys with thirty or more armed men," he said. "You can see that the government officials have secured the route for them, and next week the local police will have new clothes or motorcycles."[115]

Some police officials even cooked up a way to earn money when they have completely lost control of a district they were assigned to protect. "Sometimes, they'll just 'sell' districts to Taliban," complained a senior Interior Ministry official in Kabul. "They'll tell us that they lost control of the area because they are outgunned, but it will be a case of where there aren't more than ten Taliban in their region, and we have posted a hundred police to that district. We all know the game."[116]

The corruption doesn't stop at Afghanistan's borders. Iran, which battles one of the world's highest opium addiction rates, has made concerted efforts to stop Afghan opium from entering its territory, spending more than $400 million a year to fight the problem. It's erected massive ramparts along the border to block smugglers, and lost some 3,400 soldiers and police in battles with drug convoys over the past five years.[117]

However, Iran, like Afghanistan and Pakistan, battles a corruption problem. Multiple sources and western intelligence cables seen by the author report corrupt Iranian intelligence agents are helping to move drug shipments in their vehicles, which have special plates and don't get searched by Iran's anti-drug police. Sources along the border identified a handful of major traffickers, mainly ethnic Baluch, who cooperate with Iranian secret agents to coordinate Taliban attacks on NATO troops.

This would imply there is more than just an issue of corruption at stake, and may suggest a covert effort within Iran's wider strategy to disrupt NATO—and specifically American—activities in Afghanistan. This phenomenon was linked to U.S. Defense Secretary Robert Gates's June 2007 accusation that Iran is supplying weapons to the Afghan insurgency, including plastic explosives being used in deadly IED attacks.

Ever since the 9/11 attacks, when the former Pakistani President Pervez Musharraf was forced to choose between allying himself with George Bush or with Mullah Omar, there have been questions over whether Islamabad really abandoned its support for the Afghan Taliban. Nowhere is this murky issue more troubling than as it relates to the drug trade. To some extent, as in Iran, it's just an issue of corruption. Western officials and people who work in the drug trade alike identify dirty officials within Pakistan's police, intelligence agencies, military, customs, and the Anti Narcotics Force.

U.S. officials increasingly express concerns that levels of drug-related corruption in Pakistan are as bad as they were in the days of the Soviet resistance. In an October 2009 meeting in Islamabad, U.S. Secretary of State Hillary Clinton pledged $103 million in support from Washington for law enforcement and border security efforts, partially aimed at fighting the flow of narcotics.[118] But privately senior U.S. officials say they have little confidence they will see much action from the Pakistanis. "There is no political will in Pakistan to fight this problem," said a U.S. official.[119] The DEA in 2009 shut down a unit of special Pakistani investigators that it had trained and vetted, saying it could no longer vouch for the unit's reliability.

Pakistan arrests an immense number of people on drug-related offenses—more than 34,000 in 2006 alone, for example. However, the vast majority of them are low-level drug users—young men caught with a couple of joints in their pocket. Similar to Islamabad's apparent reticence to go after the Taliban, it's rare to hear of high-level drug traffickers getting apprehended. "Not arresting them is a passive form of assistance," said a Western diplomat. Many believe cooperation goes much deeper. At least one recent ceremony to destroy "heroin" seized by the ANF turned into a major embarrassment when a visiting European counternarcotics official pulled out a drug testing kit and took a sample of the "drugs" about to be burned. The white powder, it turned out, contained just bare traces of heroin, according to another western official who was present at the ceremony. "Every time I hear that Pakistani authorities have made a one-ton seizure, I assume there are ten tons moving down another highway," a European counternarcotics official told me.

As in Iran, elements of Pakistan's ISI help protect the drug trade, according to multiple smugglers who were able to identify specific agents in specific regions, and even knew the sums of money they had been paid off. Whether these cases represented individuals freelancing for profit or provided evidence of a covert state policy is less clear. Musharraf admitted that "retired" Pakistani secret agents may be supporting the insurgents, and some western officials believe these "retirees" coordinate the drug trade to keep the Taliban and other local *jihadi* groups funded. With billions of dollars of drugs moving through Pakistani territory, "it's impossible to imagine that's not happening," a senior U.S. official in Islamabad told me.

A Pakistani customs official, interviewed in Quetta, compared the scale of corruption in the western province Baluchistan to that in neighboring Afghanistan. "The vast majority of provincial officials are corrupted by the drug industry," he said. "This is the condition of our state."[120] He said smugglers who paid off high-ranking Pakistani officials drove around Baluchistan in armored vehicles, protected by well-armed bodyguards, and often wore actual police uniforms, which they obtained from corrupt officers. "Whenever we arrest someone or seize a drug consignment the traders band together and block the roads," he complained. "Before long, senior authorities order us to let them go free."

In order to understand how smuggling networks operated in Afghanistan and Pakistan, I set out to examine the region's most powerful trafficking organization, known as the Khan Group. "The drug industry is being run by businessmen," a veteran counternarcotics official in Kabul told me in 2007. "And they are the best I have ever seen."

5. THE KINGPIN

"HAJI JUMA KHAN HAS TWO HUNDRED HOUSES," SAID A skinny man outside the gate at a sprawling compound in Quetta, in western Pakistan. "And this is one of them."

I had been trying to track down South Asia's number one drug trafficker, the smuggler behind the Taliban, for more than two years. It hadn't been easy. The man known as HJK among counternarcotics agents is so shadowy that few have ever heard his name, even among regional policymakers. Yet Juma Khan's drug empire, which moves as much as $1 billion worth of opium and heroin a year, forms the backbone of the Taliban.

"He is the center of gravity for the Taliban drug trade," a western official told me in 2006. "I find it strange he's not a household name." A 2007 assessment by Afghanistan's spy agency, the National Directorate of Security, listed HJK as that country's premier smuggler. He held the same ranking next door in Pakistan and in Iran, according to officials from those nations. "Juma Khan's forces are terrorists. He pays them to protect his drugs," said General Ali Shah Paktiawal, a senior Afghan police official. "Mullah Omar. Tahir Yuldeshev. Osama bin Laden. They all work for him."[1]

I found his Quetta residence down a dusty, nondescript alley lined with piles of rotting garbage. A white Taliban flag fluttered in the breeze outside the compound next door. It hardly seemed an auspicious address for the region's most powerful kingpin. Another man appeared at the gate and introduced himself as Nematullah. "I am his clerk," Nematullah told me. "Inside this house we all work for Juma Khan." I asked if the boss was in residence, and if I could interview him. "He is on the run and we haven't seen him," said Nematullah. "But please come inside and have a cup of tea."

I briefly pondered his invitation, wondering whether I'd ever see my family again. Like the Burmese drug lord Khun Sa, who financed private armies and generated an estimated $200 million every year in gross profits, Haji Juma Khan's immense wealth made him so powerful that he operated with impunity across Afghanistan, Pakistan, and Iran. When I first asked Kamal Sadat, Afghanistan's former anti-drug police chief, about him in 2004, he rolled his eyes. "I can't find anybody in Kabul who wants me to arrest this guy," he said.

Similar to Pablo Escobar, the Colombian kingpin who packed jetliners with cocaine and maintained a private zoo, HJK, fifty-four, was notorious for his colossal drug shipments and his extravagant lifestyle. For a man who embedded himself with the Taliban and al Qaeda, HJK hardly behaved like his fundamentalist compatriots. "He has many sheep, but even more women," a Kabul police official said.[2] "Juma Khan keeps three wives and so many girlfriends," reported an Afghan diplomat, unable to be more specific. "He loves music and dancing."[3] HJK owns palatial residences in at least six different countries, and it is reported that alcohol-drenched parties hosted by Russian and Turkish prostitutes extended late into the night whenever he was in residence.[4]

Eventually, as I stood outside his gate, my curiosity got the better of me and I followed Nematullah inside. We sat cross-legged on Persian carpets, sipping warm orange Fanta. Veiled women and children peeked around the corner, giggled, and then ran off. Nematullah fetched a man he introduced as his boss, Abdul Karim, who promptly fell over himself trying to convince me he had nothing to do with the Taliban kingpin.

"I have never heard of him," claimed Karim, after I asked if he worked with HJK. When I replied that the other two men had already told me the house belonged to Juma Khan, Karim lit up a cigarette and inhaled sharply. "I don't know the guy," he said. "I just rented this place a year ago."

We chatted for a bit and I inquired about Karim's line of work. "Import-export," he said, waving his cigarette.

"What do you export from here?" I asked.

"Oh, you know," he replied, "whatever needs to be exported."

"These guys say you work for Juma Khan," I said, gesturing to the guard and the clerk, now both staring intently at their feet.

"Work for him? No! I haven't even seen him in years," said Karim.

"So you do know him," I said.

"Well, I met him once, maybe, seven years ago," he said, and then his tone turned pleading. "Who are you? Why do you want to make trouble for me?"

I said I was a journalist and I just wanted to interview his boss. Did he by chance know how to reach him? "It is difficult to find Juma Khan these days because he is hiding in the mountains," said Karim.

"So you do know him," I said again.

"Everyone knows Juma Khan," said Karim, breaking into a wide smile. "He is in the opium business. He is the biggest smuggler there is."

It's tough to pin down hard information about HJK. Part of the reason may be that he comes from a region as obscure as his background. He was born, by most accounts, in Afghanistan's Nimroz Province, the desert outpost jutting between Pakistan and Iran that was once capital of the ninth-century Saffarid dynasty.[5] He comes from a modest background, according to those who know him, and possibly worked as a shepherd in his youth. At the height of his power, the six-foot, three-inch drug lord tended a flock of smugglers, ruffians, and business associates extending from windswept Nimroz and across Iran to Turkey, down through Pakistan into the UAE, with tentacles sprouting up into Central Asia. His terrorist ties were central to his business empire, which came to rival that of the ancient Saffarids in size and reach.

HJK hails from the Mohammed-Hasani tribe of the Brahui people, a Sunni Muslim ethnic group nearly 2 million strong spanning the region between eastern Iran, western Afghanistan, and Pakistan. Historians believe Brahuis immigrated to the remote area about three thousand years ago from the populous Indus Valley region. Linguists interpret their distinct language as grammatically derived from ancient Dravidian tongues. Today, territories the Brahui inhabit are as forbidding and isolated as any on earth. Smuggling is the central livelihood in the tri-border area, where physical boundaries between the three countries scarcely exist. As my research assistants and I trolled the region in search of HJK, virtually everyone we found to be associated with him was Brahui. We found it's not an easy clan for outsiders to penetrate.

In a region where power courses down tribal bloodlines, HJK's is an atypical rags-to-riches story that resounds with tales of his cunning and insatiable lust for money. Afghan and Pakistani officials and tribal contacts say HJK personally came from a humble family. "He was not important in his tribe—not even a rich man," says a tribal elder from the border area. "Haji Juma Khan came from nowhere."[6] It's unclear how he became involved in drugs, and details of his childhood and birthday are unknown. "We know he got his start in the late 1980s," says an Afghan official. "And before that he owned some small businesses and a lot of sheep."[7]

Halfway through the Taliban regime, however, Juma Khan's wealth and influence was clearly established. He built a palatial compound in Zaranj, the barren capital of Nimroz that sits aside the Iranian border. HJK's citadel, which was heavily fortified and guarded by dozens of armed men, dwarfed even the provincial governor's mansion across the street. His massive hundred-vehicle convoys across the Iranian desert soon attracted the attention of counternarcotics officials. "Back then, he was one of the most powerful people in terms of money, people, and big drug consignments," said Hashem Zayyem, an Iranian counternarcotics official.[8]

British counternarcotics police regarded HJK as the man who moved the most contraband from Pakistan's Makran coast into the UAE, according to a former officer. HJK ferried opium and hashish along the narrow channel of the Arabian Sea separating Pakistan from the Arabian Peninsula, coming aground on the stretches of empty coastline between Oman and the UAE. "They would land along the remote beaches and bury their shipments in the sand," said the former British officer.[9]

HJK broke into an opium market fiercely protected by the Quetta Alliance. According to the local lore in southwestern Afghanistan, he has mercilessly purged the area of enemies and rivals, having them gunned down or, in a recent instance, poisoned. His authority eventually came to rival that of Haji Bashir Noorzai, and both men worked closely with the Taliban. "Haji Juma Khan was number three in the movement by the end of their regime," said a U.S. official.[10] He also became close to al Qaeda during the 1990s, according to a CIA document seen by the author. The intelligence report said Khan helped hundreds of Arabs flee Afghanistan into Iran when the U.S.-led invasion began in October 2001.

Incredibly, the towering tribesman was detained by U.S. forces in late 2001 near Kandahar, U.S. officials now admit. Although HJK was known to be involved in drug smuggling and tied to the Taliban, U.S. military intelligence believed he was not a significant threat. U.S. officials naïvely bought his promises to help them track down terrorists. "At the time, the Americans were only interested in catching bin Laden and Mullah Omar," said a European counterterrorism expert in Kabul. "Juma Khan walked."[11] It was a decision they would come to regret. Within three years, his operations expanded even further. The colossal size of his drug shipments amazed authorities. A Pakistani counternarcotics official formerly based in Baluchistan said the Anti Narcotics Force once intercepted a drug cache making its way to the Arabian Sea coast with forty metric tons of morphine base, hashish, and crystal heroin.[12]

By 2004, western intelligence agents identified HJK's drug network as a principal source of funding to the Taliban and al Qaeda and a key conduit for their weapons. He ran a massive refinery and maintained huge underground storage depots in Baramcha, the dusty smugglers town straddling the border between Helmand and Baluchistan.[13] NATO combat helicopters struck those sites in April 2005, working in conjunction with Pakistani helicopters across the border, according to locals from the area. It marked one of the few known occasions that the coalition took military action against a drug dealer.

Once Baramcha got too hot, HJK set up refineries in the remote Chahar Borjak district of southern Nimroz and along the mountainous border with Iran, according to Afghan officials. He also maintained large, hidden weapons caches there, they say. After coming under greater scrutiny, he developed mobile labs, often built on the bed of a Toyota Hilux or hastily erected in people's homes.

HJK also maintained a representative in the Girdi Jungle refugee camp, a notorious smuggling hub along the desolate border in Baluchistan, until it was sealed by Pakistani paramilitary troops in 2007. There, he stored opium grown in Helmand in giant underground bunkers. Consignments going to Iran were handled by two men identified in a U.S. intelligence document seen by the author as Haji Khodi Nazar and Haji Abdul Razzaq. They ran Juma Khan's operations in the Iranian border town of Zahedan. The two men reportedly operated a car showroom as cover for their trafficking activities.

"They would hold opiates, usually heroin, in Zahedan until they had enough to put together a large convoy that would cross Iran to Turkey," the report said. HJK also maintained a representative in Turkey to handle his business affairs at the gateway to Europe, the world's most lucrative heroin market. That associate was an ethnic Baluch named Murtaza who originally came from Quetta, the report said. "His men moved morphine base and heroin from Girdi Jungle and Dalbandin to Iran and then on to the Turkish border," said the Pakistani official.

HJK shifted his shipment tactics once western troops moved into southern Afghanistan. His caravans became more compact—just fifteen to twenty SUVs, which were guarded by fighters armed with heavy machine guns and RPGs. "We have tried to intercept his convoys," said a frustrated interior ministry official formerly posted to Nimroz, "but his connections are very good within the government and the police. He'll get a tip-off that we are coming and pass that information on to the Taliban, and they will come out in force."[14] Seven years after the U.S.-led invasion, HJK's highly equipped forces in Helmand were up against fledgling provincial police who remain "outnumbered, outgunned, and mostly untrained," complained another senior Afghan security official.[15]

In addition to working land smuggling routes, HJK continued to expand his maritime smuggling fleet, which a senior Afghan official said was still HJK's preferred method of moving dope. In May 2004, acting on a tip-off, agents in Pakistan turned up evidence he was moving a fleet of cargo ships between the Pakistani port city of Karachi and the Sharjah emirate, where HJK lived for several years after the Taliban government fell. Under pressure from the United States and the UK, Sharjah authorities eventually ejected HJK. Intelligence agents believed the boats carried contraband out of Karachi and returned laden with weapons—including plastic explosives and anti-tank mines. They would unload their cargo secretly and ship it overland to the militants.[16]

Haji Juma Khan also actively took a role in organizing the insurgency, counternarcotics officials say. "For some time, we knew HJK was meeting directly with Taliban officials who would then sit down with al Qaeda about battle plans," a U.S. official told me. Mirwais Yasini, who used to run Afghanistan's Counter Narcotics Directorate, said: "There are central linkages among Khan, Mullah Omar, and bin Laden."[17]

In May 2004, for example, the CIA station in Kabul cabled that HJK "arranged to have sixteen al Qaeda–affiliated Arabs moved to Iran through Pakistan via Nawzad," according to a document seen by the author. The intelligence report said the Arabs had been previously shifted into Helmand to assist the Taliban in taking control of the poppy-rich province, where HJK happened to be the dominant smuggler. "Haji Juma Khan supported the Taliban because his business was more lucrative under the former Taliban regime," the report noted. At HJK's bidding, the Taliban pressured farmers to increase output across the southwest, Afghan officials say.[18]

Taliban troops helped protect his drug shipments snaking through southwestern Afghanistan, but Afghan security officials say there was little distinction between the insurgents and his personal army. HJK maintained a force of up to 1,500 armed men, operating in border provinces like Farah and Nimroz, where they were often referred to as Taliban by the locals. "They pretend to be Taliban," said an Afghan police official. "But they are just Juma Khan's thugs."[19] One such "thug" is a commander named Mullah Manaf, according to Afghan security officials. He protected HJK's convoys as they headed west through the desert wasteland of southern Nimroz in return for Toyota Land Cruisers, Thuraya satellite telephones, and weapons.[20]

Using Manaf and other henchmen, Haji Juma Khan also dabbled in kidnapping, people smuggling, and extortion, security officials say. In 2005, for example, his men took two Turkish businessmen hostage in the Iranian border area and brought them to Baramcha, according to General Ali Shah Paktiawal, a senior Kabul police official. HJK demanded 1 million euros each for their release.[21] He was tied to the 2007 kidnapping of two French aid workers in Nimroz, along with three of their local colleagues, according to security officials in Nimroz and Kabul. And a recently unsealed U.S. indictment linked HJK to the January 2008 attack on the Serena Hotel in Kabul, which killed six people.[22] He also funded a large madrassa in Pakistan that schools as many as 1,500 students at a time, according to an intelligence document on his operations seen by the author, which said he uses the school to "talent-spot potential employees or militia members."

Though tied to the Taliban and al Qaeda, HJK maintained an unparalleled Rolodex of corrupt government officials he could call on for help across South Asia and the Persian Gulf. HJK's strength came not just from his ties to terrorists, but from his ability to build networks and corrupt people in power wherever he chose to operate. In Afghanistan, his network continues to pay off provincial governors, security agents, regional military commanders, and senior officials in the Highway Police, according to western officials and intelligence documents.

A March 2004 British intelligence document seen by the author suggested his influence extended even to Hamid Karzai's half-brother Ahmed Wali. The MI6 document said HJK allegedly used the president's sibling as a conduit to bribe southern governors "to allow narcotics to be processed and transported through their provinces without impediment." A 2009 *New York Times* report identifying Ahmed Wali as a beneficiary of CIA money also indicated that HJK had teamed up with the president's brother. The report said an Afghan informant to the DEA claimed that HJK and Wali Karzai took over a portion of Haji Bashar Noorzai's business after Noorzai's 2005 arrest.[23] The Afghan president and his brother vehemently deny Ahmed Wali's links to heroin. "I was never in the drug business, I never benefited, I never facilitated, I never helped anyone with the transportation of any kind," Ahmed Wali said in June 2006.[24]

Narcotics leaving southwestern Afghanistan follow three general routes. The first goes directly into Iran from Nimroz and Farah provinces. The second dips down into Pakistan's Baluchistan Province and then heads west for Iran. A third smuggles drugs south to Pakistan's Makran Coast and then by boat to the Persian Gulf. Either way, corrupt officials in Iran and Pakistan were essential to HJK's operations. He paid off a wide network of police, border guards, and intelligence agents in both countries, according to smugglers, officials, and western intelligence documents seen by the author.

A British intelligence report titled "Trafficking Network of Haji Juma Khan Mohammad Hasani," shown to the author, identified a "brother" of Haji Juma Khan named Shah Hussein who runs his operations from a nondescript travel agency on Jinnah Road, the main drag through downtown Quetta. I found the office, right where the document said it would be, walked inside, and asked if a man named Shah Hussein worked there. "He runs the place," said an agent who was ringing up a plane ticket for a customer. "He's right through that door."

I sat down with Shah Hussein, and we exchanged the customary pleasantries. He said he was a Brahui from Dalbandin and offered me a cup of tea. I said I was an American journalist and inquired about his travel agency. "Business is down," he said. "The economy is not good." I asked if he was the owner and he said he was a junior partner.

"How interesting," I said, "because, I am here looking for one of your partners. I am trying to find Haji Juma Khan."

Shah Hussein then launched into a familiar routine about how he had never heard of or met anyone named Haji Juma Khan. "But everyone says he is your business partner," I said to him.

"I have not seen him for a long time," he said. "Maybe seven years."

"So you do know him," I said.

"Know him? I mean, I have heard of him, maybe we met once, I don't really know," he said, now visibly sweating. "Who are you again?"

"I'd like to meet him," I said. "Do you know how he can be reached?"

"That's not possible," he said, then added quickly, "I mean, I don't know where he is." My local colleague Naqeeb and I pressed him for a few more minutes, and I left my business card with my phone number. "Please ask him to call me if you hear from him," I said.

"I don't know why you are asking me," he said weakly, "I just sell plane tickets."

However, the British intelligence report I saw claimed Hussein paid bribes on HJK's behalf totaling $2 million to Pakistani intelligence officers based in the capital of Baluchistan Province. "The bribes have been given to the MI [Military Intelligence] Corps Commander and the ISID [ISI] Colonel based in Quetta to ensure the safe passage of HJK's narcotics consignments transiting Pakistan," the report said.

As a result of the payoffs, Hussein had received MI and ISI identity cards so vehicles carrying drugs would not have trouble passing checkpoints manned by police and the Anti Narcotics Force, the report claimed. One frustrated Pakistani inspector called the Taliban, the smugglers, and the intelligence agencies an "evil troika," and said five close associates of HJK who had been arrested by police and ANF in Baluchistan were released on orders of the ISI within two weeks.[25]

A smuggler moving opium across the empty stretch of desert in Baluchistan leading to the Iran border explained how the teams operate once they cross out of Afghanistan. "We go on half-moon nights, putting a guy out front on a motorcycle," he said. The spotter will travel three to ten miles ahead of the convoy, helping the caravan choose its route across the shifting sands, and making sure the coast is clear. The spotter will communicate with the caravan using a wireless radio or Thuraya satellite phone. "Normally, our agents have paid off the intelligence officials and the Frontier Corps, so we know where the checkpoints are," he said. "When you hear of a drug package being confiscated by the authorities, you can be sure it was a deal fixed in advance."[26]

A similar system appears to exist in Iran. A June 2004 CIA cable from Kabul reported HJK would move his shipments to the Iranian border in small convoys where it was transferred into vehicles belonging to Iranian intelligence agents, whose cars would not get searched at police and customs checkpoints. The Iranian agents transported the contraband to Tehran or all the way to the Turkish border, the report said. When one of HJK's associates was arrested in early 2004 in Zahedan, the province bordering Nimroz, with more than a ton of hashish and three hundred tons of morphine base, HJK used his connections with the provincial intelligence chief to secure the man's release. The Iranian spy subsequently claimed the drugs to be a "seizure" and "an indication of his service's achievements" in the fight against drugs, the CIA report said.

Family ties matter greatly within HJK's Brahui-run operations. The 2004 British intelligence report detailed his most trusted representatives in Afghanistan, Pakistan, Iran, Turkey, and the UAE. The informant quoted in the report was described as "an established and reliable source with direct access." He identified HJK's two closest deputies as his "brothers" and gives their names only as Torakai and Shah Hussein. The source described Torakai as HJK's "right-hand man, who often travels with HJK and brokered contacts and meetings for him." Shah Hussein, the contact said, was based in Quetta and handled liaisons with Pakistani authorities "designed to protect HJK's illegal business interests." In interviews, Afghan officials have identified HJK's brothers by other names: Haji Sharif and Mohammed Yar. Another intelligence report also mentioned Mohammed Yar, describing him as a close associate but not mentioning family ties.

A "nephew" named Sharafuddin is another key lieutenant mentioned in several intelligence reports who oversees operations in Baramcha and "makes contacts" with Afghan and UAE authorities.

The British report and Pakistani officials also identify Haji Hafiz Akhtar as another nephew and chief of operations. "He was responsible for acquiring, processing and dispatching the opiates," the British report said. All his top deputies are relatives, "although it is not strictly clear how," according to the report, which I saw. Unraveling the family tree and discrepancies in names is complex, since many Afghans—especially those who deal in illegal activity—go by various names, nicknames, and honorific titles. "Juma Khan" itself literally translates "Mr. Friday."

The fact that his corrupt network extended across three countries—and reached down into the UAE as well—gave the organization an unprecedented ability to switch alliances in a region where loyalties shift more often than the sands. Insiders say HJK was close to the ISI during the Taliban regime but appeared to shift away from the Pakistani spy agency when the Musharraf government distanced itself from jihadi groups under post-9/11 pressure from Washington. In the weeks immediately after the fall of the Taliban—during which time HJK was briefly picked up by U.S. authorities—he apparently even traded information with CIA and U.S. military intelligence agents to secure his release, a western official says. "It is widely known they worked with people who had the capacity to get them to places. One was HJK, and another was Bashir Noorzai," the official told me. "Many now ask the question: 'When did the U.S. military and the CIA know the two men were involved in drugs?'"[27]

Afghan security officials believe HJK shifted alliances again around 2005, positioning himself as the central link between the Taliban and the subsequent surge of Iranian weapons, including shaped charges used to deadly effect against NATO troops. In June 2007,

U.S. defense secretary Robert Gates complained that Iranian-made weapons were increasingly falling into Taliban hands, admitting, "We do not have any information about whether the government of Iran is supporting this, is behind it, or whether it's smuggling."[28] In fact, Afghan military and intelligence officials have unearthed evidence that HJK set up a meeting between the late Mullah Dadullah and Iranian intelligence agents to organize the flow of weapons to the insurgency. "HJK is the link between Iranian intelligence and the recent rash of IED attacks," an Afghan official told me. "I have been telling the Americans for a year now that Iran has become a bigger worry than Pakistan for us."[29]

Despite the long-established and well-greased routes south and west, officials and smugglers say HJK also expanded northward, building new smuggling routes through the Central Asian states of Uzbekistan and Turkmenistan. That's in part due to a crackdown along the Pakistan border by NATO-led troops in Afghanistan. Pakistani authorities made it riskier to operate in the Girdi Jungle refugee camp. The new northern traffic may also indicate a greater role for the IMU, the Uzbek terrorists controlling much of the trade through the former Soviet republics. Sources say drugs tend to move north in smaller packets—often using human carriers who travel with loads no heavier than five kilograms.

In April 2004, Haji Juma Khan purchased an entire town in Nimroz Province, according to interviews with locals and a western intelligence document shown to the author. The village, known as Rudbar, is strategically located along the desert highway linking Baramcha to the tri-border area known as Rabat-e-Jali, a notorious gateway for smugglers and terrorists moving between Pakistan, Afghanistan, and Iran. The intelligence report shown to the author says HJK planned to "parcel out the land to members of his tribe," and in return they would cultivate poppy and wheat.

Rudbar's location in the forbidding "Desert of Death" did not put off the region's most powerful trafficker, according to locals. He simply ordered the construction of a massive artificial lake and dug irrigation canals. Locals say HJK's desert lair rises out of the desolate moonscape like a mirage, with hundreds of palm trees and twenty-four-hour electricity, wholly supplied by industrial generators.

HJK also maintained homes in Quetta's Satellite Town, the affluent Defense Colony of Karachi, and Wazir Akhbar Khan, the upscale Kabul neighborhood home to western embassies and NGOs. He owned other residences in Dubai, Sharjah, Iran, and Saudi Arabia, according to western and Afghan officials. He traveled between countries using as many as twelve different passports from Iran, Afghanistan, and Pakistan, which he changed often.[30] "He sometimes dressed in military uniform or wore a western suit rather than traditional Afghan clothing," says an Afghan security agent.[31] Officials and those who know him say that, despite his height, HJK is relatively nondescript-looking and a master at blending in. One contact from Baramcha described a time when he disguised himself as a shepherd—his former trade—to evade authorities.[32]

Accounts of HJK's excesses veer into the realm of hyperbole. "You go into his house on any given night, and a hundred people will be served," one local said breathlessly. "He likes Russian ladies, Iranians, and he keeps the most handsome boys."[33] The excessive lifestyle caught up with him in 2006, when, according to a former senior U.S. counternarcotics official, HJK was diagnosed with skin cancer. At the same time, he reached out to senior Afghan and western authorities and began talking about going straight. "One school of thought was that he believed he had a terminal illness and wanted to make right with his maker before he died," said the official.[34]

Negotiations advanced to a point where the kingpin actually visited the NATO-run Kandahar Air Base for talks with western officials, according to an Afghan official. The offer was that HJK would go clean and write the Kabul government an enormous check compensating for his untaxed wealth. After months of negotiations, HJK reneged. Western officials concluded he feared retribution from business partners who stood to lose money, and possibly realized his malignant lesions weren't going to kill him anytime soon. The episode forced HJK underground, according to locals in his area and officials.

On October 24, 2008, the Afghan kingpin resurfaced again— this time in the Southern District Court of Manhattan, where he appeared before a federal judge. "I am not guilty," he declared through an interpreter, before being whisked off to the Metropolitan Correctional Center, where he was put in solitary confinement.[35] Details of how he ended up in the United States remain murky. The official story given to media covering his arraignment was that Indonesian authorities had detained HJK on October 23 when he landed in Jakarta on a flight from Dubai, and then handed him over to U.S. officials.[36] But then how could the Brahui kingpin have ended up in a Manhattan courtroom half a world away barely twenty-four hours later? The timeline didn't add up. Speaking on condition of anonymity, federal officials later gave another story: HJK traveled to Indonesia believing he was about to land a major drug deal. But in fact, the men HJK was working with were counternarcotics agents working with the DEA. They lured him to Jakarta, where he was arrested, handed over to U.S. authorities, and whisked to New York. Khan's defense attorney, Steve Zissou, calls that version a fiction as well. "He is the victim of a misguided and inconsistent Bush policy against the tribal leaders of southern Afghanistan," Zissou said. "Haji Juma Khan is not responsible for distributing heroin into the United States."[37]

However, Khan is one of the first smugglers ever to be charged under the new narco-terrorism statute, meaning that federal prosecutors won't have to prove he smuggled dope to U.S. shores, only, as his indictment says, that he "supported the Taliban's efforts to forcibly remove the United States and its allies from Afghanistan by providing support in the form of drug proceeds to the Taliban."[38]

Michele M. Leonhart, the acting DEA chief, said in a press release that Khan's capture "disrupts a major line of credit to the Taliban, and will shake the foundation of his drug network that has moved massive quantities of heroin to worldwide drug markets."[39] But even that is unclear. News of his arrest barely caused a ripple inside Afghanistan or out, and months later residents in his main area of operations appeared not to even know the kingpin was behind bars. Rather, the border-straddling town of Baramcha remained in control of Taliban forces, and sources said HJK's key lieutenants, all members of his Mohammed-Hasani tribe, continued to smuggle narcotics as usual.[40]

Officials and sources on both sides of the border identified Haji Hafiz Akhtar, HJK's nephew and chief of operations, as the man who now runs the business, operating from Baramcha on the Pakistani side of the border. NATO forces briefly detained Akhtar in

2009 when he ventured into Afghan territory. But under controversial new Rules of Engagement, under which detainees must be handed over to the Afghan government within three days, Akhtar was a free man again and back in business in no time. "He was so confident he wouldn't get picked up, he continued using the same satellite phone," said a U.S. military official.[41]

Authorities in Pakistan identified Sharafuddin as another key player, saying he runs a fabric shop in the bazaar in Dalbandin, which doubles as a legal front for the business and also provides a meeting place for high-level associates.[42] A Pakistani intelligence official identified Shah Hussein, the man who runs the Quetta Travel Agency, as a critical player in coordinating onward movement of drug shipments once they leave Afghanistan.[43] Sources say Sharafuddin and Shah Hussein pay off officials in the Afghan National Army and the Afghan police, as well as Pakistani security officials who man checkpoints in the border areas. Payments are handsome—as high as 50,000–60,000 Pakistani rupees ($600–$800) even to low level guards—to get drug convoys through.[44] Critically, the sources say there has been little disruption to the network since "Juma Khan was a wise man," as one border source put it. "He only promoted his most trusted nephews, who never quarrel over the business."[45]

Like many top smugglers, HJK covered his tracks by investing in real estate and operating "legal" front companies that import cars and electronics, officials say. Unlike most Afghan drug traffickers, who rely on the unregulated *hawala* network to move funds, Juma Khan "was unusual because he used formal bank accounts in Dubai," a March 2005 western intelligence document said. Western officials

Helmand, Afghanistan, April 2006: A member of the Afghan eradication force cuts opium poppies in a field near Lashkar Gah as the villager who planted it looks on. Afghan forces were supervised by the American security contractor DynCorp. JOHN MOORE/GETTY IMAGES

Helmand, April 2006: Gretchen Peters interviews poppy farmers. JOHN MOORE

Director of Central Intelligence

National Intelligence Daily

The Taliban continues to institutionalize its involvement in narcotics trafficking activities despite their public opposition to narcotics-related activities on religious grounds and pledge to work with the UN Drug Control Program to reduce opium poppy cultivation. the Taliban are still taxing narcotics shipments moving through Taliban-controlled territory.

— Under one such agreement, the son of key Quetta Alliance member pays the Taliban about $230 for each kilogram of either heroin or morphine base being exported through the Jalalabad and Qandahar airports.

Close-up of a *Top-Secret National Intelligence Daily* by the CIA (dated May 1, 1988) titled "Taliban Endorses Increased Opium Production," declassified in September 2004. A copy of the document is held at the National Security Archive, George Washington University.

Heroin in Pakistan
Sowing the wind

Narcotics and the Military

There is disagreement among narcotics experts and investigative journalists in Pakistan about the degree of military involvement in narcotics trafficking. The more commonly held
view is that while individual officers in the armed forces have
become involved in trafficking, the Army as an institution is
not involved. During the eight year period of Martial Law under General Zia ul Haq (1977-1985), a number of officers did
become involved in narcotics. These were mostly Majors who
headed Martial Law Courts and started by taking bribes from
those accused in narcotics cases. In the early 1980s, the Army
charged thirteen Majors and two Brigadiers in narcotics corruption cases. Some of these men — Major Afridi, Major
Javed, Major Zahoor — escaped from custody and became
more deeply involved as traffickers connected to the Frontier
mafias.

Many observers believe the cases involving the Majors and
the Brigadiers was only the tip of the iceberg and that corruption in the military over narcotics and commissions on weapons sales, etc. was more extensive. There are rumors that the
previous Corps Commander at Lahore (IV Corps), Lieutenant-
General Mahsud Alam Jan, made a lot of money by facilitating
the movement of narcotics from the Frontier to Lahore and on
to India. Certainly, the substantial number of officers living
well beyond their means has been noted for well over a decade.
The previous Chief of the army Staff (COAS), General Mirza
Aslam Beg, attempted to restore the Army's professionalism after the Zia years. His successor, General Asif Nawaz Janjua,
continues this policy, including the retirement of officers who
cannot account for their sudden wealth.

The one broadly accepted exception to the Army's unin-
volvement as an institution in narcotics is the role of the Inter-Services Intelligence Directorate (ISID). Many believe
the ISI allowed Afghan Resistance groups to trade in narcotics after the cut off of US assistance and that individual ISI
officers participated in the trade, either as part of sanctioned
operations or to enrich themselves.

Above: Close-up of an undated top-secret CIA study on the heroin trade in Pakistan that
was leaked to the Lahore-based weekly newspaper *The Friday Times* and reprinted in full
in September 1993. COURTESY OF *THE FRIDAY TIMES*

Opposite: Close-ups of a U.S. State Department cable, dated December 1988, from former
U.S. ambassador to Pakistan Robert Oakley to Washington, D.C., outlining concerns the
heroin trade was being funded and supported by the mujahideen and the ISI. A copy of
the document is held at the National Security Archive, George Washington University.

2. SUMMARY: WIDESPREAD PAKISTANI BRIEF THAT AFGHAN
WAR HAS CAUSED MAJOR UPSWING IN NARCOTICS TRAFFIC AS
WELL AS AVAILABILITY OF WEAPONS IS WELL FOUNDED.
NOT ONLY HAS WAR RESULTED IN FLOW OF LARGE AMOUNT OF
WEAPONRY TO PAKISTAN, IT HAS ALSO LED TO INCREASE IN
HEROIN TRAFFIC INTO AND THROUGH PAKISTAN, THROUGH
HANDS OF AFGHAN REFUGEES AS WELL AS PAKISTANIS. WE
AND GOP BELIEVE THE SITUATION WILL BECOME MUCH WORSE
IN TERMS OF BOTH HEROIN AND ARMS ENTERING PAKISTAN
FROM AFGHANISTAN AS WAR WINDS DOWN UNLESS URGENT,
EFFECTIVE MEASURES ARE TAKEN RIGHT AWAY. THE FIGHT
AGAINST "HEROIN-KALASHNIKOV CULTURE" IS ALMOST AS
CRITICAL TO PAKISTAN'S FUTURE SECURITY AS THE FIGHT
AGAINST SOVIET DOMINATION OF AFGHANISTAN HAS BEEN.
END SUMMARY.

THE SHIPMENTS THROUGH BALUCHISTAN GO IN
HEAVILY-ARMED CARAVANS, AND OBSERVERS IN THE AREA
SAY BOTH AFGHAN RESISTANCE PARTIES AND ISI ARE
DIRECTLY INVOLVED.

12. WE AND THE GOP HAVE A CHANCE TO PREVENT THIS
GLOOMY SCENARIO FROM ECOMING REALITY IF WE STEP IN
NOW, WHILE THE POLITICAL OPPOSITION IS TEMPORARILY
OFF BALANCE AND BEFORE THE DRUG BARONS FURTHER
CONSOLIDATE THEIR POWER. THE NEW GOVERNMENT NEEDS
AND HAS REQUESTED OUR HELP IN ITS MOVE TO GET A
HANDLE ON NARCOTICS WITH MONEY, EQUIPMENT, EXPERTISE
AND MORAL SUPPORT.

13. AS THE AMOUNT OF HEROIN INCREASES, SO WILL
PRESSURES TO EXPORT IT TO WESTERN MARKETS, AND ALSO
TO USE MONEY AND ARMS TO DO IT. BOTH WILL BE
READILY AVAILABLE, WITH ARMS NO LONGER NEARLY AS
IMPORTANT FOR MILITARY USE, AND A GREAT NEED FOR
MONEY AMONG RETURNING REFUGEES TO SUPPORT THEIR
FAMILIES. UNDEREMPLOYED AFGHANS AND THEIR WEAPONS
CAN BE EXPECTED TO ADD TO ARMED BANDS ALREADY ACTIVE
IN PAKISTAN IN CRIMINAL ACTIVITIES AND PROTECTION OF
NARCOTICS TRAFFICKING. THIS COULD AGGRAVATE
SITUATION IN THOSE PARTS OF NWFP AND BALUCHISTAN
WHICH ARE ALREADY ALMOST BEYOND GOP CONTROL (EXCEPT
AS RESULT OF MILITARY OPERATIONS). IT COULD ALSO
RECREATE EARLIER SITUATION IN SIND WHERE PARTS OF
RURAL AND URBAN AREAS WERE VIRTUALLY BEYOND CONTROL
OF GOP.

14. KABUL MINIMIZE CONSIDERED.

OAKLEY

Top left: Dawood Ibrahim, the only individual designated both a "Global Terrorist Supporter" and a "Foreign Narcotics Kingpin" by the U.S. government. INTERPOL PHOTO, UNDATED

Top right: Osama bin Laden brokered a deal to smuggle drugs with Ibrahim, according to the U.S. Treasury Department. FBI PHOTO, UNDATED

Bottom left: Haji Bashir Noorzai. U.S. GOVERNMENT PHOTO, UNDATED

Bottom right: Haji Juma Khan. U.S. GOVERNMENT PHOTO, UNDATED

Haji Juma Khan's alleged travel agency in Quetta, Saleem Travels (July 2008).
GRETCHEN PETERS

A hospital in Quetta, owned by a prominent Helmand-based opium smuggler, that is known to treat Taliban soldiers (July 2008). GRETCHEN PETERS

Mullah Dadullah, the former southern commander of the Taliban killed in 2007, tried to muscle in on drug profits, according to sources close to the Taliban leadership.
OPEN SOURCE PHOTOS, UNDATED

Above and opposite: In December of 2003, a U.S. Navy boarding team operation from the guided missile destroyer USS *Decatur* (DDG 73) discovered an estimated two tons of hashish aboard this forty-foot dhow intercepted in the Arabian Gulf. The dhow's twelve crewmembers were taken into custody and transferred to USS *Decatur,* and *Decatur* sailors took control of the dhow. The smuggling routes are known to be used by al Qaeda and three of the crew members were believed to have links to the organization.

PHOTOGRAPHER'S MATE 2ND CLASS MICHAEL SANDBERG, COURTESY OF U.S. NAVY

Top: Mawlawi Jalaluddin Haqqani (born c. 1950) controls the southeastern flank of the Taliban from his base in Miramshah, in Pakistan's North Waziristan Agency. A legendary mujahideen fighter from the anti-Soviet resistance, he is widely suspected of having smuggled guns and drugs since the 1980s. ASSOCIATED PRESS PHOTO, UNDATED

Bottom: Siraj Haqqani, the son of Jalaluddin, has a $200,000 price on his head from the NATO-led coalition, which believes he has effectively taken over day-to-day operations from his father. SKETCH PROVIDED BY U.S. FORCES IN AFGHANISTAN

Top: Southern Afghanistan, January 1988: Former DEA agents Chuck Carter (second from right) and Richard Fiano (third from right) sit in front of bags of narcotics confiscated at a lab during Operation Jihad. The drug in the bags was likely morphine base that had been mixed with a bleaching agent to make it white. RICHARD FIANO

Bottom: Southern Afghanistan, January 1988: Carter (left front) and Fiano (front center) walk with mujahideen during Operation Jihad. RICHARD FIANO

Drums of chemicals cooking raw opium to refine it into morphine base (January 1988). Refineries in southern Afghanistan have not changed since the late 1980s, according to counternarcotics officials who have visited them, but most images of labs in Taliban-held areas are classified. RICHARD FIANO

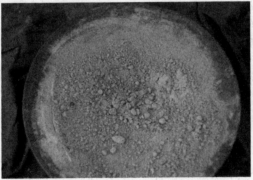

Top: Bags of heroin confiscated at a lab during Operation Jihad. RICHARD FIANO

Bottom: A bowl of chemicals found at a lab raided during Operation Jihad. RICHARD FIANO

Gretchen Peters visits poppy fields with the poppy eradication force (April 2006). JOHN MOORE

are now watching the region's financial flows more closely, trying to track patterns that may suggest where opium profits end up— and how they will be used, both by the drug kingpins and by their extremist partners.

6. FOLLOW THE MONEY ⠂⠒⠄

WE SAT IN A DUBAI CAFÉ DRINKING CAPPUCCINOS WHILE
Riaz explained to me how the boss of South Asia's underworld
launders millions of dollars of Afghan drug money.

"Every big player in dirty business will have a dozen guys like
me to make their operations look clean," Riaz explained.[1] And he
should know. For about a decade, Riaz laundered money for Dawood Ibrahim, the undisputed crime lord of South Asia.

Wanted in India for his role in the 1993 Mumbai blasts that
killed hundreds and accused of smuggling massive narcotics shipments into the UK and Europe, Ibrahim has the dubious distinction of being the only person Washington has designated both a
"Global Terrorist Supporter" and a "Foreign Narcotics Kingpin."[2]
The son of a police constable, Ibrahim started out as a small-time
hood in Mumbai, graduating to extortion, murder for hire, and
gold smuggling. He bought off Mumbai's cops, pitted Muslims
and Hindus against each other, and dabbled in Bollywood and fixing
cricket matches. In 1984, he fled India for Dubai, where he transformed his D-Company gang into a global crime conglomerate.
After the 1993 Mumbai blasts, even freewheeling Dubai wouldn't
have him anymore. Ibrahim took refuge in Karachi, reportedly under
protection of the ISI.[3]

That's when D-Company began working in the region's opium

trade. Ibrahim "traveled in Afghanistan under the protection of the Taliban" in the late 1990s and brokered a financial arrangement to share smuggling routes with "Osama bin Laden and his terrorist network," a U.S. government fact sheet says.[4] "If you want to understand what Osama bin Laden is up to," a former senior CIA official told me, "you have to understand what Dawood Ibrahim is up to."[5]

Today, Ibrahim is believed to play a major role in laundering drug proceeds from the Afghan opium market. Like bin Laden, he remains at large, reportedly spending most of his time behind the high walls of a Karachi mansion. Around the globe, agents from India, Interpol, the CIA, the DEA, and the Treasury Department are building a case against him. "Dawood's involvement in drugs and terrorism is undeniable," a senior U.S. official told me. Proving it won't be easy. As Riaz explained it, moving dirty money is hardly rocket science. D-Company and numerous organizations like it use surprisingly simple techniques to make sure that drug and terror money slips past the notice of authorities.

Two weeks after the 9/11 attacks, President Bush gathered media in the Rose Garden to declare war on al Qaeda's financing. "Money is the lifeblood of terrorist operations," he said. "Today we're asking the world to stop payment."[6] The following month, he launched Operation Green Quest, a law enforcement program to block terrorist funding. "The same talent pool and expertise that brought down Al Capone," the Treasury Department boasted in a press release, "will now be dedicated to investigating Osama Bin Ladin and his terrorist network."[7] By December, the U.S. government and allied nations had frozen the assets of 150 known terrorists, their organizations, and their bankers in the United States and abroad, blocking about $66 million.[8] However, the trail of terrorist money quickly went cold. As of 2006, bank assets frozen by U.S. authorities climbed to a little more than $300 million.[9] "Compared to what's sloshing around," one federal official complained to me, "that's a pimple on a pig's ass."

Experts in terrorism finance say the U.S. government is no closer to stopping funds reaching terror groups because it's looking for the money in the wrong places. "We look for dirty money in western institutions," says John Cassara, a former U.S. Treasury special agent and author of *Hide and Seek*. "The methods we use to track crime don't translate to what is going on."[10]

It is impossible to overstate how crucial it is to get this right. U.S. authorities so far have focused on catching high-value targets within al Qaeda and the Taliban, rather than going after the system supporting them. As Robert Charles, the former counternarcotics chief at the State Department, puts it: "It's as if we stumbled upon a combustion engine and we are reaching in trying to grab the individual pistons, and forgetting we should just cut the flow of gasoline."[11] Eight years after 9/11, the single greatest failure in the war on terror is not that Osama bin Laden continues to elude capture, or that the Taliban has staged a comeback, or even that al Qaeda is regrouping in Pakistan's tribal areas and probably planning fresh attacks on the West. Rather, it's the spectacular incapacity of western law enforcement to disrupt the flow of money that is keeping their networks afloat.

U.S. financial crime agents have suspected that drug money was helping fund Islamic extremists since the 1990s, but there has been little systematic investigation into the links between drug profits and terrorism. "We have made virtually no progress following that money," says Cassara. "I am beside myself with frustration."

It's easy to become discouraged when you start looking at the scope of the problem. The trading zone that groups Afghanistan, Pakistan, and the UAE is the financial world's Wild West, where there are disincentives to going legal. Corruption is rife, law enforcement shoddy, and tax evasion the norm. The vast majority of payments—even legal ones—for big ticket items like cars and homes are made in cash, sometimes suitcases of it. Walk into any money-changing market from Kabul to Dubai and you will see dozens of *hawaladars* counting knee-high stacks of $100 bills— literally millions of dollars in cash. The *hawaladars* balance their accounts in grimy notebooks, but keep few records of who sent what to whom for authorities to scrutinize. No one has any idea how much they transfer across borders each year, not to mention how much of it is "legal."

Since 2001, the UAE, Pakistan, and Afghanistan have adopted or at least drafted laws banning money laundering and tightened regulations on bank transfers. However, there's been limited success in tracking money flowing outside the banking system, and no effort to go after those appearing to break the law. Most Afghan opium is actually bartered for commodities, including cars and electronic goods, meaning there's virtually no money trail to follow. "None of these countries watch their trade data," an exasperated western official told me, "and more than half of the goods are smuggled anyway." Drug money flows along a different route than the opium, agents say, often bouncing through Russia and South Africa and usually passing through Dubai, the flashy free-trade emirate that's a hub for money laundering and underground banking.

The funding for 9/11 passed through Dubai, and Abdul Qadeer (A.Q.) Khan's network went there to flog nuclear technology. "Whether it's drug smuggling, people trafficking, or money laundering, all roads lead to Dubai," says Cassara. If you are a drug smuggler, it would be hard to find a more accommodating region to launder your money. And what better place to park your dirty cash than a bustling sheikdom in the oil-rich Persian Gulf?

I traveled the region's money markets, ports, stock exchanges, and border crossings to try to map out how drug money was being laundered. Here's a compilation of the most common techniques for moving or hiding dirty money (not just drug cash):

Hawala

For millions of people across the world with no access to bank accounts—most of them migrant workers—the informal money transfer network known as *hawala* is the cheapest, fastest, and easiest way to transfer money.[12] In Afghanistan, where few banks operate outside Kabul, *hawala* is crucial to the legal economy. A 2003 World Bank study calculated that international aid groups funneled $200 million in emergency, development, and reconstruction money through the *hawala* market after the fall of the Taliban, for example.[13] The informal transfer system is also heavily penetrated by drug dealers, criminals, and Islamic extremists, officials say.

Riaz, who used to move payments from D-Company's gold-smuggling proceeds, says, "Now all they do is launder drug money." No matter what the proceeds pay for, the system works the same. Say Riaz wanted to transfer $100,000 from India to Dubai to pay off a gold shipment. Through trusted *hawala* agents he would locate a group of Indian laborers in Dubai who wanted to send their salaries back home to their families. Once the agent had put together $100,000 worth of wages, plus his 20 percent commission, he would coordinate a "transfer" with another agent in India, and the two would simply zero their balance sheets. No money would ever cross borders, making it virtually untraceable.

The Indian migrant workers never knew they were tied to an illegal deal—not that records were kept anyway. *Hawala* operates on a basis of trust: the agents on either side of the transaction simply select a confirmation number, and the clients present that number to collect their cash. Just a decade ago, *hawala* agents would give their clients an open receipt, often in the form of a bank note, which had to be presented at the other end to get the cash. The serial number on the bill served as the confirmation number. "Back then," Riaz said, "the entire process took about a week. Now they just send the number by text message on their cell phones, and the whole transfer happens in seconds."

Estimates vary wildly as to how much money is pumped annually through the global *hawala* network. Economists put the total figure at about $100 billion and say most transfers are above suspicion. "Our challenge is separating the good from the bad," Noorullah Delawari, the governor of Afghanistan's Central Bank, told me.

It won't be easy, but it is critically important. The World Bank and UN calculate that *hawala* dealers in Helmand and Kandahar alone move more than $1 billion in drug money every year. Surveyors identified no less than fifty-four *hawaladars* in those provinces as "specialists" in laundering opium money. Pinpointing how much of that money benefits insurgents is impossible, with no regulatory framework in place. Most traded almost exclusively in Pakistani rupees (as opposed to the afghani, which is the currency in Afghanistan), indicating that "the large bulk of drug payments arrive in Afghanistan via Pakistan."[14]

Officials and bankers I interviewed in Pakistan are concerned, too. They believe that as much as one-third of Pakistan's overall *hawala* trade is related to drug traffic, and the sums moving back and forth are staggering. In 2002, *Forbes* reported that $8 billion was being remitted to Pakistan through the *hawala* system, more than eight times what was being transferred into the country through banks. More important, government leaders said $100 billion in capital had flowed out of Pakistan.[15]

Both Afghanistan and Pakistan have launched comprehensive programs to register *hawaladars* and establish cost-free mechanisms to identify the senders and the receivers. U.S. agents investigating *hawala* transfers praised Islamabad for its efforts to regulate informal cash flows. "Pakistan is leaps and bounds ahead of other countries in the region," one told me. "They are literally seizing bags of cash as they cross the border." However, some Pakistani officials remain frustrated. "It's proving a tough nut to crack," complained Major General Jaffery of the Anti Narcotics Force.

What has Islamabad irritated is the enormous flow of legal goods that are smuggled illegally. That old standby, the U-turn scheme, not only continues to cost Pakistan hundreds of millions of dollars in lost customs revenue, but the cross-border trade is also used to hide drug money.

Commodity Barter

Major drug traffickers in Afghanistan simply barter the opium they export for commodities. This simple con is attractive to the Afghan market, which is desperate for basic goods like vehicles, electronics, and construction materials. Take a stroll along the aptly named Smugglers Creek in Dubai, and you'll see hundreds of dhows being loaded with commodities as they prepare to sail for Pakistan. Walk through the teeming Karachi port, where tiny rowboats unload goods from larger vessels, and then visit the chaotic Chaman border crossing where brightly painted trucks from the town's 3,500 import-export firms stream into Afghanistan, and you begin to understand the complexity of trying to regulate regional trade.

The drugs-for-commodities scam provides smugglers with a "legal" front for their activities. Haji Juma Khan, for example, imported Land Cruisers to southern Afghanistan and also owns an electronics import-export firm in the UAE, according to authorities. Haji Bashir Noorzai was Afghanistan's largest tire importer until he landed himself in a U.S. jail. It is said that an empty truck never passes over the rugged Durrand Line, the disputed border between Pakistan and Afghanistan. "The Pakistanis often complain about the Afghan Transit Trade Agreement," says Cassara. "Basically, it is drugs going out and commodities going in."

Trade-Based Money Laundering

A related trick of the trade is known as trade-based money laundering: two traders agree to misprice a deal so that extra money sneaks past the authorities. Say you want to move $50,000 of drug money. You just transfer $200,000 of widgets and put their value as $250,000. "All you need is a willing buyer and a willing seller," says Raymond Baker, a Brookings scholar and author of *Capitalism's Achilles Heel.* "You can misprice anything by 10 to 20 percent and no one will notice."[16]

While he worked at the U.S. Treasury Department, Cassara proposed working with the Pakistanis and Afghans to harmonize customs duties and collection points (thus reducing the incentive to smuggle legal goods). He also wanted to establish trade transparency units, or TTUs. These computer-based stations identify mispriced trades by spotting anomalies in the cost of commodities between point A and point B. The United States has helped establish TTUs in South America, where Colombian and Mexican smugglers use similar techniques to move cocaine money, Cassara says, but to this day, there's not a single TTU operational between South Asia and the Middle East. "All the construction materials, pipes, wiring, and cement going into Afghanistan—no one is looking at this stuff," he says. "It's not sexy, but we need to start thinking like our adversaries do."

Shell Companies and Real Estate

Key to making an illegal barter scheme work is having a front company in the UAE. That's where men like Riaz come in. He established dozens of fake enterprises for the D-Company: first registering the firm, then getting an employment visa for the "director" and opening an account where the boss supposedly would receive a generous salary. For less than $20,000, Riaz said, he could set up a "totally fabricated" company to move millions of dollars in dirty money into the UAE every year. Then he'd take the firm's "earnings" and pump them into the stock market, where they come out "clean."

Shahbaz Khan, a Pakistani arrested in 2007 in Sharjah and slapped with a life sentence for drug trafficking and money laundering, operated thirteen front companies to disguise his operations, according to the U.S. government.[17] In an interview in Peshawar, Khan's son Gulbaz claimed his father was an "innocent businessman" who exported cigarettes and renovated buildings in Sharjah.[18]

U.S. counternarcotics agents have taken note of the property boom across Pakistan, Afghanistan, and the UAE. Property values soared in Afghanistan following the fall of the Taliban—although some of that climb is related to the rush of aid workers and foreign embassies to procure residences and office space. Real estate prices also mushroomed next door in Pakistan. Meanwhile, somewhere between 15 and 24 percent of the world's high-tower cranes are at work at any given time in Dubai, where skyscrapers are popping up like weeds.[19] "With just a thousand real estate transactions, you can recycle $800 million," a western official told me, and none of the countries in this region regulate real estate sales. No one suggests the property explosion in any of these countries is entirely fueled by drug money, but real estate provides a handy place to park large sums of dirty cash.

The World's Most Volatile Stock Market

The Karachi Stock Exchange (KSE) is whispered to be another good place to hide black money. The unregulated, volatile, and highly speculative Pakistani bourse has grown by an astounding 200 percent since 2002, despite market collapses that have become almost an annual event. The turnover is sky high, making analysts speculate it's being used by money launderers. More than $120 billion pumped through the KSE in 2006, a year when the country's entire economy totaled only about $130 billion, according to bankers and former Pakistani officials.[20] What makes observers most suspicious is the emergence of a handful of brokers in the last five years who now control almost 40 percent of the daily trading volume. "Their meteoric growth is hard to explain by legal means," a former senior Pakistani finance official told me.

Many wonder whose cash they are trading. "I can't prove it is drug money," said Tariq Hassan, the outspoken former chairman of Pakistan's Securities and Exchange Commission (SECP), "but there is definitely money laundering going on there."[21] Hassan lost his job after he launched an investigation into the March 2005 KSE collapse, which cost small investors $13 billion. He claims he was shown the door after he presented the Pakistani government with irrefutable evidence that a dozen major stockbrokers had deliberately triggered the crash and then reaped in billions in profits by devouring cheap shares.[22]

As the KSE swelled in the past five years, these dominant brokers raised eyebrows by expanding their operations into private banking, real estate, and even oil and gas exploration. Some observers suspect that elaborate business frameworks are laundering money, comparing the setup to the infamous Bank of Credit and Commerce International (BCCI). "These men are now power brokers in Pakistan, not just stockbrokers," Hassan said, adding that he believed top officials in the Islamabad government receive handsome payoffs to look the other way.

In April 2007, I flew to Karachi to meet Aqeel Karim Dhedhi, Pakistan's biggest stockbroker, whose firm, according to his company's website, controls about 8 percent of the KSE's daily trading volume.[23] By all accounts Dhedhi wields considerable influence in the country's political and economic circles. It has been reported in the local media, for example, that the SECP chairman who replaced Tariq Hassan used to work for him.[24] Dhedhi told me his father started the AKD brokerage house, which other bankers and Pakistani officials said was unknown until a few years ago.

Today, Dhedhi runs a multibillion-dollar empire from a nondescript office on a Karachi backstreet, where his English-speaking CEO, Nadeem Naqvi, patiently swatted away my questions about their client base.[25] Even though Pakistani law didn't require it, "AKD has a very strict 'Know Your Customer' policy," Naqvi said. "As a house we have tightened up." The firm now scrutinizes all large-volume trades, records traders' telephone calls, and employs a full-time compliance officer, he said. Still, AKD's client profile could raise eyebrows: according to records Naqvi and Dhedhi showed me, the house has only 1,500 active clients, most of whom make trades of about $2,000. That suggests only a handful of clients account for the majority of their gargantuan daily trading volume.

Since Pakistan doesn't regulate its stock trades, it's impossible to know if any of the KSE funds are tied to the Taliban or the drug traders who back them. But some U.S. officials worry that brokerage houses are moving staggering sums through the KSE and that this deserves closer scrutiny. Some financial analysts believe the KSE could mark one of the financial gateways where dirty money flows into the legitimate banking system. After all, says Baker, the Brookings scholar, "once cash has been traded through a stock market, it comes out clean."

It's important to recognize that none of the money-laundering mechanisms being used in South Asia and the Gulf are the least bit unusual. The International Monetary Fund estimates that about

$1.8 trillion of dirty money is laundered globally every year, mainly by moving it through informal markets or posing it as legitimate business. Financial crime experts say the *hawala* transfer system is equivalent to the Black Market Peso Exchange, which moves cocaine money in Latin America. In the mid-1990s, the Cali cartel was believed to recycle as much as half of its $7 billion a year in cocaine revenues using trade-based money laundering.[26]

Meanwhile, shell companies exist in tax havens across the globe, from Switzerland to the Cayman Islands. And the KSE is hardly the only financial market that appears riddled with dirty money. A 2001 report for the French parliament identified forty banks and individuals working out of Britain's City of London that were believed to maintain direct or indirect relations with bin Laden.[27] "Drug kingpins and terrorist financiers did not create this system," says Baker, who is pushing for nothing less than a global revamp of the free-market system. "They simply stepped into the mechanisms we have created to make it easy to shift money across borders." Osama bin Laden once told an interviewer that his people were as "aware of the cracks inside the Western financial system as they are aware of the lines in their hands."[28] For western law enforcement, the challenge will be closing those gaps.

To this day, surprisingly little is known about al Qaeda's financial structure: how much money the group raises through donations versus business ventures, what its annual budget is, and who decides how it gets spent. Authorities aren't entirely sure about the way in which money is shared between its network of allies, like the Taliban, the IMU, and the Pakistani jihadi groups, although some recent intelligence indicates a greater level of cooperation between them.[29] As discussed in Chapter 1, there is evidence al Qaeda cells in the West are turning to crime to raise money. As well, it's clear that the Taliban and the IMU profit from Afghanistan's booming opium trade. Yet debate continues over where Osama bin Laden stands on narcotics smuggling. According to U.S. officials, captured al Qaeda operatives have told interrogators that bin Laden banned his fighters from getting involved in the drug trade, fearing that narcotics could corrupt his movement.[30]

In its "Monograph on Terrorist Finance," the 9/11 Commission overturned the widespread belief that bin Laden funded al Qaeda from a $300 million fortune he allegedly inherited. In fact, the commission concluded, bin Laden received an annual stipend of around $1 million from his family, hardly small change but not enough to fund his terrorist ambitions. In fact, when bin Laden returned to Afghanistan in 1996 from Sudan, where he had set up construction projects and ran farms, some evidence suggests he was nearly broke.[31] What allowed him and his network to survive, U.S. investigators concluded, was his unparalleled ability to raise funds and reinvent his organization.

"Unlike other terrorist leaders, bin Laden was not a military hero, nor a religious authority, nor an obvious representative of the downtrodden and disillusioned," testified Lee Wolosky, the former director of transnational threats at the NSC. "He was a rich *financier*...distinguished by his ability to organize an effective network."[32]

The 9/11 Commission later concluded that donations from rich Arabs and Muslim charities contributed the bulk of al Qaeda's funding. "We have seen no substantial evidence," the panel added, "that al Qaeda played a major role in the drug trade or relied on it as an important source of revenue either before or after 9/11." To this day, there's still no smoking gun to prove bin Laden's link to the opium trade, officials say. "There is fragmentary evidence of their use of the criminal infrastructure," says a senior western official. "But not much more."[33] However, there is widespread evidence Uzbek insurgents linked to al Qaeda are heavily tied to drug smuggling and control as much as 70 percent of the multibillion-dollar heroin and opium trade through Central Asia.[34] Other incidents prove low-level Arab al Qaeda operatives have engaged in trafficking, including the two maritime seizures in late 2003.

There's no shortage of evidence that al Qaeda engaged in smuggling—both before and after bin Laden relocated to Afghanistan. A former operative named Jamal al Fadl testified before a U.S. court that he ferried suitcases of cash and coordinated deliveries of weapons to operatives around the globe.[35] The former *Washington Post* reporter Douglas Farah uncovered evidence that al Qaeda operatives struck a deal to purchase diamonds from rebels in Sierra Leone.[36] Farah also later reported that al Qaeda and the Taliban smuggled millions of dollars' worth of gold and bundles of U.S. currency out of Afghanistan in the wake of the 9/11 attacks. The treasure was sent via *hawala* to Dubai, where it was laundered and subsequently scattered around the globe.[37] After the U.S.-led invasion of Afghanistan, coalition troops would find an al Qaeda manual that explained how to smuggle gold on small boats and conceal it on the body.[38]

The structure of bin Laden's network, which always blended business and terrorism, was similar to large, successful criminal organizations: flexible, diversified, decentralized, and compartmentalized. While in Sudan, bin Laden ran construction businesses, imported sugar and soap, and exported sesame seeds, palm oil, and sunflower seeds. He purchased farms, some of them enormous, which grew corn and peanuts and also served as training camps.[39] In Afghanistan, he expanded his terrorist empire, allowing him to take his ambitions global. One French intelligence report compared al Qaeda's financial architecture to the disgraced BCCI, which forged a complex decentralized structure of overlapping shell companies to launder drug money, hide terrorist funds, and funnel weapons to the mujahideen. "The financial network of bin Laden, as well as his network of investments, is similar to the network put in place in the 1980s by BCCI for its fraudulent operations, often with the same people (former directors and cadres of the bank and its affiliates, arms merchants, oil merchants, Saudi investors)," the seventy-page report said. "The dominant trait of bin Laden's operations is that of a terrorist network backed up by a vast financial structure."[40]

Time and time again, as I and the local reporters who helped research this book looked for bin Laden's ties to the drug trade, our contacts suggested we would never establish clear links. The people who benefit most from the drug trade in this region never actually touch the drugs, they said. I believe that bin Laden, as well as Mullah Omar, don't sully themselves in the opium trade, but they have created an environment that has transformed Afghanistan into the world's leading supplier of opiates. Even if the Afghan opium drug trade grew without their approval or indirect involvement—an idea I find ludicrous—terrorists and insurgents are at the very least fellow travelers on the same black market circuit. "God forbid there is another major terrorist attack on the United States," says Baker, "it will absolutely use the same illicit financial structure that moves narcotics."

7. MISSION CREEP

IN OCTOBER 2006, AFTER AFGHANISTAN HARVESTED 6,100 metric tons of opium, two U.S. congressmen sat down to draft a letter. They had a bone to pick with Donald Rumsfeld.

"We all know that drugs fuel the violence and insurgency," wrote Henry Hyde and Mark Kirk, "and now we need new policy that addresses both the drugs and related terror simultaneously."[1] The U.S. lawmakers knew better than to ask the cantankerous defense secretary to take on the fight against opium. Rumsfeld had repeatedly expressed concern that Afghanistan could turn into another costly drug war like Colombia and rejected proposed engagement in counternarcotics activities as "mission creep." Five years into the war in Afghanistan, with most of Washington distracted by Iraq, the Pentagon continued to insist that the Afghan insurgency was the military's responsibility, defining the opium trade as a problem for law enforcement.

Kirk and Hyde, who chaired the Foreign Relations Committee, were receiving disturbing information from Afghanistan, however: U.S. military units would not disrupt opium bazaars, rarely stopped drug shipments moving toward the borders, and routinely rejected DEA requests to provide backup to their missions.[2] In their letter, the lawmakers suggested ways the military and the DEA could harmonize their efforts. They wanted DEA agents to ride along on military missions when there was a likelihood that drugs would be found, and urged the military to notify counternarcotics agents when they came across opium caches. "We must find a way to merge your counter insurgency mission with that of the DEA's drug-fighting mission," Hyde and Kirk wrote.

The congressmen waited almost two months to get a response from the Pentagon. The tepid reply noted that Britain, not the United States, was the lead nation on counternarcotics issues within the coalition. The U.S. government did support the British-run initiative, but that was handled by the State Department, the letter added. "Regarding your specific recommendations for DoD [Department of Defense], the Secretary has already taken such action," wrote Eric Edelman, Rumsfeld's undersecretary.[3] For frustrated counternarcotics officials and lawmakers in Washington, who felt Afghanistan drug policy was seriously adrift, the letter reflected the Pentagon's unaccommodating attitude. A congressional study found that the DEA had requested military airlifts on twenty-six occasions in 2005 and these requests were denied in all but three cases. The Pentagon improved its record in 2006, approving twelve of fourteen DEA air support requests.[4]

DoD policy itself was ambiguous: official guidance sent to commanding officers said they "could" destroy drug shipments they intercepted, but didn't say they had to.[5] Some U.S. commanders supported counternarcotics efforts, seizing and destroying drug shipments and communicating with counternarcotics agents. Others seemed to deliberately ignore them. One Green Beret complained that he had been ordered to disregard opium and heroin stashes when he came across them on patrol.[6] Meanwhile, another Special Forces officer received orders to start destroying drug labs in Nangarhar in 2003, only to have those orders abruptly re-versed several months later. "I always had a feeling I was in the middle of a pissing match between the higher-ups," he told me.[7] Contrary to what Edelman's letter said, there seemed to be no clear directive from the top to accommodate the DEA, or at least there was little awareness of it on the ground. Seth Jones, a Rand analyst traveling with U.S. Special Forces in 2006, was on hand when the elite troops obtained "actionable intelligence" that narco-traffickers were crossing from Pakistan. "Their attitude was, 'We're not getting involved,'" Jones told me.

In other cases, senior military officials discarded intelligence, or said the fragmentary evidence didn't prove the Taliban was sys-tematically exploiting the poppy trade (just as U.S. officials had said about the mujahideen in the 1980s). "We had camera work and GPS locations about the Taliban moving huge levels of opium and pocketing the cash," said a U.S. counternarcotics official posted to Kabul. "The army would just tell us, 'Oh, they just happen to hold power in that area so they take a cut.'"[8] U.S. military officials often denied there was any clear proof of a link between the Taliban and the drug trade. As one U.S. official complained to me: "You would have to find Mullah Omar on the phone trying to sell drugs and use that cash to buy weapons with which he planned to kill Americans. Only then would they believe it."

As much as anything, senior U.S. military commanders justifi-ably felt they already had enough on their plate. The initial num-ber of foreign troops deployed to Afghanistan—just four thousand peacekeepers in Kabul and another eight thousand U.S. troops fo-cused on capturing or killing Taliban and al Qaeda members—was tiny in comparison to the country's size and population. After the 2003 Iraq invasion, U.S. forces in Afghanistan were stretched even thinner. The Pentagon's hesitancy to take on the growing drug problem stemmed from three concerns: U.S. commanders feared that taking on poppy farmers would conflict with their campaign to win hearts and minds, especially in the southern countryside where the Taliban was active. An estimated 12 percent of the Afghan population is tied to the poppy industry—with much heavier population concentrations in the south and the east.

Plus, opium remains the largest sector in the Afghan economy, and it's not just the insurgents who profit off it.[9] Complicating the picture is the fact that key allies in the CIA and U.S. military–led effort to hunt down al Qaeda and Taliban are themselves known to run massive drug rings. It is clear that senior officials in the Karzai administration are involved as well, though efforts to fight corruption have stalled badly. The Afghan president raised eyebrows in 2007 when he appointed Izzatullah Wasifi as his anticorruption tsar. Wasifi was convicted two decades ago for trying to sell $2 million worth of heroin to an undercover officer in Caesar's Palace, Las Vegas. Wasifi called the bust a youthful indiscretion.[10]

There were worse cases. In June 2004, counternarcotics agents raided the offices of the twenty-something Helmand governor Sher Mohammed Akhundzada, where they found nine metric tons of opium.[11] He was removed as governor soon after, but Karzai swiftly appointed him as a member of parliament, and he never faced an investigation, much less any charges against him. Other senior Afghan officials and warlords with known ties to narcotics remain in business, according to U.S. military intelligence documents seen by the author. A number of them still work closely with the U.S. military and the CIA.

"This is the Afghan equivalent of failing to deal with looting in Baghdad," said Andre D. Hollis, a former deputy assistant secretary of defense for counternarcotics. "If you are not dealing with those who are threatened by security and who undermine security, namely drug traffickers, all your other grandiose plans will come to naught."[12]

The third issue, according to U.S. officials familiar with the Pentagon's mind-set, is an unspoken concern that individual American units deployed to drug-producing areas or along trafficking routes could become corrupted. "There's just too much money sloshing around out there," a senior Republican aide who works closely on drugs matters told me. The Pentagon's attitude infuriated counternarcotics officials, not least since it gave many Afghans the impression that Washington is unopposed to the poppy trade, and may even condone or partake in it. Besides, no one was asking the U.S. military to take on the drug trade itself—just to support operations by the DEA, the British-led Task Force 333, and the Afghan counternarcotics police. "In the war environment, you don't get from point A to point B without military assistance," says a Washington-based official. Adds Jack Lawn, the former DEA chief: "You can't drop a team into a troubled area without military backup."

Part of the problem was systemic: efforts to fight drugs in post-Taliban Afghanistan were divided among donor nations with no framework for coordination. From the start, levels of commitment were highly skewed and priorities conflicted. Washington pledged more than $4 billion in equipment alone for the new Afghan National Army, for example, while Germany sent just forty police trainers who trained cadets in a Kabul police academy. Tens of thousands of Afghan police in the countryside got no training until

2004, when the United States opened seven regional training centers.[13] Washington's commitment to Afghanistan was greater than any of the other foreign donors', but it still paled in comparison to the funds dedicated to rebuilding Iraq (which wasn't half as destroyed). The United States allocated $909 million in reconstruction assistance to Afghanistan in 2002, compared to $20 billion for postwar Iraq.[14] Aid money was slow to arrive in Afghanistan in general, and very little trickled out to remote areas like Helmand and Nimroz.

Within the newly reopened U.S. embassy in Kabul, fighting narcotics was secondary to hunting terrorists, just as it had been during the Soviet resistance. Beverly Eighmy, who had worked for USAID in Pakistan and Afghanistan during the 1980s, was brought out of retirement in late 2001 to serve as the crime and narcotics adviser on a six-month contract. "That was the length of the tour," she said. "It was pretty brutal, seven days a week, fourteen hours a day—the hardest job I ever loved. And it was just me."[15] When the spring 2002 planting season began, it quickly became apparent that the opium crop was going to be enormous. "I kept telling people at the embassy: 'At some point, somebody has got to get serious on this,'" she said. But for another three years, there would only be one counternarcotics officer posted to the Kabul embassy at any given time, all of them on temporary duty contracts. The DEA didn't open an office in Afghanistan until 2004, and even then most agents were on temporary duty rotations.[16]

Back home in Washington, Rand Beers, who ran the State Department's Bureau of International Narcotics and Law (INL), was tasked to come up with ideas for fighting the opium problem. In fall of 2002, he sat down with British counterparts and they hammered out a plan blending forced eradication of poppy fields, interdiction of traffickers, and alternative livelihood programs to wean farmers off poppy. "The British said they would be responsible if we gave them some forms of support, including military airlift for drug operations," he said. "This was the most prominent thing we did not agree to 100 percent, but in principle, we agreed to it whenever possible."[17]

Beers drafted a cable that got signed off by the relevant officials in Washington—including the Pentagon. "Then I dispatched a senior counternarcotics Foreign Service officer to Kabul with the paper in hand, and the United States military told him they had never heard of it," Beers told me. "It would appear Central Command sat on it, whether on their own or with orders from the Pentagon. Effectively, they put a stop to the program then and there."

Unable to pursue its plans to wipe out the poppy crop or arrest drug traffickers, the British government instead launched a three-year, $140 million crop substitution program that would amount to a spectacular and costly failure. As more farmers planted poppy to receive the easy money, opium production skyrocketed past three thousand metric tons. "It was well-intentioned," a western official based in Kabul told me. "But the Brits got snookered. The Afghans took them to the cleaners." The program, hastily dropped after its first year, was a major embarrassment for the British government and built friction with U.S. officials, who wanted to use crop dusters to spray herbicide on the poppy fields. Privately, both sniped about each other's proposals.

Publically, the Bush administration continued to tout Afghanistan as a major success story. On May 1, 2003, just a day before President Bush made his historic tailhook landing onto the USS

Abraham Lincoln and declared Iraq "mission accomplished," Rumsfeld traveled to Kabul, where he announced an end to major combat operations there as well. Acknowledging that "pockets of resistance" continued to make trouble along the Pakistan border, the defense secretary said, "The bulk of this country today is permissive. It's secure."[18] Girls were back in school, aid groups were pouring into Kabul, and the country held its first-ever democratic presidential election. But by the time the new government was in place, reports were flowing into the U.S. embassy indicating the insurgency was profiting richly from the booming opium trade.

The Pentagon continued to refuse to target drug labs, even as counternarcotics officials became more and more convinced it would weaken the Taliban. In January 2004, a U.S. Air Force A-10 bomber was called in to support a British Special Forces team that was locked in a firefight at a major drug lab. Within days, opium prices nationwide climbed by 15 percent.[19] "We found that if we had a successful raid in Nangarhar [in eastern Afghanistan], within twenty-four hours our snitches in the south would tell us that the price had shot up," a U.S. official told me. "Opium prices were phenomenally sensitive."

After the 2003 harvest produced 3,600 tons of opium, even the Pentagon couldn't avoid the problem entirely any longer. It dedicated $73 million to anti-drug efforts in 2004, up from nothing in 2003. The State Department, meanwhile, increased its funding from $30 million to $50 million.[20]

In 2004, President Karzai told American diplomats he feared Afghanistan "had only two or three years to solve the [drug] problem or risk dissolving into a classic narco-state."[21] According to a cable sent by the U.S. embassy in Kabul in March 2004 and seen by the author, Karzai believed Pakistan was encouraging the Taliban to get involved in the opium trade. He charged that Islamabad was "using profits from the drug trade to finance armed opposition" to his government. Some former U.S. officials believe Karzai's reticence to go after tribal allies who engage in drug trafficking stems from a belief that he needs to compete with his Taliban rivals, who are backed by Pakistan. The same year, the outgoing CIA station chief in Kabul dispatched a message home warning of the growing link between the Taliban and the drug trade. "His cable said there was a direct causal link between insurgent funding and the opium trade," according to a U.S. official who saw the document. "If we do not do something about this, he wrote, we will win the battle and lose the war."[22]

Back home in Washington, Robert Charles, who had replaced Rand Beers as INL chief, got nicknamed "Cassandra" in his office for his routine tirades about the Afghan drug problem. When he delivered downbeat testimony on the matter to Congress, a White House official warned he was becoming "inconvenient."[23] Charles wanted to launch an aggressive spraying campaign across the south, matched with alternative livelihood packages for farmers, and he believed he could get the Afghan government to sign on. Charles put together a team of experts and scientists whom he planned to accompany to Kabul to pitch their case to President Karzai. U.S. ambassador Zalmay Khalilzad, an Afghan American envoy known to his colleagues as Zal, denied Charles country clearance, even though as INL chief he had assistant secretary of state status. "I had a knock-down drag-out with Zal over this," Charles said. "I said, 'Zal, I know all the great things you are doing, but if you do not tackle this dragon it will ultimately consume you.'"[24]

Khalilzad opposed the aggressive program Charles was advocating, but the U.S. envoy was nonetheless pushing for stronger measures on the narcotics front. He characterized the British approach to fighting drugs as "inadequate both conceptually and operationally" in an April 2004 cable classified secret and titled: "Counternarcotics: Rethinking our Strategy."[25] Asking Washington to increase the number of staff dedicated to counternarcotics matters, Khalilzad warned: "There is a growing danger that the rapidly growing illegal drug industry will sweep away all the other things we are doing to rebuild Afghanistan." There was evidence that "money from the illegal drug industry finds its way into the coffers of the Taliban and other terrorist groups. Disrupting this connection should be our first priority in the counternarcotics area," he wrote.

There may have been growing consensus within the U.S. embassy that Afghanistan's opium trade urgently needed to be tackled, but by 2004 there was considerable friction between the Americans, the British, and the Karzai administration over how to approach the problem. The British and Afghan governments vehemently opposed U.S. proposals to spray the crops. They wanted the focus put on arresting "bad guys," not targeting poor Afghan farmers, according to British and Afghan officials. Interdiction was easier said than done, however, especially in a country where there was no functioning police force or judicial system. Extraditing Afghan drug lords was tricky, too. Britain does not have extraterritorial drug laws, meaning their agents couldn't arrest an individual for committing narcotics crimes outside British territory. The DEA had similar legal limitations developing cases against Afghan smugglers, because until 2005, they had to prove the drugs ended up on U.S. streets, which it rarely did. Eventually, diplomats and counternarcotics agents came up with a target everyone could agree on. "Zal wanted to find a superficial solution that was high-profile and made everyone happy," a former embassy official told me. "That ended up being the arrest of Haji Bashir Noorzai."

As I detailed in Chapter 3, the powerful Noorzai tribe had been known to the U.S. government since the 1990s, when DEA agents began to track Bashir's father Mohammed Issa, a leading member of the Quetta Alliance of smugglers. Bashir himself fought as a mujahideen fighter in the early 1980s, eventually forming his own five-hundred-strong militia known as the Haji Bashir Front. After the Soviets withdrew, he cooperated with CIA agents to recover Stinger missiles. In his 2007 sworn deposition before the federal court at the Southern District of New York, Noorzai testified that he recovered about a dozen missiles working with two agents he knew as Mike and Sam. The agency paid him approximately $50,000 for his work.[26]

The State Department was aware of Bashar Noorzai's role in financing the early Taliban movement, and the CIA reported on deals he brokered with Mullah Omar to export crystal heroin.[27] Federal agents believed Noorzai's smuggling profits reached their pinnacle when he bought up large stockpiles of cheap opium just ahead of Mullah Omar's ban on poppy cultivation. In an apparent bid to protect his own drug interests by snitching on his rivals, the burly tribesman even became a DEA informant, providing U.S. agents in Pakistan with information about Turkish smugglers.[28] Long before the September 11 attacks, Bashir Noorzai walked a fine line with the U.S. government, simultaneously serving as a shadowy asset to American agents while engaging in large-scale drug trafficking activities that could have landed him in a U.S. prison.

His long journey from the poppy fields of Kandahar to a Manhattan prison reads like a John Grisham novel, highlighting the complexities that U.S. law enforcement faces when building cases against shadowy Afghan drug networks, and exposing the sometimes conflicting interests among U.S. government agencies. After 9/11, the U.S. military initially included Bashir Noorzai on a list of "high-value targets." Not that Noorzai let such trifles worry him.[29] Ever the opportunist, he promptly made contact with American troops after they invaded Kandahar and told them he wanted to help form the new Afghan government. "I am a tribal leader," he said, according to his own testimony. "And I want to bring stability to Afghanistan."

American officials held Bashir in custody in Kandahar for six days, interrogating him about the whereabouts of Mullah Omar and the Taliban's financial setup, according to Bashir's testimony and U.S. officials familiar with the meetings. He offered to bring his one-million-strong tribe—traditional allies of the Taliban—into the new political order and to collect weapons the Taliban had stashed in his territory in Maiwand district. The soldiers let him go, and two weeks later he lived up to his word. Noorzai returned to the Kandahar Air Field with more than a dozen trucks piled with weapons, including four hundred antiaircraft missiles.

Within months, Noorzai had become a major power broker in the new regime. Mark Corcoran, a correspondent for the Australian Broadcasting Corporation, reported on his luxurious mansion and his twelve-thousand-man private army.[30] "He's the most powerful drug lord in southern Afghanistan," Corcoran reported. "With each new administration that comes to Kandahar, they have to face the choice of either taking on Haji Bashar or making a deal with him." The U.S.-appointed Kandahar governor, Gul Agha Sherzai, had moved into Noorzai's mansion, the story said, and even U.S. Special Forces appeared to be working with him. "The Americans, for their part, received intelligence on a level that I do not believe they had been receiving before," said Michael Ware, a reporter, then for *Time* magazine, who was interviewed in the story. "Haji Bashar intimately knows senior members of the Taliban," Ware said. "He more than anyone has information on where these leaders went, how they got away, and is now proving pivotal in negotiating the surrenders of countless Taliban commanders."

Several months later, however, his dealings with the Americans would sour. Noorzai convinced the former Foreign Minister Wakil Ahmed Muttawakil to come out of hiding, and the Americans promptly shipped the senior Taliban official off to Guantánamo Bay. Noorzai then tried to secure the surrender of Haji Birqet Khan, another Kandahari close to the Taliban. U.S. warplanes attacked Birqet's home shortly after the pair met, having apparently received information they were hatching a plan to attack U.S. troops. Noorzai later claimed the Americans had bad information. Regardless, the air strike killed Birqet, one of his wives, and two of his grandsons.[31] Fearing he, too, would be killed, either by the Americans or in a revenge attack, Noorzai fled to Pakistan, according to his own testimony.

There, the DEA believes he swiftly returned to the heroin trade, reportedly with the help of Pakistani intelligence agents who gave him a new passport.[32] Noorzai traveled between Pakistan and the Gulf—mainly Dubai—but stayed out of Afghanistan, according to a 2004 U.S. intelligence report seen by the author. The scale of his business remained enormous. According

to testimony given to the House International Relations Committee, Noorzai was smuggling about two metric tons of heroin out of
Kandahar every eight weeks, moving it west with the help of al
Qaeda operatives based in Pakistan.[33] Hussein Karimi Rikabadi, a
convicted Iranian smuggler, testified in Noorzai's 2008 trial that
he had personally conducted five drug deals with the Kandahar
tribal leader totaling about two metric tons. The 2004 intelligence
report said Noorzai processed opium grown on his family lands at
eighteen heroin refineries in Registan, a desert district in southern
Kandahar.

In 2004, President Karzai's half-brother Ahmed Wali and
Khalid Pashtun, a Kandahar parliamentarian, traveled to Quetta to
ask Noorzai to sit down with the Americans again. Noorzai agreed
and in August he flew to Dubai for talks with two investigators,
identified in transcripts of their meetings as Mike and Brian.[34]
Those talks would continue in Pakistan the following month. Mike
identified himself to Noorzai as an employee of the Defense Intelligence Agency, and said Brian worked for the Federal Bureau of
Investigation, according to Noorzai's deposition. In fact, the two
men weren't government agents at all. They were part of an unusual three-man private intelligence firm called Rosetta Research
and Consulting that was trying to collect sensitive information and
sell it to the U.S. government for a profit.

Rosetta formed in 2003, founded by a former Treasury Department researcher, Michael Patrick Jost. Its original mission was to
assist in a mammoth lawsuit filed on behalf of 9/11 victims to
track terrorist money flows. Investors, who put more than $1 mil-
lion into Rosetta's start-up, thought their money was going toward creating a database of terrorist financiers, not capturing an

Afghan opium kingpin.[35] Throughout their work, the three Rosetta investigators maintained high-level contacts with officials in the Defense Department and the FBI, where at least one employee reportedly searched government databases and forwarded information to the firm.[36]

In their meetings with Noorzai, Mike and Brian appeared to have only a passing interest in the opium trade, in which Noorzai denied having any involvement. Throughout hundreds of documents reviewed by the author, covering four separate meetings in August and September 2004, their line of questioning focused on "our money flow of funds project," as Mike called it. The investigators appeared to be trying to identify how *hawala* traders sent money to al Qaeda, and wanted Noorzai to secure them meetings with prominent moneychangers close to the terror group. "These are people who can give us information and educate us on how money moves," Mike said at one point. From their first encounter, Mike and Brian told Noorzai that they had access to high-level U.S. officials and tried to convince him that, if he flew to the United States to meet their superiors, he would have nothing to fear from the long arm of the law.

After four meetings where this message was systematically repeated, Bashir Noorzai apparently came to believe it would be okay to "take a vacation," as Mike put it, to the United States. In their final session on September 16, 2004, Mike said his superiors wanted to sit down with Noorzai in New York:

> "It would be like a vacation. He would be interviewed. He
> would be talked to about a lot of subjects, but the goal would
> be to position him very appropriately to assist us with opening

dialogues with some of the people there. Then he is coming back here, like he was just away for a couple of weeks on vacation. . . . The goal of the trip would be that no one will really know that he made the trip to the United States. It will be kept very, very quiet. . . . I think quite frankly the way our government prefers to do it is to take him quietly to the United States."

In fact that was not the way it was going to work at all. A U.S. grand jury had issued a sealed indictment against Noorzai three and a half months earlier.[37] Even if there were some members of the U.S. defense and intelligence community who believed Noorzai might be willing to help them track down terrorist financiers and Taliban leaders, the Department of Justice considered him a criminal. U.S. federal agents had spent four years methodically building their case against Noorzai.

The investigation began in 2001 in Manhattan, just months before hijacked passenger jets smashed into the World Trade Towers. Detectives with New York's Organized Crime Drug Enforcement Strike Force, which includes NYPD and DEA agents, developed an Afghan informant who claimed he could purchase heroin from Kandahar, according to federal officials and court documents. Following the money trail up from street-level dope peddlers, the investigation eventually led to the arrest of eleven heroin wholesalers in the New York area. One agreed to cooperate, identifying a supplier from Afghanistan named Mohammed Essa who coordinated heroin shipments into the United States and other countries, smuggling the white powder in secret compartments tucked inside suitcases. The agents tracked Essa, who liked to gamble in

Atlantic City during his U.S. stopovers, back to a wholesale supplier in Pakistan named Haji Baz Mohammed, according to federal officials and court records.[38] After DEA agents in Pakistan picked up Baz Mohammed's trail, they discovered that Haji Bashir Noorzai was one of his main suppliers. Both Essa and Baz Mohammed were eventually arrested in Afghanistan, and brought to the United States to face justice.

Meanwhile, in a separate investigation half a continent away, DEA agents and Romanian officials were tracking Hussein Karimi Rikabadi, an Iranian smuggler based in Bucharest who was moving multiton shipments of morphine base through Iran and Turkey into Eastern Europe, and then on to Holland, Austria, and Germany. Investigators learned that Rikabadi was getting his dope from three main suppliers in Afghanistan, one of them a Kandahari. When Romanian authorities agreed to wiretap Rikabadi's phone, it turned out that the Kandahari on the other end of the line was none other than Haji Bashir Noorzai. "What happened to the four hundred tires?" Rikabadi asked him in one intercepted phone conversation, using a fairly flimsy code since Afghanistan does not produce tires. "God willing, that is ready," Noorzai responded. "But it needs a day or two." Rikabadi later admitted to a New York jury that terms like tires and cigarettes were in fact code for heroin and morphine base.

Once federal agents had locked sights on Bashir Noorzai from three separate continents, the case against him began to congeal. "Now we had a trail, and we had a target," said a U.S. official. Rikabadi, who was arrested in 2007 and extradited to the United States, would later testify that the two met periodically in places like Dubai, Karachi, and Quetta over a period of about six years.

And over that time, Rikabadi said Noorzai supplied him with roughly two metric tons of morphine base.

In January 2005 the two men were hatching plans to smuggle ten kilos of heroin toward Europe, according to court documents. "Don't forget the number two," said Rikabadi in an intercepted phone conversation that took place on January 10. "Ten kilos of the number two." Noorzai responded: "Why should I forget?"

At the same time the two smugglers were finalizing their dope deal, U.S. federal agents half the world away were pressing Rosetta's Patrick Jost to hand over his firm's most prized asset. Jost reportedly learned that Noorzai had been indicted during a January 2005 meeting in Washington with U.S. federal officials.[39] He and his colleagues at Rosetta, who have declined to comment on the case, reportedly worried that handing over Noorzai to the feds would compromise their network of informants.[40] But they also apparently expected to earn a $2 million reward for helping the U.S. government snare Noorzai.

On April 13, 2005, a jetliner touched down at JFK airport in New York carrying Mike, Brian, and Haji Bashir Noorzai, each man believing he was going to get something he wasn't. Noorzai thought he had been guaranteed safe passage. U.S. federal agents—real ones this time—met him as he deplaned and drove the Kandahari tribesman to the Embassy Suites Hotel in lower Manhattan, where he was put up in a suite and grilled for thirteen days by DEA and FBI agents. According to Noorzai's attorney, the kingpin wondered why they told him he had a right to a lawyer at the start of each meeting, but he didn't comprehend the significance of these offers until the day he tried to return home. The moment a DEA agent present told him he was under arrest, Noorzai demanded they provide legal counsel.

Rosetta, meanwhile, never ended up receiving that $2 million reward. Instead, the firm's interaction with an FBI agent, along with payments Rosetta made to at least one Afghan diplomat, resulted in a Justice Department investigation.[41] The firm eventually went bankrupt.

In his meetings with the feds, Noorzai admitted knowing that drugs cultivated on his family lands were later processed into heroin and exported to New York, according to court documents. When his case came to trial three years later, Noorzai's deposition said he believed he was cutting a deal with U.S. agents to put an end to poppy cultivation and drug smuggling that originated from his tribal territory. The agents' notes from those meetings, along with the testimony of Baz Mohammed and Rikabadi, both of whom copped a plea and testified for the government, resulted in a jury handing Noorzai a guilty verdict on September 23, 2008. He was sentenced to two life terms.

Noorzai's lawyer, Ivan Fisher, one of the most prominent defense attorneys in New York, seeks to argue in an appeal that U.S. agents violated Noorzai's Miranda rights.[42] As Fisher put it: "Whenever they told him he had a right to a lawyer, Noorzai told them, 'I am a guest. For what would I need a lawyer?' "[43] For thirteen days, none of the federal officials he spoke to bothered to mention that he had been indicted. In the 2008 trial, judge Denny Chin ordered the jury to ignore the circumstances of Noorzai's arrival and subsequent arrest, saying they were immaterial to the smuggling charges against him. It's fair to say that Noorzai might have saved himself some hefty legal fees, not to mention years in jail, had he bothered to check the DEA's Web site before he boarded his flight to New York in 2005. Earlier that year, Washington had added his name to its top-ten list of targeted drug kingpins.

In the end, the biggest impact of *United States of America vs. Bashir Noorzai* may have been that it proved that Afghan drug smugglers could no longer escape the long arm of American law. Still, as Afghanistan has no formal extradition treaty with the United States, and since Pakistan and the UAE have also proved reticent to hand over major drug suspects, U.S. federal agents have often had to operate in murky legal territory to get suspected smugglers onto American territory. In 2005, Baz Mohammed became the first and only Afghan drug smuggler ever officially extradited to the United States, using a 1988 UN trafficking convention. He pled guilty the following year.[44] Mohammad Essa, who was arrested in Afghanistan and originally held in jail there, "consented to his removal to the United States" in 2007, according to a DEA statement.[45] Essa faces charges of conspiring to smuggle $25 million worth of heroin into the United States.[46]

On December 22, 2008, Taliban commander Khan Mohammed became the first Afghan ever to be put away for life under a new statute in the Patriot Act that makes it a crime to traffic drugs in order to finance terrorism. Eight years, two months, and eighteen days after the U.S.-led invasion of Afghanistan, it was the first time a Taliban fighter was convicted on narco-terrorism charges. An elaborate sting operation brought down Mohammed, with the help of an Afghan farmer, secretly working with DEA agents, who recorded the Taliban commander using a hidden camera. The recordings captured Mohammed discussing past attacks he had carried out against the Afghan government and NATO forces in Afghanistan, and showed he was trying to purchase rockets and other munitions with which to launch further attacks. He also agreed to supply the farmer several kilos of heroin, which he did in the presence of his four-year-old son. A videotape played at Mohammed's trial showed him repeatedly expressing how pleased he was to hear that the dope was being exported to the United States, saying he hoped it would kill infidels. "Whether by opium or by shooting, this is our common goal," he said.[47] As with Essa, Mohammed waived his right to an extradition trial and consented to be brought to the United States.

No doubt all these cases are success stories. But given the way corruption plagues the Afghan justice system, some foreign law enforcement officials remain frustrated by the legal hurdles slowing down U.S. law enforcement efforts there. "With the Afghan justice system the way it is, we should be extraditing twelve or more of these guys every month," said a former U.S. counternarcotics official.[48] Few expect that to change much until there is actual resolve among senior authorities in the region to stamp out the drug problem.

That said, the NATO-led coalition has dramatically increased the number of counternarcotics missions it undertakes, going after drug labs, storage depots, and smuggling hubs. One of the most colossal seizures took place in May 2009, when NATO and Afghan troops launched a major offensive to clear militants out of Marjah, a Taliban hub in central Helmand Province, ahead of a suspected assassination plot being launched against the provincial governor.[49] After three days of intensive fighting, sixty Taliban lay dead and the troops had seized a stunning ninety-two metric tons of heroin, opium, hashish, and poppy seeds, making it the second largest drug haul in global history. In addition, they captured hundreds of gallons of precursor chemicals from the market, which also housed a Taliban command center, complete with elaborate communications systems, suicide vests, and a large weapons cache.[50]

The sheer size of Afghanistan's drug economy, coupled with the lack of resources to fight it, has always been a drag on progress, however. When I visited Ahmadullah Alizai, the Kandahar counternarcotics police chief, in 2004, his entire force comprised himself and a rusty motorcycle. "I have made a request for a police force," he told me shrugging. "We need at least two to three hundred well-trained anti-drug police for this province alone." Four years later, the DEA was importing Colombian counternarcotics police who used mock AK-47s made of wood to instruct Afghanistan's fledgling anti-drug force. "This is kindergarten," said Vincent Balbo, the DEA chief in Kabul. "This is Narcotics 101." Another DEA agent added: "We are at a stage now of telling these recruits, 'This is a handgun, this is a bullet.'"[51]

The biggest problem facing law enforcement efforts is widespread corruption and lack of capacity in the Afghan government, judiciary, and police. Almost eight years since 9/11, amid fresh calls to build a bigger Afghan army, what the nation really needs is a functioning police and judiciary. The Afghan National Police remain largely untrained, underequipped, poorly funded, and riddled with graft. Regional warlords who stepped into rural power vacuums often installed their private militias as the provincial police. The international community, with Germany as the lead nation on police reform, got off to a slow start transforming these ragtag groups into a 62,000-strong national force.

In 2004, Washington accelerated the effort with a $1.1 billion program, contracted in part to Virginia-based DynCorp International, to put provincial police through eight-week crash courses, using retired American police as trainers. Even this massive investment failed to make much of a difference, however, in part because there were so few trainers per province, and eight weeks was not nearly enough time to turn militia fighters—70 percent of them illiterate—into respectable, trusted law enforcement officers.

A joint 2006 report by the Pentagon and the State Department found most of the program's graduates were incapable of carrying out even routine law enforcement work.[52] The initiative was also chronically mismanaged. Two years into the initiative, its directors couldn't say how many police were on duty or locate thousands of vehicles and other equipment the program had purchased.[53] Police commanders were widely known to put "ghost" employees on the payroll, while their forces reportedly worked with smugglers and extorted money from truckers and local businessmen.

Some of the most insecure regions received the fewest trainers. DynCorp initially sent two former sheriff's deputies to Lashkar Gah, the capital of Helmand, to train the entire province's three thousand police. Security was so poor the two Americans couldn't visit any of the districts, however. They described their students as eager to learn, but pitifully underequipped. In one class, forty police officers shared just fifteen rifles.[54] In the volatile south, U.S. and Afghan officials estimate police are dying at a rate six times that of the Afghan National Army. The U.S. military is now implementing a $2.5 billion overhaul of the Afghan police that aims to retrain the country's entire 72,000-member force and embed 2,350 American and European advisers in police stations across the country. Entire police units are to be pulled from districts, retrained as a group for eight weeks, and then sent back in a "top-to-bottom" effort to eliminate corruption.[55]

A top-to-bottom overhaul of the interior ministry will also be necessary. A U.N. study found drugs corruption has penetrated the highest levels of the ministry, with senior officials and police commanders earning tens of thousands of dollars every month in kickbacks and bribes. The study found senior officers "purchase" plum positions along lucrative drug smuggling routes, and then pay monthly fees to their seniors not to get fired.[56] Delays in training judges and prosecutors for Afghanistan's faltering judicial system have slowed progress in convicting drug criminals, and so far courts have mainly only gone after small-time crooks and drug addicts.[57] Meanwhile, a gleaming new $4.4 million prison, built with British funds to house major smugglers, sits virtually empty on the outskirts of Kabul.[58] At least four convicts already escaped, prompting UNODC chief Antonio Maria Costa to remark that the prison's greatest weakness was its front door.[59]

Perhaps most troubling of all, in the light of President Karzai's notorious reluctance to take on the drug trade, are persistent reports that his immediate family members are taking an active role in coordinating it, and that members of his Popalzai tribe, his half brother and other cronies, have been posted to positions along trafficking routes around Afghanistan. In May 2005, American diplomats cabled back to Washington that Karzai "has been unwilling to assert strong leadership" on the narcotics issue "even in his home province of Kandahar."[60] Afghan technocrats who populated the Karzai regime at the outset of his government had mostly resigned or been sacked. Regional warlords and tribal chiefs with dubious records on drugs continue to populate the administration. "Karzai's record with counternarcotics is even worse than his record of going after corruption," a western official complained to me. Widespread graft within the Kabul administration is what gives the insurgency space to grow. "Afghanistan's biggest problem isn't drugs," said Doug Wankal, a former DEA agent who later ran the Counternarcotics Task Force at the U.S. embassy in Kabul. "It's corruption."[61]

Major campaigns to wean Helmand's farmers off of poppy have been expensive failures. A sizable portion of Washington's $600 million Afghan counternarcotics effort is now spent on "alternative livelihood" programs. More than $200 million in U.S. and British funding was designated for Helmand in 2007, a year when poppy output there still increased by 45 percent.[62] In early 2008, the World Bank estimated donor nations would need to invest more than $2 billion in irrigation, roads, and other development projects to entice Afghan farmers away from poppy cultivation.[63] That will be challenging logistically to implement in the south, given NATO and the Kabul government's inability to quell the violence there. A number of facilities built with aid money already sit empty and crumbling. One western-funded school on the edge of Lashkar Gah was turned into a poppy field after it closed in a shower of Taliban threats.[64]

In other cases, projects have been unsustainable or just plain pointless. In 2006, I visited a cash-for-work project to build a cobblestone road between Lashkar Gah and the ancient fortress of

Qala-e-Bost on the outskirts of the provincial capital. I was accompanied to the worksite, where half a dozen Afghans hammered stones into the earth, by four Humvees each full of U.S. soldiers and bodyguards from the security contracting firm Global. I pointed out to the USAID organizers that the last thing Afghanistan needed was more bumpy roads. They agreed, but said the project was "labor-intensive," and that cobblestone roads lasted centuries. It looked more security-intensive to me, and the stone workers who lined up to tell me they had given up the poppy habit seemed disingenuous. On the way back into town, a British bodyguard in my armored vehicle confirmed my suspicions. "Come back in six weeks and you won't see any of these workers here," he said. "They'll all be off harvesting poppy."

Aid projects were built to suit U.S. deadlines and values—including political time lines and priorities in Washington—rather than meeting the needs and realities of poor Afghan farming families. Despite poor roads, a shortage of electricity, and deteriorating security, USAID planned to launch an apricot and raisin industry, a flour mill, Internet cafés, and a dairy-processing plant. One aid worker I met was doing a feasibility study for an industrial park. A separate plan would have Helmand's produce exported by plane, despite rising fuel costs.[65] Although I believe these groups are genuinely trying to help, most plans I have come across have been utterly unrealistic.

In 2007, aid worker Joel Hafvenstein, contracted by USAID to help set up Helmand's cash-for-work program, published his memoirs, *Opium Season*. His vivid account of his treacherous stint in southern Afghanistan revealed the pressure his team came under from the Bush administration to meet arbitrary quotas they set. Washington dispatched advisers—hired by the Defense Department but answerable to the State Department—to get Afghanistan's faltering reconstruction effort off the ground. The advisers ordered Hafvenstein's team to create 2.5 million workdays in Helmand during their first year, a Herculean task that meant employing thousands of people. They appeared to be unconcerned about the nature of the work, but worried about accusations that too much USAID money went to pay high-priced foreign advisers. The advisers wanted 70 percent of the cash to be spent on Afghans. "Condoleezza Rice will be getting weekly updates on this project," one of the advisers told Hafvenstein, who wondered to what extent the targets were for "Condi's benefit," as he put it, and not based on on-the-ground realities.[66]

Ultimately, none of Washington's goals would be met. Hafvenstein and his colleagues fled Helmand after pro-Taliban assailants killed eleven of their local colleagues and guards. Hafvenstein's experience, while tragic, nonetheless evokes the old adage that the U.S. government is the world's last communist institution, with five-year plans, risk aversion, and targets everyone pretends to meet. Planned economies are doomed to failure when their goals are shaped to meet the political priorities of their planners instead of the needs of the people who live under them.

Deteriorating security and the day-to-day pressures it brought, coupled with the demanding work schedules and Afghanistan's general lack of comfort, has made it hard to keep aid programs and embassies staffed. The country's complex environment presented a steep learning curve for even the most highly dedicated people, especially when tours of duty for diplomats, aid workers, and foreign troops rarely lasted more than one year. As often as not, former officials have complained to me, short-termers tended to bury problems rather than try to solve them. It was a policy the former INL chief Robert Charles dubbed "not-on-my-watchism."

The most spectacular case of this phenomenon came in 2003, when President Bush and Donald Rumsfeld, under domestic pressure to show they were bringing U.S. troops back home, handed the Afghan conflict over to NATO. The changing of command, which came months after the U.S. invasion of Iraq, led many officials in Pakistan and Afghanistan—not to mention the Taliban—to conclude that the United States was looking for an exit strategy. "This decision was made for political impact back home," a former senior U.S. commander in Afghanistan told me. "It reinforced everyone's opinion in the region that we were unreliable."

Afghanistan is the most complex mission NATO has ever taken on, and the first outside the Euro-Atlantic region. Cracks in the twenty-six-nation alliance began to appear immediately. European nations bickered over every troop and aircraft deployment, while lawmakers in Germany, Italy, and Spain have refused to deploy soldiers to dangerous southern regions. American, Dutch, Canadian, and British soldiers do most of the heavy fighting, and have sustained by far the most casualties. Some national forces only take part in combat missions once they have permission from home, making it hard for commanders in Kabul to react rapidly. Some fear the NATO alliance itself may be crumbling. Washington is now seeking a total revamp in strategy, and boosting its forces with thirty thousand more troops. But President Obama has said they will start to pull out in mid-2011.[67]

Within the shaky coalition, the fight against the opium trade remains one of the most divisive issues of all. Washington finally "got religion" on the Taliban's ties to the drug trade, according to senior U.S. officials, but convincing the Europeans they have to help fight it has been a tougher sell. "Diplomatically, my biggest challenge was finding unity," said Thomas Schweich, who formerly led the State Department's efforts to address Afghanistan's opium problem. "I spent far more time in Europe than in Afghanistan."[68]

Washington put forward a five-pillar strategy to fight the opium trade in 2007, with a focus on aerial eradication, alternative livelihoods, interdiction and law enforcement, justice reform, and public information.[69] The Kabul government and most European nations rejected it as too heavily focused on aerial eradication using the herbicide glyphosate, which is commonly sold in the United States under the trade name Roundup. Senior U.S. officials insist their real priority is arresting opium kingpins but admit that the policy also creates divisions since it will mean going after top officials in the Karzai administration.

"I'm a spray man myself," quipped President George W. Bush, summing up his depth of understanding of the controversial and complex issue in two meetings with stunned Afghan officials. U.S. ambassador to Afghanistan William Wood was far less flippant in his messages to Afghan officials, threatening to cut off aid from Washington if they didn't agree to allow crop dusters to wipe out the 2008 harvest.[70] When the 2007 opium harvest soared past $4 billion in value, even the normally impartial UN issued a call for alliance members to take military action against the problem. "Destroy the drug trade and you cut off the Taliban's main funding source," said UNODC director Antonio Maria Costa in an open letter to NATO.[71]

At the end of the day, the biggest problem in coalition building may come not from NATO but from across the border. Counternarcotics officials publicly praise Pakistan's efforts, but privately gripe that Islamabad has done little to shut down the command and control centers for the Afghan drug trade, which are in Baluchistan Province and the southern port city of Karachi. In 2007, Pakistan was quietly slipped onto the State Department's list of major trafficking countries, a designation that in the past could have cut off millions of dollars of aid to Islamabad. "No matter what we do in Afghanistan, we won't touch the problem if we can't get to Pakistan," one senior U.S. official told me. "What keeps me up at night," said a senior western envoy, "is that I don't see a way out of this."[72]

8. ZERO-SUM GAME ⸫⸫

IT'S EASY TO TRACE HOW AFGHANISTAN REACHED THE state it is in today, and to finger all those responsible. It's a lot tougher to try and formulate a way forward.

After reading the data field researchers compiled for this book, readers could perhaps be forgiven for concluding (as the Bush administration did) that the best strategy would be an aggressive aerial spraying campaign to wipe out Afghanistan's poppy crop. That way the insurgents and terrorists are denied much-needed funds, right?

Wrong. Wiping out Afghanistan's poppy fields would actually drive up poppy prices and put *more* money in the pockets of drug dealers and terrorists. It's basic economics (the Taliban used it themselves when they banned poppy in 2000). When supplies go down, prices go up. Due to major overproduction in Afghanistan for several years now, poppy prices have plummeted to the point one actually hears opium smugglers saying they *hope* the West launches an aggressive spraying campaign: "I'll be very happy if the eradicators are successful," said a trafficker in Helmand. "I have lots of poppy stored. If they don't destroy [poppy fields], I'm afraid the price will come down."[1] The United Nations estimates that there are now more than 12,000 metric tons of Afghan opiates stockpiled in the region, and since Afghan farmers do not report storing major quantities of opium, it appears that insurgents and traffickers are holding them. Those stockpiles would sky-rocket in value if there were widespread eradication.

There's another camp suggesting that the best way forward is to "just buy" the entire opium crop. First of all, that's easier said than done in a country where the Taliban control about one-third of the territory. Second of all, the British government already tried a version of that plan in 2002, offering to pay farmers to cut down their poppy crops. It backfired completely: Thousands more farmers planted poppy the following year, just to get their hands on the easy money. The international community should not inadvertently give farmers another incentive to plant poppy, especially because in non-Taliban zones of the country, the area planted with poppy has decreased steadily from 2007 to 2009. Plus it's a terrible idea to get into a bidding war with drug traffickers and the Taliban. Unfortunately, they would probably be able to outspend the international community.

Still others want to legalize the crop. Personally, I'm intrigued by proposals to start small-scale operations that would legally harvest cannabis and opium in Afghanistan for use as biofuel. The idea stems from an Australian program, launched in 2005, in which farmers in Tasmania began using biodiesel produced from poppy seed to run their tractors.[2] I can also visualize the day when narcotics grown in Afghanistan could produce cheap, hygienically harvested pharmaceuticals, as has also been proposed by the International Council on Security and Development.[3]

However, if Afghanistan's drug crop were legalized tomorrow, there would exist neither the infrastructure nor the resources to regulate it. Who would make sure the opium got sold to pharmaceutical companies and biofuel firms and not to drug traffickers?

Probably not Afghanistan's notoriously corrupt police, many of whom also profit off the drug trade. Opium grown for medicine must be harvested under hygienic conditions, using clean water and sterilized farm tools. Who would ensure it was harvested hygienically in dusty southern Afghanistan? Afghanistan's Food and Drug Administration? There isn't one.

On top of that, it would be impossible in the current security vacuum to account for the legal distribution of poppy. India grants licenses to more than 70,000 farmers to grow opium for medicinal purposes, and monitors their activities using Smart Identity Cards, farm patrols, and satellite imagery. Despite Delhi's efforts, it's estimated that one third of its poppy crop is sold illegally, since drug traffickers pay about five times more for opium than drug companies. If poppy were legalized in Afghanistan, Afghan farmers would stand to earn about the same selling it on the legal market as they earn from selling wheat.[4] In other words, there would be no financial incentive to sell it on the legal market.

Afghanistan needs good governance and rule of law before there can be earnest conversations about legalizing its drug crop. And that is something that will not emerge overnight. It's important to remember that people don't go into the narcotics business because they enjoy gardening. They do it to make money—lots of money. The more difficult it becomes to profit from the drug trade, the greater the chances of defeating it. That means targeting drug refineries, convoys carrying opium, and the multiton stockpiles stored at Taliban hideouts. That means interdicting people tied to the drugs trade—whether they support the Afghan government or the Taliban—and bringing them to justice. This will have to be handled by the international community until Afghanistan's judicial system and police are functioning effectively. It also means supporting farmers in the effort to shift onto a broad array of legal crops, and helping to open global markets for those farm products. It means educating the Afghan public about the dangers and pitfalls of trading narcotics, and conducting selective eradication programs only in areas where all the other options fail.

A successful counternarcotics strategy would be like a four-legged table, supported by interdiction, alternative livelihoods, public education, and eradication. Just as a table will wobble if its legs are uneven, there must be balance between the four pillars for a counternarcotics strategy to succeed. Raise incentives for people to function within the law, while simultaneously raising the risks of operating outside of it. It's less a matter of being tough than persistent.

Currently, NATO and the Taliban are fighting a zero-sum game: the West wants to wipe out the insurgents and their al Qaeda allies; the Taliban want to drive foreign non-Muslims out of Afghanistan. The best strategy against the Taliban is not to fight them but to make them irrelevant. NATO has not lost ground in Afghanistan because Afghans like the Taliban (they don't). The coalition has failed until now because it hasn't offered Afghans a better alternative, and in many areas, the Taliban have outgoverned the local government. Fixing Afghanistan—and the greater region—is going to be costly, slow going and it will require an enormous amount of manpower. Since the Bush administration failed to complete the job in 2001 and beyond, defeating the insurgency and the drug trade will now take years—possibly decades—of sustained investment and effort. The Obama administration has taken steps in the right direction, but there remains concern among Afghans and Pakistanis that the United States might abandon the effort before it is complete. A successful approach would be broad and long-term, and recognize that there is no silver bullet.

A complete counternarcotics strategy would combine nine pillars: diplomatic initiatives for regional peace and free trade; effective governance and rule of law; a properly implemented counterinsurgency strategy; blended intelligence and law enforcement efforts; military strikes against drug lords, labs, and opium convoys; the isolation and disruption of drug and terror funds; a public relations campaign; and the creation of a farm support network and alternative livelihoods program. Eradication, the foundation of Bush's strategy, would be used in limited cases, and only when all the other efforts have failed.

Together, it would work like the drug cocktail administered to HIV patients, mounting a simultaneous, multipronged attack. The effort should be holistic, not prioritized. Washington is wary of *state building*. Well, this problem requires *region building*. As the biggest donor with the largest number of troops deployed to Afghanistan, the United States should take the lead in revitalizing strategy.

Support Regional Peace

Afghanistan was center stage in the nineteenth century for the "Great Game," when Tsarist Russia and the British Empire jockeyed for influence and control over resources in Central Asia. In the 1980s, it was the final battleground of the Cold War. Now the front line in the Global War on Terror, Afghanistan again finds itself the victim of regional and global power plays having little to do with Afghans themselves. Overcoming the India-Pakistan rivalry as well as finding common ground between the United States and Iran are among the numerous regional barriers preventing sustainable peace in Afghanistan. At first glance, many of these issues seem totally unrelated to the poppy problem, but boundary and trade disputes, along with global geopolitics, are at the heart of the region's security problems.

Former U.S. envoy Peter Tomsen suggests a regional conference based on the Helsinki talks of 1975, which attempted to improve relations between the Communist bloc in Eastern Europe and the West. A South Asian peace confab would address broader goals of regional peace that could give regional leaders cover with their domestic audiences. Located at the center of Eurasia, Afghanistan sits at the crossroads of trade, transportation, and energy corridors— it's the modern day Silk Route. Instead of trying to appease bilateral rivalries, like the one between India and Pakistan, a broad peace conference would examine the benefits for all if the region began to think as one. "Bold creativity and thinking big could produce lasting benefits," Tomsen said.[5] U.S. President Barack Obama could set an example for India and Pakistan by having senior American diplomats sit down with their counterparts in Tehran. I'm not suggesting Washington overlook Iran's apparent nuclear ambitions, but the United States and Iran share a common interest in stopping the flow of opiates from Afghanistan. It's a good place to start.

As well, Southwest Asia remains one of the few parts of the world without a free-trade grouping like NAFTA, ASEAN, or Mercusur. A free-trade zone could one day expand to include the isolated Central Asian states. Opening markets and surmounting border, ethnic, and religious divides plaguing the region since British colonialists departed would bring stability and increase prosperity—two factors vital to easing the dependence on smuggling illegal drugs and other commodities. Afghanistan must have access to Pakistani seaports, and could harmonize its customs duties with Pakistan to cut down on the smuggling of legal goods. Islamabad loses as estimated $2 billion a year in tax revenues because of goods transported to Afghanistan from Karachi and then smuggled back into Pakistan, according to Sardar Shaukat Popalzai, president of the Baluchistan Economic Forum. Afghanistan, for its part, has one of the lowest tax bases on the globe. Helping both countries harmonize and better regulate customs collection would weaken smuggling groups and strengthen the federal governments in both Pakistan and Afghanistan.

Implement a Proper Counterinsurgency Strategy

For four months of 2009, officials in the Obama administration debated about whether or not to send General Stanley McChrystal the troop increase he requested. In the end the U.S. president decided to surge 30,000 soldiers and marines, putting them on a tight eighteen-month timetable. There are two problems with this decision, as well as opportunities to correct them down the line. One is that counterinsurgency requires a large force presence, and even with 30,000 more U.S. troops, certain regions of Afghanistan will remain under-resourced. The general rule of thumb is that there should be one reliable and trusted soldier or law enforcement officers for every fifty inhabitants (meaning about 20,000 foreign and local forces for Helmand province alone). The second issue is that counterinsurgency takes time, certainly more than eighteen months. That said, there is a decent chance it will be evident whether or not the tide is turning before President Obama's mid-2011 deadline. By the time the surge is complete, for example, Helmand province will have roughly the appropriate ratio of local and foreign troops to civilians. If General McChrystal's strategy is showing signs of success there, President Obama may choose to expand it. If not, he has given himself an out date. The biggest drawback to underresourcing the overall mission is that counterinsurgency—like counternarcotics—is comparable to squeezing a balloon. You squeeze it in one place, and it pops up somewhere else. The Taliban have proven to be nimble and adaptable, moving north in 2009 when Marines flowed into Helmand. The coalition has not.

I support the notion that protecting the local population will help defeat the Taliban and al Qaeda, but I don't suggest it will be easy, especially given the cultural and language barriers. Say a company of U.S. Marines moves into a district in southern Helmand dominated by the Taliban. Until reliable local officials come on stream and begin to govern effectively, those 120 or so Marines will not only be fighting battle-hardened insurgents, they will also effectively become policemen, aid workers, and diplomats, with their company commander as the town mayor. If they're well prepared, the Marines will have good local interpreters. If they're very well prepared, one or two people in their unit will have trained in Pashto. But what Washington is expecting its armed forces to achieve in Afghanistan is in no way simple. Building trust takes time and patience. There are measurable benefits to providing security, according to a 2007 *ABC News* poll. The national survey found Afghans rated American efforts twice as high in areas where they described security as "very good." Meanwhile, in areas where there was heavy U.S. troop deployment, 73 percent of respondents held positive views of America as a nation and 67 percent said they thought U.S. troops had done a good job.[6]

Ironically, security appears to improve for foreign forces only once they move outside the comfort zone of their bases and armored vehicles, and interact with ordinary civilians. Unlike American and British fortresses looped with razor wire, Dutch soldiers in Uruzgan province have had some success from operating out of small, mud-walled compounds known as "qalas," the Pashto word for house, which have a visitor's room where locals can come for impromptu meetings. The Dutch make house calls in the province they patrol, making sure the locals' needs are met.[7] As to be expected, they have encountered push back from the Taliban, especially along strategic drug smuggling routes.[8] But some analysts credit the Dutch strategy—and their decision to stay neutral in local tribal conflicts—with a casualty rate that is lower than those suffered by other foreign forces deployed in the south.[9] In 2010, Canadian troops plan to copy the Dutch technique by moving out of their heavily armed bases and into Kandahar city and other provincial towns.[10]

Interaction with the local community is vital to building trust, especially in Afghanistan, where personal trust forms the basis of all relationships—whether in business, politics, or elsewhere. "You have to hunker down with the Afghan people to get stuff done," says Beverly Eighmy, the former USAID counternarcotics official. "You have to have credibility. You can't go out there with seventy-five bodyguards looking confrontational." There should be less attention paid to how many insurgents are killed in battle. Kill ratios make little difference when the local population despises you. Better metrics of success include an increase in the number of locals tipping off the coalition about militant activity, a sustained reduction in poppy cultivation, drug trafficking, kidnapping, and extortion over a five-year period, and a correlative growth in alternative industry and crops.

Support Good Governance and Fight Corruption

A counterinsurgency campaign is only as good as the government it supports, making state corruption in Afghanistan a major obstacle to success. If Mexico and Colombia are anything to go by, there won't be real improvement in Afghanistan until the president himself decides it's time to stamp out corruption and the narcotics trade. Hamid Karzai is under immense pressure to show progress on these issues. How he responds will be critical to the success of the NATO mission and the future of his country.

Efforts to degrade the Taliban's ability to earn from drugs and crime have failed in part because so many individuals within the Kabul government are also profiting from narcotics and wrongdoing. The fact that interdiction of officials tied to crime has never been a priority has created the impression among many Afghans that U.S. leaders not only condone the opium trade, but are even participating in it, or simply helping their allies within the Karzai regime get rich on the side. A few major arrests, jointly carried out by the Afghan government and international community, would help change that impression, and they should not just focus on traffickers linked to the insurgency. Foreign and Afghan law enforcement officials working in Kabul should jointly and thoroughly investigate the reports that high-level officials in the Karzai administration, including the president's half-brother, Ahmed Wali, are tied to the opium trade. They should present Karzai and the Afghan National Assembly with finished evidence, not just rumors, and press for prompt judicial action where necessary, recognizing that those trials will probably occur outside Afghanistan. It may never be possible to cut off Karzai from his drug-corrupted cronies, but at the very least Washington should ban U.S. government agencies from keeping Afghan officials found to be tied to drugs and crime on their payroll, as is the case with Ahmed Wali and several key warlords.

Washington should also implement better oversight of its aid and development money, putting more focus on community-driven projects that give Afghans a sense of ownership over the changes taking place around them. When ordinary Afghans get to help decide how their communities grow, and when that growth also provides opportunities for local employment, there is a correlative reduction in graft and violence. There's a fairly simple principle behind this: You don't steal, damage, or destroy what you already own. Instead, you protect it.

Blend Counterterrorism and Counternarcotics Efforts

In the wake of 9/11, it became painfully clear that better cooperation between America's intelligence and law enforcement agencies might have prevented those attacks. Lack of coordination has also hampered U.S. efforts in Afghanistan post-2001. "We get so wrapped around the axle about who has what responsibility: is this for the military, the DEA, or law enforcement," one U.S. military official complained to me. "The terrorist doesn't worry about any of that. You never hear him say, 'I'm not working with that guy. He's a drug dealer.'"[11] One positive focus of McChrystal's new command structure is that he is trying to ensure direct and open lines of communication between the military, law enforcement, intelligence, and aid communities, according to people on the ground. Now there is an interagency task force tracking threat finance and insurgent criminal funding, while Special Forces teams work closely in southern and western Afghanistan with paramilitary teams from the DEA. More such cooperation is needed to combat a fast-changing and flexible enemy.

As well, there is growing recognition among senior NATO officials that the model for attacking organizations such as the Taliban and al Qaeda is no different than the method used to bring down drug cartels and organized crime groups. The biggest challenge still seems to be changing the military mind-set to accept that there is wartime value to good old-fashioned police work. As thousands more U.S. troops fan out around Afghanistan, pushing into insurgent-held zones in the south and southeast, they could benefit from increased interaction with American law enforcement professionals who know how to walk the beat, identify criminal elements in local communities, and collect evidence at a crime scene or after a bomb has exploded. Soldiers don't necessarily have to turn into detectives, but at the very least they should support police work in their zones. Counternarcotics agents piecing together information about the major regional smuggling cartels have embedded with some NATO forces. That should continue.

A number of Marine infantry units have benefitted from the Law Enforcement Professional or LEP program, which has placed retired police officers with experience fighting gangs as advisers into about a half-dozen infantry units in Afghanistan. "We can't just drop thousand-pound bombs all over the place," says Ralph Morten, who worked for the Los Angeles Police Department for twenty-nine years, serving both on the bomb squad and fighting gangs. "The bad guys live among the citizens, and we have to go in and dig them out, just like we do in gang work in Los Angeles."[12] The LEP program teaches infantry troops to seek out criminals and insurgents in the communities where they operate, and to establish how insurgents communicate and acquire supplies like IED components and precursor chemicals. Then it shows them how to disrupt those activities. The LEP program boosts force protection and helps make local communities safer. It should be expanded to every infantry unit.

Target Criminals, Not Farmers

The UNODC and counternarcotics officials estimate that less than two dozen Pashtun and Baluch traffickers control the majority of the Afghan opium market. "Everyone knows who they are and where they are," a western official complained to me. "Why aren't they being arrested?"[13] But in a region where corruption is rife and political will almost nonexistent, the capture and prosecution of major traffickers is not as simple as it sounds, especially since the masterminds of the opium trade related to the insurgency tend to reside in Pakistan or the UAE, neither of which has a positive track record for apprehending and handing over powerful crime lords.

That said, there have been some remarkable success stories, including the arrest of Haji Juma Khan and the convictions of Bashir Noorzai and Khan Mohammed, showing that the long arm of U.S. law can reach Afghan drug traffickers with ties to the Taliban. In cases where such individuals remain out of reach, they can still be "named and shamed" by the international community. As the UNODC has argued, U.N. member states should add top traffickers who work with the insurgency to the Security Council's list of al

Qaeda and Taliban members "in order to seize their assets, ban their travel, and facilitate their extradition."[14] Naming and shaming won't land anyone in jail, but over time, it can build up pressure on a government, like Pakistan or the UAE, that fails to respond to repeated complaints about the individuals it shelters.

Inside Afghanistan and the Pakistan border areas, the U.S. military has put fifty traffickers known to cooperate with the insurgency on its "kill or capture" list. In addition to targeting drug traffickers—a strategy that will significantly raise the risk for engaging in the drug business inside Afghan territory—there should be stepped-up military efforts to intercept drug convoys, and to destroy heroin labs and drug stockpiles, using infrared technology. This will hit the traffickers where it hurts—in their wallets—and reduce the amount of narcotics leaving the region. It will also take the focus off of poor poppy farmers, who need support in moving onto legal crops.

Create a Farm Support Network

Any plan to rid Afghanistan of its drug crisis will fail until the Afghan government and international donors can come up with a farm support network for legal alternatives. There has been much talk of legalizing the poppy crop, a plan I don't support until there is good governance in Afghanistan. Instead, why not subsidize *legal* crops? The United States and Europe subsidize their farmers, why should Afghan farmers be expected to survive with less support? Because actually, they don't. The traffickers have established their own, predatory farm support system, and it's one of the reasons so many farmers grow poppy. Poor farmers need the small loans opium merchants provide in the fall to make it through the winter months. But those loans are geared to trap the farmers in debt come the spring harvest. A nonpredatory, internationally funded microcredit program for legal crops would create another incentive for farmers to shift off of poppy.

A support team inside Afghanistan's Commerce Ministry to source regional buyers and form partnerships with international produce firms could yield further positive results. By determining what subsidies are needed to make crops viable for farmers and buyers alike, a farm support plan based on market needs and in consultation with Afghan tribal councils would benefit locals. William Byrd, a World Bank expert on Afghan poppy, suggests donors invest in a broad portfolio of fruit and nut orchards instead of annual crops like wheat and rice. Pomegranate, orange, and grape orchards take longer to mature, meaning there would have to be a sizable initial investment on the part of international donors, but once planted, it would become harder for farmers to shift back to poppy.

There should be focus on identifying and gaining entrance to new markets. This will be challenging and expensive. Experts suggest an effective agricultural replacement strategy will cost $1 billion a year over the next five years, which sounds like a lot until you consider that the United States was spending $5 billion *every month* to fight the Taliban by the end of 2009.[15] It's not beyond the realm of possibility that Afghans could turn away from drug crops. Before the Soviet invasion in 1979, Afghanistan not only fed itself, it exported $100 million worth of food and farm products a year.[16]

Since personal trust plays a vital role in Afghan business deals, farm support programs working closely with tribes and local leaders—trying to meet their needs and connect them with international or regional investors—would have a better chance at winning public support. "It has to be a one-to-one thing with the Afghans," said Eighmy, who negotiated alternative crop programs with tribal leaders in Nangarhar in the late 1980s. "They knew me, so I could go out to the countryside and I could sit down with the tribal elders and say, 'We can do this and this for you, but I can not see any poppy come next spring.' And I would get their personal guarantee and it worked." As the number of NATO troops expands across the poppy-rich south, there is a need to deploy agricultural experts and Commerce Ministry teams to negotiate new markets. The idea, as another U.S. official puts it, is "to come upon enemies and leave behind friends."[17]

Improve the Public Relations Campaign

Ninety-five percent of the Afghans surveyed for this book opposed the poppy trade, and virtually every farmer interviewed by local researchers expressed a desire to grow something else. Afghan people in poppy-growing and opium-refining areas loathe the insurgents and traffickers, but they don't hold the Afghan government or NATO in high esteem either. A public relations campaign should strive to convince the Afghan public that the Kabul government and the international community are trying to make their lives better. The campaign would only succeed if it occurred in conjunction with the other eight pillars of this strategy, in particular the anticorruption drive.

Radio and local television will be pivotal to creating awareness about the policies of NATO troops and alternative livelihoods on offer for the Afghan people. The militants use religion to justify their cause. To counteract the militant propaganda, the Koran can be an ally in the war against drugs, as Islam forbids the use, cultivation, and traffic of narcotics. Islamic law experts and Muslim clerics supporting a call to stamp out poppy could prove useful in broadcast media.[18] Aid workers say Afghans also respond to messages from doctors that heroin addiction—an increasingly common affliction there—is not curable. Moreover, NATO and the Afghan government should go public with their knowledge of the links between insurgents, opium, and other crime, holding up a mirror to the illegal economy that hides behind their veneer of piety and religion.

Isolate and Obstruct Drug Money

Afghanistan has created a Financial Supervision Unit within its central bank to monitor money transfers in and out of the country's financial institutions. Any transfer above $20,000 must be reported to a banking oversight agency, and suspicious activity gets investigated with the cooperation of more than twenty countries, much as bank transfers get monitored in the United States. Finance agents in Kabul say there are suspicious amounts of funds bouncing between Afghanistan, Russia, the UAE, and South Africa, but they are starting to develop the ability to separate the good from the bad. "We are ahead of the game," the Central Bank Governor Noorullah Delawari said, "because we have to be. We are in the front line in both the wars on terror and drugs."

Since the majority of money transfers through Pakistan and Afghanistan pass through the informal *hawala* system, better efforts also must be made to separate the minority of dirty money from the majority of innocent funds. In Afghanistan, there is already a program underway to license the *hawaladars* and install a cost-free reporting system, allowing financial agents to track money flows and identify who is sending what where. It has already helped isolate various money traders who appear to be tied to dirty money. Financial experts say it would be unfeasible—not to mention pointless—to try and transfer a U.S.-style regulatory system onto Afghanistan.

Donor nations should subsidize efforts to help Afghanistan and Pakistan establish cost-free reporting mechanisms for regulating the *hawala* network, and use the vast databank of information the *hawaladars* have to help *fight* crime, rather than move criminal money. Financial incentives—such as discounts—must be offered for moneychangers and customers who agree to regulate their transfers within the legal market. "Only when we can make the regulated systems more attractive to customers than the unregulated, will we win," said a western official. NATO governments should press the UAE to implement such programs as well.

Regulating the region's trade is of even greater importance. Afghanistan and Pakistan should be encouraged to harmonize their customs duties and to collect the taxes together at the Karachi port. This would increase badly needed tax revenue for both countries and reduce the smuggling of legal commodities that's closely tied to the export of opiates. The establishment of Trade Transparency Units, or TTUs, between Afghanistan, Pakistan, and the UAE would monitor commodity flows and try to isolate cases of trade-based money laundering. Eventually, this system could be expanded to include Central Asian states.

John Cassara, the former U.S. Treasury Special Agent, believes a small team of specially trained financial agents could target major Afghan traffickers—not to mention insurgent cash flows—and interrupt them relatively quickly. If it becomes difficult to make money in the Afghan region, traffickers will move elsewhere. That won't necessarily slow narcotics supplies to the West, but it may break their ties to the Taliban and al Qaeda in this region.

Stamping out the drug trade will weaken the Afghan economy in the short run, and that is something the donor community must prepare and accommodate for financially. Once drugs are replaced with legal commerce, exactly the opposite is true. The export value of the 2007 opium harvest was $3.1 billion, with approximately 25 percent of the opium's value, or $755 million, paid to Afghan farmers, and the remainder going to traffickers who mainly live out of Afghanistan. "Drugs drain money from a country, and they don't bring the profits back home," says Raymond Baker, author of *Capitalism's Achilles Heel.* Governor Delawari, at Afghanistan Central Bank, put it another way, "We get called a narco-state and the money ends up outside the country."[19] The net outflow of drug money offsets inflows of investment and aid, making it impossible to drag Afghanistan out of poverty. One often hears the argument that fighting the drug trade will create instability. I believe there is no way to build a stable Afghanistan until the criminal economy is dismantled and replaced.

Eradicate Only When Everything Else Fails

Wide-scale eradication will disrupt peace-building strategies, and since insurgents and traffickers earn the bulk of their profits beyond the poppy fields, it won't succeed in weakening them. That said, there are some large landowners who will likely resist going legal, and in those cases, there may need to be some eradication. Spy satellites, for example, have found cases where desert reclamation projects have taken place in southern Helmand—traffickers are creating farmland in order to grow more poppy. Poor farmers do not have the means to fund such large-scale projects, and eradicating these crops would not disrupt efforts to build peace and win broad public support. But these are very rare cases. In general, U.S. funds earmarked for eradication could be far better spent on alternative livelihood programs and efforts to build Afghanistan's domestic security and law enforcement capability.

Zero-Sum Game

Criminal and terrorist groups take root and flourish where there is an absence of good governance and security. The international community must stop thinking about Afghanistan's drug and insurgency problems as isolated issues and understand that this country—and the region as a whole—will remain a problem until a comprehensive, holistic strategy is adopted. The nexus of terrorists and traffickers is as much a threat to the West as it is to South and Central Asia. The campaign against it must be global in scope, reach, and purpose. The ultimate goal should not be the end of the Taliban and al Qaeda, but the creation of a prosperous and stable Afghanistan and greater region. The United States owes it to the citizens of Afghanistan, and it will make the United States safer, too.

Since the first edition of this book was published, I have held dozens of meetings with American military planners, law enforcement officials, and intelligence analysts. I tell them: Treat each village as a unique campaign. Listen to what the villagers want, and help them achieve it. Keep it simple. Start small. Think big. This won't be easy, but in every area, there is a solution.

AFTERWORD

There are two common justifications given for engaging in the drug trade in Afghanistan. Both of them are completely false.

One is that the Koran gives a pass in times of jihad to profit off narcotics. In fact, Islam's holy book defines drugs as "the filth of Satan's handiwork."[1] The other is that it is permissible to traffic in drugs so long as you only sell them to non-Muslims. But that isn't the case either. Anyone who thinks infidels are the main consumers of Afghan dope is fooling himself.

Measured by volume, Muslims consume more than half the opiates grown and refined in Afghanistan, according to eye-popping 2009 data released by the United Nations Office on Drugs and Crime. Addicts in Iran, Afghanistan, and Pakistan alone accounted for 55 percent of the 1,100 metric tons of opium consumed worldwide in 2008. Users in Central Asia, Iran, and Pakistan smoked, snorted, or injected another 17 percent of the heroin produced that year.

A tsunami of addiction, accompanied by rising incidence of HIV and Hepatitis C, is washing over Afghanistan and the countries around it. One 2009 study calculates that Afghanistan now has more than two million drug addicts, a plight aggravated by poor security in the southern poppy belt, where villagers are forced to self-medicate in the absence of hospitals and health clinics.[2] There are stomach-churning photos of Afghan mothers exhaling opium smoke into the mouths of their colicky babies, bringing them temporary comfort perhaps, but also a lifetime of drug dependence. And on the streets of Afghanistan, there are small children pushing heroin.[3]

The problem is equally severe for Afghanistan's neighbors. Iran has 1.4 million opium users and Pakistan 4 million addicts, according to government estimates in those countries.[4] Heroin constitutes about 70 percent of the drugs seized in Central Asia, where it costs no more than two dollars a hit. Although there are only vague estimates of addiction rates in countries like Tajikistan, Uzbekistan, Turkmenistan, and Kazakhstan, intravenous drug use has contributed to one of the world's fastest-growing infection rates of HIV, the virus that causes AIDS.[5]

Meanwhile, it's quite clear that European nations and Russia (countries that have done considerably less to stem the flow of narcotics from Afghanistan than the United States) consume a stunning 47 percent of the heroin produced there. The UNODC report puts the toll in perspective:

- The number of people who die from heroin overdoses in NATO nations is five times higher than the number of NATO soldiers killed since military operations began there in 2001.

- More Russians die every year from drug overdoses (an estimated 30,000–40,000 annually) than the total number of Red Army soldiers who died during the seven-year Soviet occupation of Afghanistan.

There's little doubt that making addicts of non-Muslims in the West is part of the insurgent and terror groups' strategy. And there are indications that insurgents on the battlefields in southern Afghanistan have direct links to criminal gangs in the West. For some time, British spy planes have picked up radio communication between Taliban fighters in Helmand who speak with thick accents from Manchester, Birmingham, West Bromwich, and Bradford, all cities with large populations of British Muslims of South Asian origin. Western law enforcement officials have come to suspect those British Taliban fighters may have links to criminal gangs whose members are Muslim and who have been connected to selling heroin on British streets. At least one other captured Taliban fighter was found to have British gang tattoos on his arms, according to a western law enforcement adviser to the Marines, and there is evidence that various British Muslim gangs have sent fighters to Afghanistan, or sell Afghan heroin on British streets. Roughly 90 percent of the heroin sold in Britain comes from Afghanistan.

The Gambinos, a group of gangsters of Pakistani origin who take their name from the New York crime family, have been linked to selling Afghan heroin in north London and Luton. So have the South Man Syndicate and the Muslim Boys (who are also known as the PDC, or Poverty Driven Children). "The big bosses have Taliban and al Qaeda connections and we're often told only to deal it to non-Muslims. They call it chemical jihad and hope to ruin lives while getting massive payouts at the same time," said a street dealer interviewed by a British newspaper.[6]

British officials admit it is hard to tell how much is bravado and how much is a sign of a concrete relationship between extremists in South Asia and the Muslim gangs of the United Kingdom. British law enforcement officials believe the link is there—and a cause for concern. Lee Jasper, the chair of the Lambeth Police Consultative Group has expressed concerns that Muslim gangs could be morphing into a criminalized front for terrorist extremists in Britain.[7]

And although the DEA says that less than 5 percent of the heroin sold on U.S. streets comes from Southwest Asia, some American law enforcement authorities fear Afghan heroin could be headed to the United States. Currently, Latin American gangs control most heroin smuggled into the United States. But that may be changing. Canada's Royal Mounted Police has warned that more than 60 percent of the heroin sold in Canada now comes from Afghanistan.[8] And U.S. authorities have tracked a moderate increase in the number of Afghan heroin seizures in cities near the Canadian border, including Chicago, Detroit, and Minneapolis.[9]

Criminal gangs with links to extremism are spreading their tentacles ever more globally. Recent events prove that al Qaeda has taken lessons learned facilitating the heroin trade in Afghanistan and applied them on an even more global scale.

In November 2009, investigators in the West African country of Mali discovered the smoldering wreckage of a Boeing 727 near a remote Sahara airstrip.[10] It appeared the jet crashed shortly after takeoff, and may have been torched to destroy evidence. U.S. and European intelligence and law enforcement officials who examined it agreed on one thing: the cargo plane had carried large quantities of cocaine from South America into Europe, and the narcotics were probably destined for the European market.[11]

Investigators knew there was a drug route from South America to West Africa prior to the discovery of the plane, but they had believed that traffickers were using small planes or skiffs. The fact that smugglers were using Boeing jets came as "a complete surprise," said Alexandre Schmidt of the UNODC.[12] The Boeing appeared to have been carrying between two and three metric tons of cocaine—a huge amount given that the U.N. estimates about 250 tons of cocaine enters western Europe every year.[13]

More worrisome still were claims that the airstrip in Mali was under the control of al Qaeda in the Islamic Magreb, a Sunni radical group from Algeria that has allied itself with Osama bin Laden.

On December 18, 2009, the U.S. Department of Justice confirmed suspicions that al Qaeda was providing protection for drug traffickers moving cocaine through West Africa into Europe. Three men arrested in Ghana after allegedly agreeing to transport drug shipments as large as 1,000 kilos appeared before the federal court of the Southern District of New York to be arraigned on narco-terrorism charges. Oumar Issa, Haroune Touré, and Idriss Abelrahman identified themselves as members of al Qaeda in the Islamic Magreb, according to court documents made public the same day.

An elaborate sting operation brought down the three men, using a confidential informant to the DEA posing as a member of the Colombian rebel group, the FARC. The three al Qaeda men agreed to transport drugs from West Africa through the Canary Islands into Europe. When the informant asked the three extremists if they had the manpower and connections to transport the cocaine safely, Abelrahman just smiled, according to the court papers. "We are everywhere," he said.

NOTES ∴

1. The New Axis of Evil

1. Information for this passage was recounted to research assistant 1 in Ghazni, Afghanistan, July 2008.

2. Richard Oppel, "More U.S. Forces for Afghanistan Will Be Sent to Taliban Stronghold in South," *New York Times*, December 2, 2009.

3. "Karzai Sworn in as Leader," *BBC News*, December 7, 2007. http://news.bbc .co.uk/2/hi/south_asia/4074175.stm.

4. U.S. Central Command, "Coalition Forces Make Second Major Drug Seizure in Five Days," news release, December 20, 2003; U.S. Central Command, "USS *Decatur* Captures Possible Al Qaeda Associated Drug-Smuggling Dhow in Arabian Gulf," news release, December 19, 2003.

5. Interview with U.S. official, Kabul, March 2004.

6. Yusufzai, "Taliban Aims to Regain Power," and Peters, "Hostilities Flare in America's Other War."

7. Interviews with U.S. military officials in Afghanistan and the United States; Nick Meo, "The Spoils of War: Hate and Heroin," *Sydney Morning Herald*, November 21, 2004.

8. Interview with U.S. official, Kabul, March 2004.

9. For a full transcript of Bush's speech see http://archives.cnn.com/2001/ US/09/20/gen.bush.transcript/.

10. In a 2009 statement, for example, the Taliban's number two Mullah Brader Akhund said: "This pious and patriotic people have offered tremendous material and soul sacrifices in the way of their sacred objectives. The mujahideen have not chosen this path of strife between the truth and the evil to obtain material goals. They have lofty Islamic and nationalist aims." For the full transcript of Brader's comments, see http://www.nefafoundation.org/ miscellaneous/nefaAkhund1109.pdf.

11. Telephone interview with DEA spokespersons Garrison Courtney and Mary Cooper, August 30, 2007.

12. Michael Braun, "U.S. Counternarcotics Policy in Afghanistan: Time for Leadership."

13. Sedat Laciner, "Drug Smuggling As the Main Financial Source of PKK Terrorism," *Turkish Weekly*, December 30, 2008.

14. Cilluffo, "Threat Posed from the Convergence of Organized Crime, Drug Trafficking and Terrorism."

15. Fearon, "Why Do Some Wars Last So Much Longer Than Others?"

16. http://www.unodc.org/documents/crop-monitoring/Afghanistan/Afghanistan_opium_survey_2009_summary.pdf.

17. For more detail, see David Kaplan and Alec Dubrow, *Yakuza: Japan's Criminal Underworld*, Berkeley: University of California Press, 2003.

18. For more detail, see John Dickie, *Cosa Nostra: A History of the Sicilian Mafia*, New York: Palgrave Macmillan, 2004.

19. Interview with a senior U.S. official, Islamabad, February 5, 2008.

20. Information for this paragraph comes from Rabasa and Chalk, "Colombian Labyrinth," and Hanson, "FARC, ELN: Colombia's Left-Wing Guerrillas."

21. Aryn Baker, "How Crime Pays for the Taliban," *Time* magazine, September 7, 2009.

22. Interview by author, Kabul, March 2006.

23. Using local assistants, I conducted surveys in Arghastan, Dalbandin, Gereshk, Kandahar, Musa Qala, Now Zad, Panjway, Registan, Sangin, and Spin Boldak in Afghanistan and among Afghan populations residing in Chaman and Quetta, Pakistan.

24. Interview by author with David Kilcullen, COMISAF advisor, Washington D.C., October 27, 2009.

25. A full version of the assessment is available at www.media.washingtonpost.com/wp-srv/ . . . /Assessment _Redacted_092109.pdf.

26. An August 2009 report to the Senate Foreign Relations Committee claimed the UN had reduced its estimates of insurgent drug earnings, quoting the figure of $128 million. But in my subsequent communications with the UN-ODC, senior officials there said the $128 million figure referred to direct taxation of farmers and traffickers only, with the overall estimated total remaining at between $200 million and $400 million.

27. Data for this paragraph comes from United Nations Office on Drugs and Crime 2009 Opium Survey in Afghanistan (http://www.unodc.org/documents/crop-monitoring/Afghanistan/Afghanistan_opium_survey_2009_summary.pdf) and my interviews with UN and U.S. officials.

28. "Afghan Drug Raid Nets 50 Tons of Opium," Associated Press, October 9, 2009.

29. I am using $64/kilo, the average wholesale price for dry opium listed in the UNODC's 2009 Opium Survey in Afghanistan, and $2405/kilo, the average wholesale price for heroin listed in the 2009 World Drug Report. http://www.unodc.org/documents/wdr/WDR_2009/WDR2009_Statistical_annex_prices.pdf.

30. Interview by author with U.S. official, Washington, D.C., November 12, 2009.

31. Telephone interview with U.S. official, August 20, 2009.

32. Interview by author with U.S. officials, Washington, D.C., October 2009.

33. Interview with Taliban commander by research assistant, July 3, 2009.

34. Interviews with families by research assistants 1, 5, and 6, July 2009.

35. For details see Lawrence, Ed. *Messages to the World*, 98, 167.

36. Interview by author, Washington, June 18, 2007.

37. Tenet, "Statement by the Director of Central Intelligence on the Worldwide Threat in 2000."

38. Beers, "Narco-Terror: The Worldwide Connection Between Drugs and Terrorism."

39. Hutchinson, "Narco-Terror: The International Connection between Drugs and Terror."

40. McCraw, "International Drug Trafficking and Terrorism."

41. Interview by author, Washington, D.C., May 23, 2007.

42. Telephone interview, June 7, 2007.

43. "Afghanistan's Narco War: Breaking the Link between Drug Traffickers and Insurgents," A report to the Committee on Foreign Relations. U.S. Senate, August 10, 2009.

44. The statements can be read here: http://www.nefafoundation.org/documents-aqstatements.html.

45. Interviews by research assistants in FATA and NWFP, September 2009.

46. For more detail see www.intelcenter.com.

47. The video is posted at http://counterterrorismblog.org/2009/03/nefa_foundation_a_un-ique_look.php.

48. Craig Whitlock, "Flow of Terrorist Recruits Increasing." *The Washington Post*, October 19, 2009.

49. Whitlock, "Flow of Terrorist Recruits."

50. "Pakistan Seizes 7 Militants with Explosives, Drugs," Associated Press, August 24, 2009.

51. Interview by author, Kabul, March 2004.

52. Kaplan, "Paying for Terror."

53. Kaplan, "Paying for Terror" and Haven, Paul, "Madrid Bombings Show No al Qaeda Ties." Associated Press (March 9, 2006); Haven Paul and Mar

Roman, "Madrid Bomb Suspects face 40 Years in Jail," *The Scotsman* (February 14, 2007).

54. Kaplan, "Paying for Terror."

55. Kaplan, "Paying for Terror."

56. Interviews by author with western and Afghan officials, March 2004, October 2006, and March 2007.

57. Tenet, "Converging Dangers in a Post 9/11 World," testimony, Select Committee on Intelligence; Tenet, "Challenges in a Changing Global Context," testimony, Select Committee on Intelligence.

58. "Afghanistan Pullout 'Daunting': Defence Chief," *CBC News*, December 8, 2009.

59. James Risen and Mark Landler, "Accused of Drug Ties, Afghan Official Worries US," *New York Times*, August 26, 2009; Graeme Smith, "Afghan Officials in Drug Trade Cut Deals Across Enemy Lines," *Globe and Mail*, March 21, 2009.

60. Matthieu Aitkins, "The Master of Spin Boldak," *Harper's Magazine*, December 2009.

61. Farah Stockman, "Karzai's Pardons Nullify Drug Court Gains," *Boston Globe*, July 3, 2009.

62. Dexter Filkins, Mark Mazetti, and James Risen, "Brother of Afghan Leader Said to be Paid by CIA," *New York Times*, October 27, 2009.

63. For a detailed account of one NATO operation in which traffickers and insurgents appeared to coordinate closely from Quetta, see "Afghanistan's Narco War," a report to the Senate Foreign Relations Committee.

64. Interviews by author with officials in Washington, D.C., and Islamabad.

65. Telephone interview by author, December 16, 2009.

66. Mark Mazzetti and Eric Schmitt, "Afghan Strikes by Taliban get Pakistan Help, U.S. Aides Say," *New York Times*, March 25, 2009.

67. Telephone interview by author.

68. Telephone interview by author, January 30, 2007.

2. Operation Jihad

1. This segment is drawn from interviews conducted in Washington, D.C., with former DEA administrator Jack C. Lawn, retired DEA special agent Richard Fiano, and former CIA chief of station Milton Bearden on July 19 and October 4, 2007. Retired special agent Charles Carter was interviewed by telephone on May 25.

2. Or at least the longest anyone will admit to. I interviewed various former intelligence officials and diplomats, as well as Fiano and Carter, on the subject.

3. Information from this paragraph compiled from http://www.opiods.com/ timeline/index.html; Macdonald, *Drugs in Afghanistan*; Booth, *Opium*.

4. See, for example, "GOP Begins Cleanup of Smugglers Den at Sohrab Goth," U.S. State Department cable.

5. Lowinson and Musto, "Drug Crisis and Strategy."

6. It's important to note two external factors simultaneously contributed to a rise in opium production in Afghanistan. First, counternarcotics efforts in the Golden Triangle, which includes Thailand, Laos, and Burma, started to show a decline in production from that region. As well, the new Khomeini regime in neighboring Iran banned all forms of narcotics production and usage, thus shifting a lively economy over the border into Pakistan and Afghanistan.

7. See "National Narcotics Intelligence Consumers Committee Report for 1985–1986."

8. Bonner, "Afghan Rebel's Victory Garden: Opium."

9. Ibid.

10. Ibid.

11. Ibid.

12. Telephone interview with a former U.S. official, July 28, 2007.

13. For more information, see Rubin, *The Fragmentation of Afghanistan*; Coll, *The Ghost Wars*; and Yousaf and Adkin, *The Bear Trap*.

14. Akhundzada was a member of the Revolutionary Islamic Movement, one of the less centralized mujahideen parties. Some former U.S. officials believe he turned to the opium trade for spare cash because there was no organized mechanism within his party to distribute funds received in Peshawar.

15. Telephone interview with Peter Tomsen, former U.S. special envoy, July 28, 2007.

16. Rubin, *The Fragmentation of Afghanistan*, 263.

17. Ibid.

18. Griffin, *Reaping the Whirlwind*, 148.

19. Macdonald, *Drugs in Afghanistan*, 89.

20. The original Hizb-i-Islami split in 1979. Today Hekmatyar's faction is known as Hizb-i-Islami Gulbuddin, or HIG, and is considered a terrorist organization and trafficking group by coalition forces in Afghanistan.

21. Rupert and Coll, "U.S. Declines to Probe Afghan Drug Trade; Rebels, Pakistani Officers Implicated."

22. Rubin, *The Fragmentation of Afghanistan*, 257.

23. Telephone interview with Edmund McWilliams, May 3, 2007.

24. Telephone interview with a former U.S. official, July 28, 2007.

25. Lifschultz, "The Death Toll of Educated Afghans in Peshawar Is Now More Than One Thousand," 61.

26. Macdonald, *Drugs in Afghanistan*, 88.

27. Griffin, *Reaping the Whirlwind*, 142.

28. Mujahideen commanders were known to switch allegiance between the Peshawar Seven parties depending on access to funds and weapons. There is evidence Mullah Omar fought under Khalis and also with Mohammad Nabi Mohammadi and his party, the Harakat-i-Inqilab-i-Islami.

29. Interview with a U.S. military official, Bagram Air Base, August 2006.

30. In another case of history repeating itself, the supply line bringing weapons to the Afghan National Army, which the U.S. military is training and equipping, also appears riddled with graft. One weapons supplier with a $300 million contract was sending aged munitions made in China and the former Soviet bloc and working with a middleman on a U.S. federal list suspected of illegal arms trafficking. For details, see C. J. Chivers, "Supplier Under Scrutiny on Aging Arms for Afghans," *New York Times*, March 27, 2008. So far, however, no one has publicly accused any U.S. suppliers of also smuggling drugs.

31. Lawrence Lifschultz, "Pakistan, the Empire of Heroin," in McCoy and Block, eds., *War on Drugs*, 320; Lifschultz, "Heroin Empire," 71–72.

32. Yousaf and Adkin, *The Bear Trap*, 100.

33. Hussein, "Narco Power," 15; Rupert and Coll, "U.S. Declines to Probe Afghan Drug Trade; Rebels, Pakistani Officers Implicated."

34. Information for this passage comes from Hussein, "Narco Power," 14, and Lifschultz, "Inside the Kingdom of Heroin," 495.

35. "Narcotics Trafficking and the Military," Near East and South Asia briefs, CIA.

36. Rupert and Coll, "U.S. Declines to Probe Afghan Drug Trade; Rebels, Pakistani Officers Implicated." Bugti remained in opposition for decades, leading a resistance against the government of President Pervez Musharraf. He was assassinated in an air strike in August 2006.

37. For examples, see Lifschultz, "Inside the Kingdom of Heroin," and Rupert and Coll, "U.S. Declines to Probe Afghan Drug Trade; Rebels, Pakistani Officers Implicated."

38. Lawrence Lifschultz, "Pakistan, the Empire of Heroin," in McCoy and Block, eds., *War on Drugs*, 321.

39. Telephone interview with Edmund McWilliams, May 3, 2007.

40. Sciolino, "U.S. Urging Afghan Rebels to Limit Opium."

41. Telephone interview with William Piekney, former CIA agent, September 24, 2007.

42. "HFAC International Narcotics Control Task Force Hearings, May 22," U.S. State Department document.

43. "UN Striving for Tact in Its Fight on Drugs," *New York Times,* July 25, 1987.

44. Telephone interview with a former CIA official, September 5, 2008.

45. Until the war began in Afghanistan, most of the opium produced there was exported to Iran. Opium grown in Pakistan, meanwhile, was more likely to be processed into heroin and smuggled to the West, according to former DEA officials and declassified government documents.

46. "Pakistan's Narcotics Control Program," letter from Edward Fox, Asst Secretary of Legislative and Intergovernmental Affairs, to the Chairman of the Foreign Affairs Committee, U.S. House of Representatives.

47. Interview with Teresita Schaffer, Washington, D.C., May 11, 2007; also see http://www.csis.org.

48. "Pakistan: Countering an Expanding Drug Industry," Intelligence assessment, CIA.

49. "Daily Muslim Article on Balochistan Heroin Seizure," U.S. Embassy (Islamabad) cable. The tribes running the Quetta Alliance were the Noorzai, the Rigi, and the Notezai, according to counternarcotics officials and local media reports from the time.

50. "Afghanistan, Iran, Pakistan Country Profiles," Office of Intelligence Drug Enforcement Administration.

51. "Visit of INM Assistant Secretary Wrobleski: Meeting with President Zia."

52. Lifschultz, "Inside the Kingdom of Heroin," 495; Haq, *Drugs in South Asia,* 200–201.

53. Alexiev, "Inside the Soviet Army in Afghanistan," 49. Another passage from this report reveals the lengths Soviet soldiers would go to create intoxicants: "You cannot imagine what they drink. They will drink shaving lotions and cologne. That's the good stuff. Then they will drink toothpaste. The best one is the Bulgarian Pomorian brand. They will simply squeeze four or five tubes in a jar, dilute it with water and drink it. They also drank truck antifreeze, glue and brake fluid. The brake fluid, they used to heat up and put some nails in it for some reason. I don't know why. They will also take shoe polish and smear it on a piece of bread and leave it in the sun until the alcohol separates from the shoe polish. Then you eat the bread and get drunk."

54. Bonner, "Afghanistan's Other Front: A World of Drugs."

55. Information and quotes in this paragraph come from Cooley, *Unholy Wars,* 128–129, and Sancton, "Dispatches."

56. Interview with Mohammed Yousaf, Wah Cantonment, October 2006.

57. Telephone interview with William Piekney, September 24, 2007.

58. Coll, *The Ghost Wars*, 103–105.

59. Yousaf and Adkin, *The Bear Trap*, 102. Corruption along the pipeline was reportedly rife. The Federation for American Afghan Action, a support group for the resistance, concluded that 70 percent of the $342 million appropriated by Congress for weapons between the fiscal years 1980 and 1984 had never reached the mujahideen in the field.

60. Coll, *The Ghost Wars*, 105.

61. Interview with Zamir Kabulov, Russian ambassador to Afghanistan, Kabul, March 4, 2008.

62. Telephone interview with a former CIA agent, October 3, 2007.

63. Interview with a former CIA agent, Washington, D.C., May 21, 2007.

64. Telephone interview with a former CIA agent, October 2, 2007.

65. Telephone interview with Robert Oakley, May 21, 2007.

66. Frederick Hitz, "Obscuring Properiety? The CIA and Drugs," *International Journal of Intelligence and Counter-Intelligence* 15, no. 4 (November 2002): 565–579.

67. Interview with Richard Fiano, former DEA agent, Washington, D.C., June 2007.

68. Telephone interview with Larry Crandall, former USAID official, September 20, 2007.

69. "Narcotics and the New Government," U.S. Embassy (Islamabad) cable.

70. "Heroin, Guns and the War in Pakistan," U.S. Embassy (Islamabad) cable.

71. The main highway from Baluchistan also snakes into Sohrab Goth, passing right by the Karachi office of the NLC before entering into the port. To this day, the road is crowded with colorfully painted trucks, many of them festooned with the Afghan flag, lumbering into the seaside slum. There appear to be no authorities checking their contents.

72. "Pakistan: Countering an Expanding Drug Industry."

73. Coll, *The Ghost Wars*, 182–183.

74. Interview with Milton Beardon, former CIA agent, Washington, D.C., July 19, 2007.

75. Coll, *The Ghost Wars*, 180–183; Rubin, *The Fragmentation of Afghanistan*, 182–183.

76. Rubin, *The Fragmentation of Afghanistan*, 183.

77. "Narcotics Trafficking from Afghanistan," U.S. Embassy (Islamabad) cable.

78. Sciolino, "U.S. Urging Afghan Rebels to Limit Opium"; telephone interview with Peter Tomsen, July 28, 2007.

79. Alfred McCoy, "Fallout: The Interplay of CIA Covert Warfare and the Global Narcotics Traffic," paper delivered at the Institute for African Studies, Columbia University, November 14, 2002, 19.

80. "Request for Afghan Opium Crop Figures," U.S. Embassy (Islamabad) cable.

81. "Narcotics Production/Trafficking in Northern Helmand," U.S. Embassy (Islamabad) cable.

82. Telephone interview with a former U.S. official, July 28, 2007.

83. Telephone interview with Robert Oakley, former U.S. diplomat, May 21, 2007.

84. Rubin, *The Fragmentation of Afghanistan*, 264. USAID's program in Nangarhar suffered a similar fate. Then governor Haji Abdul Qadir accepted a $200,000 USAID program to cut production in half, but when U.S. funds disappeared, he ordered farmers to grow crops again, according to former U.S. officials.

85. David B. Ottaway, "GAO Asked to Probe Alleged Diversion of Afghan Rebel Aid," *Washington Post*, March 13, 1987; Tolchin, "CIA Admits It Failed to Tell Fed About BCCI."

86. Lifschultz, "Pakistan, the Empire of Heroin," 350.

87. Rubin, *The Fragmentation of Afghanistan*, 182–183.

88. Ibid.

89. Interview with a former CIA officer, Washington, D.C., August 18, 2007.

90. Griffin, *Reaping the Whirlwind*. After the Taliban took over Kabul in 1996, they hanged Najibullah in Kabul's Ariana Square.

91. "Request for Afghan Opium Crop Figures."

92. "Afghanistan: U.S. Interests and U.S. Aid," letter to U.S. State Department.

93. For more on this, see Napoleoni, *Terror Incorporated*, 119–120.

94. Ibid., 119.

95. Griffin, *Reaping the Whirlwind*, 142.

96. McCoy, *The Politics of Heroin*, 483.

97. Hussein, "Narco Power."

98. That Afridi worked with Zia's government comes from "Heroin in Pakistan: Sowing the Wind," a CIA report leaked to Pakistan's *Friday Times*, which published it in full on September 3, 1993.

99. Zahid Hussein, "Three Major Drug Syndicates in Pakistan," *Newsline*, May 1993.

100. Haq, *Pakistan*, 34–35.

101. "Pakistan." DEA country analysis.

102. "The Narcotics Issue and Contacts with Politicians." U.S. State Department letter to U.S. Embassy (Islamabad).

103. "Request for Afghan Opium Crop Figures." U.S. State Department cable to U.S. Embassy (Islamabad).

104. "Narcotics—FY 90 Budget." Robert Oakley, U.S. Embassy (Islamabad) cable.

105. Coll, *The Ghost Wars*, 220–221.

106. Interview with a former U.S. official, Washington, D.C., July 18, 2007.

107. "Heroin in Pakistan: Sowing the Wind," CIA report.

108. Knut Royce, "Country Run on Drugs: CIA Report Says Heroin Is Pakistan's Lifeblood," *Newsday*, February 23, 1993.

109. John Ward Anderson and Kamran Khan, "Heroin Plan by Top Pakistanis Alleged," *Washington Post*, September 12, 1994.

110. Interviews of former airport workers by research assistant 1, Jalalabad, June 2007.

111. Interview with a Pakistani police official, Islamabad, June 2007.

112. "Interview with Zbigniew Brzezinski," *Nouvel Observateur*, January 15, 1998.

3. Narco-Terror State

1. Peters, "Taliban Stamping Out Hashish but Opium Production Continues to Flourish."

2. Rashid, *The Taliban*, 25; Anthony Davis, "How the Taliban Became a Military Force," in Maley, ed., *Fundamentalism Reborn?* 44; multiple interviews.

3. Interview with Mullah Roketi, Kabul, January 2006.

4. Marquand, "The Reclusive Leader Who Runs the Taliban."

5. Multiple interviews with former Afghan, Pakistani, and U.S. officials.

6. Griffin, *Reaping the Whirlwind*, 153.

7. See documents 1–8, *The Taliban File*, 9/11 Sourcebook, national security archive electronic briefing book no. 97, Sajit Ghandi, ed., NSA/GWU, especially document 1, "New Fighting and New Forces in Kandahar," U.S. Consulate (Peshawar) cable; document 3, "The Taliban—Who Knows What the Movement Means?" U.S. embassy (Islamabad) cable; document 5, "[excised] Believe Pakistan Is Backing Taliban," U.S. embassy (Islamabad) cable; document 6, "The Taliban: What We've Heard," U.S. embassy (Islamabad) cable. The collection is available online at http://www.gwu.edu/~nsarchiv/NSAEBB/NSAEBB97/index.htm.

8. These quotes come from Ghandi, ed., *Sourcebook*, documents 3 and 6.

9. Ibid., document 6.

10. Ibid., "Meeting with the Taliban in Kandahar: More Questions Than Answers." U.S. embassy (Islamabad) cable.

11. The U.S. embassy cable documenting this meeting has excised the name of the Afghan official, but describes him as a native of Maroof district, where Ghaus is from, and someone tipped to be a senior foreign ministry official in the new Taliban government.

12. He died in 2000.

13. That Issa Noorzai was a major smuggler and a member of the Quetta Alliance comes from multiple interviews with Afghan and Pakistani officials, as well as Noorzai tribesmen. Another alleged member of the Quetta Alliance, "Sakhi Jan" Dost Notezai, was briefly arrested in October 1990 in connection with the multiton seizure of heroin, hashish, and opium referenced in Operation Jihad. Notezai, through a combination of legal maneuvering and wielding his significant political influence, largely avoided incarceration. Today his son, Amanullah Notezai, is a provincial minister in the Baluchistan government and a member of the Pakistan Muslim League faction, which supported former president Pervez Musharraf.

14. "TKO Proposal," [name exised] Islamabad Country Office, Drug Enforcement Administration.

15. Bob Clark, a former DEA agent posted to Islamabad in the 1990s, says most TKO designations were given to Latin American drug smugglers, since Southwest Asian drugs "weren't seen as something that made its way into the U.S. market."

16. This is according to an Afghan who accompanied Noorzai to one of the meetings and who was able to accurately identify DEA agents serving in the Islamabad embassy at the time.

17. Ghandi, ed., *Sourcebook*, document 8, "Finally, a Talkative Talib: Origins and Membership of the Religious Students' Movement," U.S. Embassy (Islamabad) cable.

18. "First Heroin Kingpin Ever Extradited from Afghanistan Pleads Guilty to Smuggling Heroin into the United States," news release from U.S. Attorney's Office, Department of Justice, Southern District of New York, July 11, 2006.

19. Interview with an Afghan official, Peshawar, January 2008.

20. Davis, "How the Taliban Became a Military Force," 44; Ghandi, ed., *Sourcebook*, document 3. Abdur Ghaffar was the younger brother of Nasim, the Helmand strongman who was assassinated and succeeded by his brother Rasul (see Chapter 2). When Rasul died of cancer in the early 1990s, Abdur Ghaffar took over the business.

21. Davis, "How the Taliban Became a Military Force," 50–51.

22. The DEA document is cited in Griffin, *Reaping the Whirlwind*, 154.

23. Interview with a U.S. official, Kabul, March 2005.

24. Ahmed Rashid, "Pakistan and the Taliban," in Maley, ed., *Fundamentalism Reborn*, 77.

25. Ghandi, ed., *Sourcebook*, document 5.

26. Davis, "How the Taliban Became a Military Force," 45–46; Coll, *The Ghost Wars*, 291.

27. Rashid, *The Taliban*, 28–29.

28. Ibid., 29.

29. Information for this paragraph comes from Rashid, *The Taliban*, 27–29, and multiple interviews.

30. For more detail, see Barbara Elias, ed., *Pakistan: "The Taliban's Godfather"? Documents Detail Years of Pakistani Support for Taliban, Extremists*, national security archive electronic briefing book no. 227, NSA/GWU, at http://www.gwu.edu/~nsarchiv/NSAEBB/NSAEBB227/index.htm.

31. Coll, *The Ghost Wars*, 293.

32. Rashid, "Pakistan and the Taliban," 88.

33. Elias, ed., *Pakistan*, "Afghanistan: Russian Embassy Official Claims Iran Interfering More Than Pakistan," U.S. Embassy (Islamabad) cable.

34. Coll, *The Ghost Wars*, 293.

35. Ghandi, ed., *Sourcebook*, document 15, "A/S Raphel Discusses Afghanistan," U.S. Embassy (Islamabad) cable.

36. Coll, *The Ghost Wars*, 332.

37. Transnational Institute, "Afghanistan, Drugs and Terrorism: Merging Wars," TNI briefing series no. 2001/2, December 2001, http://www.tni.org/reports/drugs/debate3.pdf.

38. Both the U.S. government and UNODC perform annual surveys of Afghanistan's poppy crop. The U.S. government uses satellite technology, while the UN conducts ground surveys, which is why there are discrepancies in their total estimates. The drop-off in opium production in 2001 is due to the Taliban's decision to ban poppy cultivation, a subject to be discussed later in this chapter.

39. Rubin, "The Political Economy of War and Peace in Afghanistan," 1795.

40. Telephone interview with Bernard Frahi, UNODC official, August 2007. This is also cited in Rubin, "Political Economy," 1796.

41. Rashid, *The Taliban*, 118.

42. Interview with a former Pakistani counternarcotics official, Islamabad, April 2007.

43. Jeffrey Bartholet and Steve Levine, "The Holy Men of Heroin," *Newsweek*, December 6, 1999.

44. Director of Central Intelligence, "National Intelligence Daily," Central Intelligence Agency, May 1, 1998, 7, NSA/GWU. In this document, yet to be assigned to a collection at the NSA, Haji Bashir Noorzai's name has been redacted. It reads: "Under one such agreement [name excised]—the son of key Quetta Alliance member [name excised] pays the Taliban about $230 for each kilogram of either heroin or morphine base being exported through

the Jalalabad and Qandahar Airports." Other public reference documents on Noorzai specifically refer to his export deal with the Taliban.

45. Telephone interview with Julie Sirrs, former U.S. official, June 5, 2007.

46. Interview with a retired ISI agent, Islamabad, June 2006.

47. Macdonald, *Drugs in Afghanistan*, 102.

48. Interview with David Macdonald, Kabul, September 26, 2007.

49. Macdonald, *Drugs in Afghanistan*, 51. Various Afghan officials believe the Taliban today gives drugs to young soldiers—and specifically suicide bombers—to make them fearless. Several have raised the issue with U.S. officials, asking for kits to perform blood tests on attackers captured before they self-detonate. "When we have captured suicide bombers before they could set off their charge, they often seem to be high on drugs—really out of it and wild," a former governor told me in 2007.

50. "National Intelligence Daily," 7.

51. Ibid.

52. Interview with Bob Clark, former DEA agent, Islamabad, February 2, 2008.

53. Interview with a former UN official, Islamabad, November 18, 2007.

54. Telephone interview with a former CIA official, September 5, 2008.

55. Jonathan Oliver, "West Will Hit the Taliban's Opium Trade," *Mail on Sunday*, September 30, 2001.

56. Perl, "The Taliban and the Drug Trade."

57. Benjamin and Simon, *The Age of Sacred Terror*, 155.

58. Barry Meier, "Super Heroin Was Planned by Bin Laden, Report Says," *New York Times*, October 4, 2001. Bin Laden's only two known public statements on opium can be found in Lawrence, ed., *Messages to the World*, 98, 167. In one statement, bin Laden praises Mullah Omar for "the prohibition of growing opium," calling it a "great Islamic decision." In a separate diatribe against Americans he says, "You are a nation that permits the production, trading and usage of intoxicants. You also permit drugs, and only forbid the trade of them, even though your nation is the largest consumer of them."

59. Perl, "The Taliban and the Drug Trade," 4.

60. Mary Anne Weaver, "Hunting with the Sheikhs." *The New York*, December 14, 1992.

61. Multiple interviews. This subject also gets a mention in Rubin, "Political Economy," 1796, and in Coll, *The Ghost Wars*, 613, footnote citing a Human Rights Watch report.

62. A copy of Bashir's deposition was given to the author by his American lawyer, Ivan Fisher. In it, Noorzai went on to claim the Emirati sheik sought to continue the lease arrangement after the Taliban government collapsed, and,

curiously, invited HBN to help smooth the process. Other public documents from the trial report on meetings between HBN and two American investigators on August 9, 2004, in Dubai, in which HBN described in detail a trip he had made to Dubai in 2001 with Gul Agha Sherzai, the man who took over Kandahar following the U.S. invasion. HBN said Sheikh Mohammed had sent a plane for them in Kandahar, and they had met with the sheik's Afghan representative, Rahim Balouch. In the written testimony he said Balouch had given Sherzai a suitcase with 1 million dhirams ($270,000) and said, "This is your gift."

63. Multiple interviews.
64. Mary Anne Weaver, "Hunting with the Sheikhs."
65. Farah and Braun, *Merchant of Death*, 141.
66. Braun and Pasternak, "Long Before Sept. 11, Bin Laden Flew Aircraft Under the Radar."
67. Interview with Mohammad Fedawi, former president of Ariana Airlines, Kabul, March 2007.
68. Interview by research assistant 1 with Hayat Zalmay, Jalalabad, June 2007.
69. Farah and Braun, *Merchant of Death*, 117, 139.
70. Ibid., 121. Fedawi also described Ahmed in an interview with the author.
71. Ibid., 117–118.
72. Braun and Pasternak. "Long Before Sept. 11."
73. Benjamin and Simon, *Sacred Terror*, 289.
74. This information is compiled from Farah and Braun, *Merchant of Death*, 63–64; Brunwasser, "The Embargo Buster"; and Phillip Van Niekerk and André Verlöy, "Africa's Merchant of Death Sold Arms to the Taliban," Washington, D.C.: Center for Public Integrity, January 31, 2002, http://www.publicintegrity.org/assets/pdf/pi_2002_02.pdf.
75. Interview, July 2007.
76. Farah and Braun, *Merchant of Death*, 64.
77. Van Niekerk and Verlöy, "Africa's Merchant of Death."
78. Farah and Braun, *Merchant of Death*, 128.
79. Ibid., 140.
80. Interview with a U.S. official, Washington, D.C., May 8, 2007.
81. Van Niekerk and Verlöy, "Africa's Merchant of Death."
82. Farah and Braun, *Merchant of Death*, 146; Brunwasser, "The Embargo Buster."
83. Telephone interview with Julie Sirrs, former DIA analyst, June 5, 2007.
84. Telephone interview with Karl Indurfurth, May 10, 2007.
85. "Taliban File Update: U.S. Pressed Taliban to Expel Usama bin Laden Over 30 Times," news release, State Department, January 30, 2004, NSA/GWU, http://www.gwu.edu/~nsarchiv/NSAEBB/NSAEBB97/index3.htm.

86. Transnational Institute, "Afghanistan, Drugs, and Terrorism: Merging Wars."

87. Ibid.

88. Martin Jelsma, "Learning Lessons from the Taliban Opium Ban," *International Journal on Drug Policy* 16, no. 2 (March 2005), http://www.tni.org/detail_page.phtml?page=archives_jelsma_taliban.

89. Jelsma, "Learning Lessons from the Taliban Opium Ban"; House Government Reform Committee Subcommittee on Criminal Justice, Drug Policy, and Human Resources, statement of Asa Hutchinson, 107th Cong., 1st sess., October 3, 2001, http://www.usdoj.gov/dea/pubs/cngrtest/ct100301.html.

90. The estate is described in Coll, *The Ghost Wars*, 549. The author has also reviewed photos of the compound.

91. William Sami and Charles Recknagel, "Iran's War on Drugs," *Transnational Organized Crime* 5, no. 2 (Summer 2002).

92. Transnational Institute, "Afghanistan, Drugs and Terrorism: Merging Wars."

93. Ibid.

94. Rashid, *The Taliban*, 122.

95. "Worldwide Drug Threat Assessment: A Joint Intelligence Report," Committee on Narcotics Intelligence Issues.

96. Pakistan had 3 million addicts by 1996, 5 million by 1999, according to Rashid, *The Taliban*, 122.

97. Interview with a former Pakistani official, Islamabad, October 2006.

98. Interview with a Pakistani counternarcotics official, Rawalpindi, September 13, 2007.

99. Hannah Bloch, "A Skirmish Over Drugs," *Time*, June 2, 1997, 25.

100. Ibid.

101. See document collection at Elias, ed., *Pakistan*.

102. Ibid., document 15, "[excised]/Pakistan Interservice Intelligence/Pakistan (PK) Directorate Supplying the Taliban Forces," from [excised] to DIA, [excised] cable; document 17, "IIR [excised] Pakistan Involvement in Afghanistan," from [excised] to DIA.

103. Interview with a western official, Kabul, September 26, 2007.

104. Telephone interview with William Milam, former U.S. diplomat, August 2007.

105. In a subsequent interview, Chamberlain retreated from the testimony she made under oath, saying aggressive questioning backed her into an assessment based on "unclassified reporting—what you know." She added, "I regretted it the moment I said it." The full transcript of her testimony is available at http://commdocs.house.gov/committees/intlrel/hfa85841.000/hfa85841_0f.htm.

106. Interview with a western official, Kabul, September 26, 2007.

107. Elias, ed., *Pakistan*, document 34, "Pakistan Support for Taliban," U.S. Embassy (Islamabad) cable.

108. Musharraf, *In the Line of Fire*, 209.

109. Interview with a U.S. official, Washington, D.C., May 2007.

110. Coll, *The Ghost Wars*, 560.

111. National Commission on Terrorist Attacks upon the United States, Kean and Hamilton, *The 9/11 Commission Report*, 259.

112. Coll, *The Ghost Wars*, 552.

113. House Government Reform Subcommittee on Criminal Justice, Drug Policy, and Human Resources, statement of Asa Hutchinson.

114. "Another Powder Trail," *Economist*, October 18, 2001.

115. Woodward, *Bush at War*, 212.

116. Risen, *State of War*, 154.

117. Interview with Robert Charles, former INL chief, Washington, D.C., May 23, 2007.

118. Telephone interview with Dana Rohrabacher, U.S. congressman, October 2006.

119. Woodward, *Bush at War*, 228.

120. Risen, *State of War*, 154.

4. The New Taliban

1. In a January 9, 2007 e-mail, a U.S. military spokesman, Colonel Tom Collins, confirmed Osmani was killed with two associates and identified one of them as Mullah Zahir. Separately, three Afghan officials in Helmand identified the third man as Haji Masooq, a major heroin dealer, to two research assistants.

2. Michael Smith, "Taliban Leader 'Killed' After RAF Tracks Phone," *Sunday Times*, December 24, 2006.

3. For more on Centcom's refusal to dispatch U.S. Marines who were also in theater to Tora Bora, see: Mary Ann Weaver, "Lost at Tora Bora," *The New Yorker*, September 11, 2005. Weaver accurately blames the U.S. Special Forces' reliance on two corrupt warlords—Hazrat Ali and Haji Zaman—both of whom are suspected of ties to opium trafficking—for bin Laden's escape. U.S. and Afghan officials believe a multimillion-dollar bribe was paid to the warlords secure bin Laden's great escape. "It was more of a great release," a senior Afghan security official complained to me.

4. Telephone interview by author, October 10, 2007.

5. Gary Schroen, *First In*, Presidio Press (New York: 2005), p 92.

6. Peter Maass, "Gul Agha Gets His Province Back," *New York Times Magazine*, January 6, 2002.

7. "Countering Afghanistan's Insurgency: No Quick Fixes," International Crisis Group, Asia Report No. 123, November 2, 2006.

8. Interview by author, New York City, August 11, 2007.

9. Patrick McDowell, "As Disruption from War on Taliban Ends, Traffickers Moving Big Heroin Shipments," Associated Press, March 3, 2002.

10. Barry Bearak, "Unreconstructed," *New York Times Magazine*, June 1, 2003.

11. Interview by the author, Islamabad, March 2003.

12. Matt Pennington, "Afghanistan Stops Paying Farmers to Give Up Growing Opium," Associated Press, August 25, 2003.

13. Elizabeth Rubin, "In the Land of the Taliban," *New York Times Magazine*, October 22, 2006.

14. Drug dealers in at least one instance may have aided a senior Taliban commander in securing his escape from the U.S.-led invasion. A March 2004 intelligence report seen by the author says Mullah Dadullah paid northern smuggler Shamuk Haq $1 million to escape Mazar-e Sharif when the Taliban fell from power there. Haq was a dealer based in northern Balkh provinces who allegedly smuggles heroin and weapons between the north and Helmand.

15. Interview by the author, Washington, D.C., July 25, 2007.

16. Gretchen Peters, "Hostilities Flare in America's Other War," *Christian Science Monitor*, March 31, 2003.

17. Rahimullah Yusufzai, "Taliban Aims to Regain Power," www.news.bbc.co.uk.

18. Rahimullah Yusufzai quoted in ICG's "No Quick Fixes." He names the original 2003 members as Jalaluddin Haqqani, Saifur Rahman Mansoor, Mullah Dadullah, former Taliban army chief Akhtar Mohammad Osmani, Akhtar Mohammad Mansoor, former Taliban defense minister Mullah Obaidullah, Kandahar's ex-security chief Hafiz Abdul Majeed, former Nimroz provincial governor Mullah Mohammad Rasul, Mullah Barodar, and former Taliban corps commander in northern Afghanistan Mullah Abdur Razzaq Akhundzada.

19. E-mail interview with author, October 16, 2007.

20. Liz Sly, "Opium Cash Fuels Terror," *Chicago Tribune*, February 9, 2004. Prices calculated from UNODC World Drug Report, www.unodc.org/pdf/WDR_2006/wdr2006_chap5_opium.pdf, p. 4.

21. From a U.S. Department of Homeland Security report cited in Angel Rabasa et al, "Ungoverned Territories," 66.

22. A kilo of refined heroin might sell for $1,000 along the border. On the streets of Europe and the United States, it will fetch as much as $130,000 according to the UNODC.

23. "Coalition Forces Make Second Major Drug Seizure in Five Days," story number: NNS031220-01, U.S. Naval Forces Central Command/Commander,

U.S. 5th Fleet Public Affairs, December 20, 2003; "USS *Decatur* Captures Possible Al-Qaida Associated Drug-Smuggling Dhow in Arabian Gulf," story number: NNS031219-09, U.S. Naval Forces Central Command/Commander, U.S. 5th Fleet Public Affairs, December 19, 2003.

24. Interview by author, Kabul, March 2004.

25. John Mintz, "15 Freighters Believed to be Linked to Al Qaeda," *Washington Post*, December 31, 2002.

26. Interview by author, Islamabad, October 25, 2007.

27. Owais Towaid, "Bumper Year for Afghan Poppies," *Christian Science Monitor*, July 24, 2003.

28. MacDonald, *Drugs in Afghanistan*, 103.

29. Interviews with Maj-Gen Khaled Jaffery, Director General of Pakistan's Anti-Narcotics Force, in Rawalpindi on September 13, 2007; General Kamal Sadat, the former Chief of Afghanistan's Counter Narcotics Police in Kabul, February 28, 2007, and Hashem Zayyem, Iranian Drugs Liason Officer at the Iranian Embassy in Kabul, March 1, 2007.

30. Interview by author in Rawalpindi, September 13, 2007.

31. The author was shown dozens of still classified State Department, DoD, and CIA documents; many of them, like this one, were raw intelligence reports outlining links between the drugs trade and terrorist groups which were cabled back to Washington from the U.S. Embassy in Kabul. Various U.S. officials told me the U.S. military and the CIA resisted doing "finished analysis" on the raw intelligence, which would have required them to take a stand on the nature of the drug trade. "It allows them deniability," said one official. I will discuss this issue further in Chapter 7.

32. Interview by author, Islamabad, August 2, 2006.

33. Telephone interview by author, May 12, 2007.

34. In Afghanistan, Iran, and Pakistan, some users smoke or consume unrefined opium gum. The most common product on the regional market is partially refined opium base—known as "brown sugar." Crystal heroin, the more potent white powder produced from boiling opium base with acetic anhydride, is what gets smuggled to the West.

35. Victoria Burnett and Mark Huband, "UK Trains Afghans in Anti-Drugs Drive," *Financial Times*, January 10, 2004.

36. Telephone interview by author, June 12, 2007.

37. Interview by research assistant 1, Ghazni, July 2008.

38. Molly Moore, "NATO Confronts Surprisingly Fierce Taliban," *Washington Post*, February 26, 2008.

39. Interview by author, Washington, D.C., July 2007.

40. A copy of the night letter was shown to the author.

41. Interviews by research assistant 3, Helmand, July 2007.

42. Interview by author, Kabul, March 4, 2008.

43. Interview by research assistant 2, Lashkar Gah, July 2007.

44. Both men interviewed by research assistant 3, Sangin, July 2007.

45. Hayatullah Gaheez, "Daughters Sold to Settle Debts," *Institute for War and Peace Reporting* ARR No. 155, December 30, 2004.

46. Tom Coghlan, "Even the School Playground Has Been Turned into a Poppy Field," *Telegraph*, February 8, 2007; and author's interviews with local farmers in Helmand.

47. Graeme Smith, "Air Strikes and Drug Eradication," in "Talking to the Taliban: Globe Special Report," *Globe and Mail*, March 24, 2008. See: www.theglobeandmail.com/talkingtothetaliban. The figure of 8 percent comes from the UNODC 2007 Opium Survey, 6.

48. For example, see David Mansfield and Adam Pain, "Opium Poppy Eradication: How to Raise Risk When There is Nothing to Lose?" Afghanistan Research and Evaluation Unit Briefing Paper, August 2006.

49. Abubakar Siddique and Muhammad Salih, "Afghanistan: Poor Helmand Farmers Find Themselves in Eye of Drug Storm," Radio Free Europe/Radio Liberty, October 10, 2007.

50. Interview by research assistant 2, Sangin, July 2007.

51. Tony Perry, "Afghanistan: Marines Bring Some Calm to Afghanistan," *Los Angeles Times*, November 9, 2009.

52. Ibid.

53. When U.S. troops moved into new districts, asking villagers to name their biggest concern, they were often surprised that "the Taliban" wasn't the answer, but "lack of water." In fact, decades of war have destroyed irrigations systems on which these communities depended to grow traditional crops like wheat, melons, and pomegranates. Although a variety of factors contribute to a farmer's decision to grow poppy, one of them appears to be the lack of viable irrigation, since the opium poppy flower flourishes with little water.

54. UNODC Afghan Opium Survey 2009, 8.

55. Telephone interview by author, December 17, 2009.

56. Siddique and Salih, "Poor Helmand Farmers," and authors' interviews.

57. For their full reports, see: iwpr.net/?p=arr&s&=f&o&=340973&apc_state henfarr340968.

58. Aziz Ahmad Tassal, "Winning Hearts and Minds," *Institute for War and Peace Reporting* ARR No. 275, November 27, 2007.

59. Aziz Ahmad Shafe, "Taliban Ghost Town," *Institute for War and Peace Reporting* ARR No. 275, November 27, 2007.

60. Tassal, "Winning Hearts and Minds."

61. Information in this paragraph is from Noor Khan, "Taliban Collected Taxes, Ran Heroin Labs, Had Own Judge in Afghan Town," Associated Press, December 12, 2007; Noor Khan, "Taliban Hang Three Alleged Afghan Informers," Associated Press, April 1, 2007.

62. Jean MacKenzie, Aziz Ahmad Tassal, Mohammad Ilyas Dayee, "What Next for Musa Qala?" *Institute for War And Peace Reporting* ARR No. 277, December 12, 2007.

63. Laura King, "Afghan Civilian Deaths in 2009 Were Most Since Invasion," *Los Angeles Times*, January 14, 2010.

64. MacKenzie et al., "What Next?"

65. One of the key commanders to lose his position was Mansoor Dadullah, the brother of the late military commander Mullah Dadullah Lang. According to some sources close to the Taliban, Mansoor Dadullah was purged not simply for reasons of excessive violence, but because he was caught holding onto funds that were supposed to be sent back to his superiors in Pakistan.

66. The Quetta Shura is so named because the Taliban leadership is widely believed to operate from the western Pakistani city of Quetta, in Baluchistan province. The NATO acronym for the Taliban is now QST, standing for Quetta Shura Taliban. In late 2009, media reports suggested that the Taliban leadership had shifted to Pakistan's populous southern port city Karachi out of fear that an intensive U.S.-led drone campaign in the FATA would be extended to Baluchistan to target QST leaders. Pakistani officials routinely deny there are any Afghan Taliban leaders inside Pakistan. See for example: Ron Moreau, "Sheltered in Karachi," *Newsweek*, November 28, 2009.

67. Kathy Gannon, "Taliban's Shadow Government Poses Challenge to Election, US Troops," Associated Press, August 18, 2009.

68. For a longer analysis of this subject, see Gretchen Peters, "Crime and Insurgency in the AfPak War Theater," *Combating Terrorism Center*, U.S. Military Academy at West Point, February 2010.

69. Interviews by research assistant 1 in Kabul, July 2007.

70. Interviews by research assistant 4, Quetta, October 8 and 9, 2007.

71. Peters, "Crime and Insurgency."

72. Peters, "Crime and Insurgency."

73. Aryn Baker "How Crime Pays for the Taliban," *Time* magazine, September 7, 2009.

74. Baker, "How Crime Pays."

75. Multiple businessmen and sources said the Roshan network has refused to pay Taliban fees, and as a result suffers more frequent attacks and the resulting service outages.

76. Peters, "Crime and Insurgency."

77. Laurie Ure, "Winning Hearts and Wallets in Afghanistan," CNN, December 8, 2009.

78. Author's interviews and "Afghanistan's Narco War," a report to the Committee on Foreign Relations.

79. Interviews by research assistant 1, March 2008.

80. Interviews by research assistant 1, March 2008.

81. Interviews by research assistant 1, July 2009.

82. Before his death, Mullah Dadullah was known to visit the Haqqani *madrassa* in North Waziristan regularly for the purposes of coordination, and the HiG even posted a senior commander, Haji Abdul Ghafour, to Wana, in neighboring South Waziristan for similar purposes, according to U.S. intelligence and military intelligence documents seen by the author.

83. Personal interviews by author in Washington, D.C. and by research assistant in Kabul, July 2009.

84. Interview by author, Washington, D.C., July 13, 2008.

85. Peters, "Crime and Insurgency."

86. David Rohde, "'You Have Atomic Bombs, but We Have Suicide Bombers'," *New York Times*, October 19, 2009.

87. Telephone interview by author with Rohde, November 2009. It's important to note that on several occasions, lower ranking militants wanted to kill Rohde and his Afghan colleagues as a matter of principle or in revenge from U.S. drone strikes in the FATA, but their commanders always intervened.

88. Author's interviews with officials and with relatives of kidnap victims in Pakistan and Afghanistan, 2009.

89. Terrorist violence in Pakistan soared 70 percent in 2008, claiming 2,239 lives, according to the U.S. State Department. Monthly violent acts, tracked by the Pak Institute for Peace Studies, indicated that 2009 would easily eclipse the 2008 record.

90. Owen Bennett-Jones, "Tide Turns Against the Militants," *British Broadcasting Corporation*, May 21, 2009.

91. Zubair Torwali, "From Swat with No Love," *News Newspaper*, January 8, 2009; Jane Perlez and Pir Zubair Shah, "Taliban Exploit Class Rifts in Pakistan," *New York Times*, April 16, 2009. The *New York Times* article provides a useful analysis of the efforts by the Taliban in Swat to rupture the

traditional feudal power structure in Swat and to exploit grievances among the poor to attract supporters. Militants in many areas partnered with local criminal gangs to push out feudal lords, although most locals eventually came to resent the new power structure.

92. Declan Walsh, "Video of Girl's Flogging as Taliban Hand out Justice," *Guardian*, April 2, 2009.

93. Animesh Roul "Resourceful Taliban Milk the Land," *Asia Times Online*, May 5, 2009; Interviews by research assistant in Swat, August 2009.

94. "Militants Torch Pakistani Ski Resort," *Reuters*, June 26, 2008.

95. Peters, "Crime and Insurgency."

96. Interviews by research assistant in Swat, August 2009; Animesh Roul, "Resourceful Taliban."

97. Animesh Roul, "Resourceful Taliban."

98. Peters, "Crime and Insurgency."

99. Telephone interview by author with Waziristan native, August 2009.

100. "Dir Lashkar Pushes Taliban to Last Hideout," *News Newspaper*, June 11, 2009; "Lashkar Struggles to Dislodge Holed-up Militants," *News Newspaper*, June 13, 2009.

101. Peters, "Crime and Insurgency."

102. Rahimullah Yusufzai, "Hakimullah Mehsud Unveils Himself to Media," *News Newspaper*, November 30, 2008.

103. The sketch is online at http://www.nefafoundation.org/miscellaneous/Hakimullahnote-translation.pdf.

104. "Baitullah's Death Finally Confirmed by Taliban," *News Newspaper*, August 26, 2009.

105. "Taliban Video Production Developments & Bugs," www.IntelCenter.org, November 17, 2009.

106. Imtiaz Ali, "Military Victory in South Waziristan or the Beginning of a Long War?" *Terrorism Monitor Volume*: 7 Issue: 38, *Jamestown Foundation*, December 15, 2009.

107. Griffe Witte and Joby Warrick, "Insurgents Forced out of Pakistan's Tribal Havens Form Smaller Cells in Heart of Nation," *Washington Post*, December 19, 2009.

108. Aamir Latif, "Pakistan Militant Groups," *Islam Online*, February 6, 2008.

109. Ahmed Rashid, *Jihad*, Vanguard Books (Lahore: 2002), 165. Steven Catseel, "Narco-Terrorism: International Drug Trafficking and Terrorism—a Dangerous Mix," Statement of the Assistant Administrator for Intelligence before the Senate Committee on the Judiciary *DEA Congressional Testimony* (Washington, D.C.: May 20, 2003); and Tamara Makarenko, "Central

Asia's Opium Terrorists," Wide Angle Productions, *Public Broadcasting System.* www.pbs.org/wnet/wideangle/printable/centralasia_briefing_print.-html.

110. Rashid, *Jihad,* 165.

111. Mark Burgess, "Profile of the IMU," The Terrorism Project. The Center for Defense Information www.cdi.org/terrorism/imu.cfm; Rashid, *Jihad,* and Makarenko.

112. Author's interviews with western and Pakistani officials and from Tohid, Owais. "Al Qaeda's Uzbek Bodyguards," *Christian Science Monitor,* September 28, 2004.

113. Peters, "Crime and Insurgency."

114. Interview by author in Kabul, February 25, 2007.

115. Interview by research assistant, July 3, 2007.

116. Interview by research assistant 2, in Lashkar Gah, July 2007.

117. Interview by author in Kabul, February 26, 2007.

118. For details, see: http://www.america.gov/st/texttrans-english/2009/October/20091028171105eaifas2.144587e-02.html.

119. Telephone interview by author, December 18, 2009.

120. Interview by author in Quetta, July 10, 2008.

5. The Kingpin

1. Interview with General Ali Shah Paktiawal, Kabul, May 2005.

2. Interview with an Afghan police official, Kabul, July 2007

3. Interview with an Afghan official, Peshawar, February 2007.

4. Interviews by research assistant 1 with Afghan officials and tribal sources, Kabul, July and August 2007.

5. The short-lived Saffarid dynasty was led by a coppersmith, Ya'qub bin Laith as-Saffar, who like HJK rose from humble origins to became a powerful warlord. With his base in modern-day Zaranj, the capital of Nimroz Province, he eventually conquered all of Afghanistan and what are today parts of eastern Iran and western Pakistan. At its height, the Saffarid dynasty nearly conquered Baghdad but was defeated.

6. Interview by research assistant 5 with a tribal elder, Dalbandin, October 3, 2007.

7. Interview with an Afghan police official, Kabul, September 26, 2007.

8. Interview with Hashem Zayyem, Kabul, March 1, 2007.

9. Interview with a former British official, Kabul, November 2007.

10. Interview with a U.S. official, Kabul, June 30, 2005.

11. Tim McGirk, "Terrorism's Harvest," *Time,* August 9, 2004.

12. Interview with a Pakistani official, Islamabad, March 12, 2008.

13. Baramcha is spelled Baramshah in some intelligence reports shown to the author.

14. Interview by research assistant 1 with an Afghan interior ministry official, Kabul, July 2007.

15. Interview with an Afghan security official, Kabul, September 2006.

16. McGirk, "Terorism's Harvest"; multiple interviews.

17. Ibid.

18. Multiple interviews by research assistant 1 with Afghan officials.

19. Interview by research assistant 1 with an Afghan official, Kabul, July 2007.

20. Ibid.

21. Interview with General Ali Shah Paktiawal, Kabul, May 2004.

22. Interviews by research assistant 1 with an Afghan interior ministry official, Kabul, July and August 2007; http://www.usdoj.gov/usao/nys/pressreleases/October08/usvkhansignedindictment.pdf.

23. Dexter Filkins, Mark Mazzetti, and James Risen, "Brother of Afghan Leader Said to Be Paid by CIA," *New York Times*, October 27, 2009.

24. Gretchen Peters and Brian Ross, "U.S. Military Links Karzai Brother to Drugs," ABC News, June 22, 2006, http://blogs.abcnews.com/theblotter/2006/06/us_military_lin.html.

25. Interview with a Pakistani officer, Islamabad, March 12, 2008.

26. Interview by research assistant 5 with a smuggler, Quetta, October 2, 2007.

27. Interview with a western official, Kabul, September 2006.

28. Robert Burns, "Gates: Taliban Fighters Use Iranian Weapons," Associated Press, June 4, 2007.

29. Interview with an Afghan official, Peshawar, December 2007.

30. Interviews by research assistants 1 and 2 with Afghan officials, Kabul and Helmand, July 2007.

31. Interview by research assistant 2 with an Afghan security official, Helmand, July 2007.

32. Interview with a smuggler, Quetta, April 2006.

33. Interviews by research assistants 1 and 2 with tribal sources, Kabul and Helmand, July 2007.

34. Interview with a former U.S. official, Washington, D.C., June 16, 2007.

35. Author's interviews and Larry Neumeister, "Afghan Man Arrested in New York Narco-Terrorism Case," Associated Press, October 24, 2008; "Afghan Charged in N.Y. Drug-Terrorism Case," Associated Press, October 24, 2008.

36. "Suspected Afghan Drug Smuggler Arraigned in New York," *Agence France-Presse*, October 24, 2008.

37. Interview by author, Bayside, N.Y., December 5, 2009.

38. Read the full indictment at http://www.nefafoundation.org/miscellaneous/ FeaturedDocs/US _v_ Juma-Khan_dojprspcind.pdf.
39. http://www.usdoj.gov/dea/pubs/pressrel/pr102408.html.
40. Telephone interview with border resident by research assistant 6, December 2008.
41. Interview by author, Alexandria. V.A., November 13, 2009.
42. Interview by research assistant 6, Quetta, December 2008.
43. Telephone interview with Intelligence Bureau official by research assistant 6, December 2008.
44. Interview by research assistant 6, Quetta, December 2008.

6. Follow the Money

1. Interview with Riaz, Dubai, December 10, 2007.
2. See http://newdelhi.usembassy.gov/pr060206.html and http://www.ustreas .gov/press/releases/js909.htm. Groups like the FARC and the United Self-Defense Forces of Colombia also have double designations.
3. Mehta, *Maximum City Bombay Lost and Found*, 134–140; Kaplan, "Paying for Terror."
4. See http://www.ustreas.gov/press/releases/reports/fact_sheet.pdf.
5. Telephone interview with a former CIA official, September 5, 2008.
6. Carolyn Lochhead, "Bush Goes After Terrorists' Funds," *San Francisco Chronicle*, September 25, 2001.
7. See http://www.ustreas.gov/press/releases/po727.htm.
8. For a transcript of the speech, go to http://edition.cnn.com/TRANSCRIPTS/ 0112/20/se.05.html.
9. See http://www.treas.gov/offices/enforcement/ofac/reports/tar2006.pdf, 15.
10. Interview with John Cassara, Washington, D.C., June 29, 2007.
11. Interview with Robert Charles, Washington, D.C., May 23, 2007.
12. It's also known as "Hundi" in Pakistan, where it specifically refers to a balancing of trade accounts.
13. Maimbo, "Money Exchange Dealers of Kabul: A Study of the Hawala System in Afghanistan," 9.
14. Edwina Thompson, "The Nexus of Drug Trafficking and *Hawala* in Afghanistan," in Byrd and Buddenberg, eds., *Afghanistan's Drug Industry* (report), 177–179.
15. Behar, "Kidnapped Nation."
16. Interview with Raymond Baker, Washington, D.C., July 17, 2007.
17. "U.S. Designates Suspects in Pakistani Drug Lord's Ring."

18. Interview with Gulbaz Khan, Peshawar, January 2008.
19. "Dubai Has 30,000 Construction Cranes," *Gulf News*, June 18, 2006.
20. Interviews with bankers and former Pakistani officials, Karachi, March 2008.
21. Telephone interview with Tariq Hassan, February 18, 2008.
22. Sherbaz Khan, "Big Fish Allowed to Escape the Net: Tariq, Ex-SECP Issues White Paper," *Dawn*, July 8, 2006.
23. See http://www.akdsecurities.net.
24. "Investors Lost $13bn in 2005 Stock Crisis," *Dawn*, July 8, 2006.
25. Nadeem, curiously, is the son of Swaleh Naqvi, the former chief executive of BCCI, according to other brokers and bankers in Karachi.
26. Mark Smith, "With Vast Sums in Transit, Even Entire Nations Put at Risk," *Houston Chronicle*, December 3, 1995.
27. Jon Henly, "City 'Haven' for Terrorist Money Laundering," *Guardian*, October 10, 2001.
28. Patrick Radden Keefe, "Quartermasters of Terror," *New York Review of Books*, February 10, 2005, 2.
29. Office of the Director of National Intelligence, "The Terrorist Threat to the U.S. Homeland," news release, July 17, 2007, 6, http://www.dni.gov/press_releases/20070717_release.pdf.
30. As well, there is evidence that bin Laden banned his supporters and trainees in his camps, not just from using alcohol and hashish, but even from smoking tobacco. For example, see Sifaoui, *Inside al Qaeda*, and http://cns.miis.edu/pubs/reports/.pdfs/binladen/060201.pdf.
31. "Monograph on Terrorist Financing," 9/11 Commission.
32. Lee Wolosky, "Statement to the National Commission on Terrorist Attacks upon the United States," April 1, 2003, http://govinfo.library.unt.edu/911/hearings/hearing1/witness_wolosky.htm.
33. Interview with a U.S. official, Islamabad, February 5, 2008.
34. Rashid, *Jihad*, 165; Catseel, "Narco-Terrorism: International Drug Trafficking and Terrorism—a Dangerous Mix"; Makarenko, "Central Asia's Opium Terrorists."
35. See http://cns.miis.edu/pubs/reports/pdfs/binladen/060201.pdf.
36. Radden Keefe, "Quartermasters of Terror," 5.
37. Farah, "Al Qaeda's Road Paved with Gold."
38. Cassara, *Hide and Seek*, 178.
39. Benjamin and Simon, *The Age of Sacred Terror*, 112.
40. Farah, "Al Qaeda's Road."

7. Mission Creep

1. The author was given copies of the correspondence by staff at the Foreign Relations Committee.

2. Multiple interviews; Meyer, "Pentagon Resists Pleas for Help in Afghan Opium Fight."

3. A copy of the letter was given to the author by staff at the Foreign Relations Committee.

4. Meyer, "Pentagon Resists Pleas."

5. Risen, *State of War*, 157.

6. Ibid.

7. Interview with author, Los Angeles, C.A., June 29, 2009.

8. Interview with a U.S. official, Washington, D.C., May 14, 2007. GPS stands for "global positioning system."

9. Meyer, "Pentagon Resists Pleas"; Blanchard, "Afghanistan, Narcotics and U.S. Policy"; see also UNODC's *Annual Drug Survey 2004*, 206, http://www.unodc.org/afg/reports_surveys.html.

10. Declan Walsh, "How Anti-Corruption Chief Once Sold Heroin in Las Vegas," *Guardian*, August 28, 2007.

11. David Kaplan and Aamir Latif, "A Stash to Beat All," *U.S. News & World Report*, August 10, 2005. Sher Mohammed was the nephew of Nasim Akhundzada (cited in Chapter 2). As with his uncle, Sher Mohammed appears to have set poppy quotas for Helmand. Antonio Maria Costa, the executive director of the UNODC, blamed Sher Mohammed specifically for Helmand's soaring poppy crop. President Karzai, meanwhile, has repeatedly pressed for him to be restored to power.

12. Quoted in John Risen, "Poppy Fields Are Now a Front Line in the Afghan War," *New York Times*, May 16, 2007.

13. David Rohde, "The Afghanistan Triangle," *New York Times*, October 1, 2006; Gretchen Peters, "Law Lessons for Afghan Police," *Christian Science Monitor*, January 7, 2003.

14. David Rohde, "Afghan Symbol for Change Becomes a Symbol of Failure," *New York Times*, September 5, 2006.

15. Telephone interview with Beverly Eighmy, May 15, 2007.

16. Karen Tandy, "Statement Before the Committee on Armed Services." U.S. House of Representatives, 66–73; Michael Braun, "U.S. Counternarcotics Policy in Afghanistan," testimony, Committee on International Relations.

17. Telephone interview with Rand Beers, August 5, 2007.

18. "Rumsfeld: Major Combat Over in Afghanistan," CNN, May 1, 2003, http://www.cnn.com/2003/WORLD/asiapcf/central/05/01/afghan.combat/.

19. Risen, *State of War*, 158.

20. Victoria Burnett, "Crackdown on Afghanistan's Cash Crop Looms," *Boston Globe*, September 18, 2004.

21. A copy of the cable was shown to the author.

22. Interview with a U.S. official, Washington, D.C., July 25, 2007.

23. Risen, *State of War*, 153.

24. Interview with Robert Charles, Washington, D.C., May 23, 2007.

25. A copy of the cable was shown to the author.

26. A copy of his testimony was given to the author by Bashar's American lawyer, Ivan Fisher.

27. The details on this can be found in Chapter 3, "Narco-Terror State."

28. Author's interview with an Afghan who accompanied him to a meeting with DEA officials in Pakistan, and who was able to correctly identify the DEA agent in charge of the U.S. embassy at the time.

29. Bill Powell, "Warlord or Druglord?" *Time* magazine, February 8, 2007.

30. Corcoran, "America's Blind Eye."

31. According to Noorzai's testimony, author's interviews, and local news reports from the time.

32. Risen, *State of War*, 164.

33. Gregg Zoroyya and Donna Leinwand, "Rise of Drug Trade Threat to Afghanistan's Security," *USA Today*, October 26, 2004.

34. A copy of the transcripts was obtained by the author from Noorzai's lawyer. The story is also reported in: Richard Lieby, "Tangled Objectives Bring Down Spy Firm," *Washington Post*, December 27, 2008.

35. Lieby, "Tangled Objectives."

36. Joseph Goldstein, "Justice Dept. Eyes U.S. Firms' Payments to Afghan Diplomat," *New York Sun*, January 29, 2008.

37. Powell.

38. Interviews by author, December 4 and 16, 2009.

39. Author's interviews and Joseph Goldstein, "Justice Dept. Eyes U.S. Firms' Payments to Afghan Diplomat," *New York Sun*, January 29, 2008.

40. Lieby, "Tangled Objectives."

41. Goldstein, "Justice Department Eyes."

42. Fisher's client list reads like a who's who of smugglers, crime bosses, and other ne'er-do-wells. As a young lawyer, he defended Jack Henry Abbott against murder charges, arguing that the best-selling author of *In the Belly of the Beast* stabbed an actor in a moment of "extreme emotional disturbance." In addition to representing Afridi, Fisher also worked on the so-called "French

Connection" case, served as lead counsel for Mafioso Salvatore Catalano in the "Pizza Connection Trial," and represented Michele Sindona, an Italian financier dubbed "the Vatican's banker," whose financial empire collapsed amid charges of fraud, bribery, and murder.

43. Interview by author, New York, December 4, 2009.
44. See www.usembassy.gov/pakistan/h05102402.html.
45. See www.usdoj.gov/dea/pubs/states/newsrel/nyc051107a.html.
46. See www.usdoj.gov/usao/nys/pressreleases/May07/essaarrivalpr.pdf.
47. See http://www.justice.gov/opa/pr/2008/December/08-crm-1145.html.
48. Interview by author, Washington, D.C., July 13, 2008.
49. For a detailed account of the offensive, confirmed by military officials who took part in it, see "Afghanistan's Narco-War," a report to the Committee on Foreign Relations, U.S. Senate, August 10, 2009, 19.
50. Personal interviews by author and Heidi Vogt, "Troops Make Large Drug Seizure in Afghanistan," Associated Press, May 23, 2009.
51. Risen, "Poppy Fields."
52. James Glantz and David Rohde, "Report Faults Training of Afghan Police," *New York Times*, December 4, 2006.
53. Ibid.
54. Rohde, "Afghan Symbol for Change."
55. Rohde, "Overhaul of Afghan Police Is New Priority."
56. Multiple interviews with UN and Afghan officials, March 2007.
57. Constable, "Poor Yield for Afghans' War on Drugs."
58. Jeremy Page, "Wanted for Empty Prison: Some Convicted Afghan Drug Barons," *Times* (London), February 23, 2008.
59. Moore, "Struggling for Solutions as Opium Trade Blossoms."
60. Gall and Cloud, "U.S. Memo Faults Afghan Leader on Heroin Fight."
61. Interview with Doug Wankal, Helmand, May 2006.
62. David Rohde, "Taliban Raise Poppy Production to a Record Again," *New York Times*, August 26, 2007.
63. Joseph Coleman, "World Bank Urges Counter Opium Measures," Associated Press, February 5, 2008.
64. Coghlan, "School Playground."
65. Burch, "Afghan Airport to Help Switch from Drugs to Fruit."
66. Hafvenstein, *Opium Season*, 64–65.
67. Ed Johnson, "Gates Wants NATO to Reorganize Afghanistan Mission," *Bloomberg*, December 13, 2007; Thomas Harding, "Canadians to Quit Afghanistan," *Telegraph*, February 22, 2008.

68. Interview with Thomas Schweich, Washington, D.C., June 1, 2007.

69. Read the full report at http://www.state.gov/documents/organization/90671 .pdf.

70. Hollbrooke, "Still Wrong in Afghanistan"; multiple interviews.

71. "UN Urges NATO to Stop Afghan Opium Trade," CNN, November 17, 2007, http://www.cnn.com/2007/WORLD/asiapcf/11/17/afghan.opium/index.html.

72. Interview with a western official, Islamabad, February 5, 2008.

8. Zero-Sum Game

1. "Helmand Heads for Record Poppy Harvest," *Institute of War and Peace Reporting*, February 9, 2007.

2. See http://www.ft.com/cms/s/0/f1a58a50-c242-11dc-8fba-0000779fd2ac .html?nclick_check&equals$1.

3. This group was previously known as the Senlis Council, and is funded by the Mercator Fund.

4. See www.state.gov/p/inl/rls/nrcrpt/2007/vol1/html/80858.htm; and Pierre-Arnaud Chouvy, "Licensing Afghanistan's Opium: Solution or Fallacy?" *Asia Times*, February 1, 2006.

5. Peter Tomsen, "Statement on Afghanistan: In Pursuit of Security and Democracy."

6. See http://abcnews.go.com/images/PollingUnit/1049a1Afghanistan -WhereThingsStand.pdf.

7. Graeme Smith, "Doing It the Dutch Way in Afghanistan," *Globe and Mail*, December 2, 2006.

8. Molly Moore, "NATO Confronts Surprisingly Fierce Taliban," *Washington Post*, February 26, 2008.

9. With 21 troop fatalities, the Dutch casualty rate at the end of 2009 was less than 1 percent, while Britain had lost 2.6 percent of its soldiers (240 deaths) and Canada 4.6 percent (133 deaths).

10. "Canadian Troops to Leave Safety of Bases to 'Live' with Afghans," *Canadian Press*, December 13, 2009.

11. Interview by author in Islamabad, September 10, 2007.

12. Telephone interview, December 14, 2009.

13. Interview by author in Kabul, October 30, 2006.

14. Barnett Rubin and Jake Sherman, "Counter-Narcotics to Stabilize Afghanistan: The False Promise of Crop Eradication," *The Center on International Cooperation*" New York University, February 2008, 8.

15. Paul Barker, Michael Kleinman, Emily Pelton, Barnett Rubin, and Cara Thanassi, "Too Early to Declare Success."

16. Rubin, "Road to Ruin," 3.

17. Interview by author in Islamabad, February 21, 2007.

18. Molly Moore, "Struggling for Solutions as Afghanistan's Opium Trade Blossoms," *Washington Post,* March 21, 2008.

19. Interview by author in Kabul, March 27, 2007.

Afterword

1. For an online read-in on the subject, see http://www.islamweb.net/ver2/archive/article.php?lang=E&id=135424 or http://www.ediscoverislam.com/Life-Death-and-Hereafter/About-Life-and-hereafter/reason-and-questions-of-faith-unseen-world-life.

2. Barry McCaffery, "After Action Report: Visit to Kuwait and Afghanistan," *Report to Department Head Social Sciences,* U.S. Military Academy at West Point, December 5, 2009.

3. Fawad Ahmadi, "The Drug Courrier Children of Herat," *Institute for War & Peace Reporting,* December 17, 2009.

4. "Addiction, Crime and Insurgency: The Transnational Threat of Afghan Opium," UNODC report, October 2009. http://www.unodc.org/documents/data-and analysis/Afghanistan/Afghan_Opium _Trade_2009_web.pdf; "Pakistan Blighted by Afghan Drugs in Transit," *Dawn Newspaper,* April 23, 2009.

5. Golnaz Esfandiari, "Central Asia: Drug Addiction is on the Rise," *RFE/RL,* June 22, 2004.

6. Scott Hesketh, "Asian Terror Gangs Target UK with Killer Heroin," *Daily Star,* February 22, 2009.

7. "Are 'Muslim Boys' Using Profits of Crime to Fund Terrorist Attacks?" *The Independent,* August 15, 2005.

8. "Afghan Heroin Hitting our Streets, Mounties Warn," *Daily Star,* August 6, 2007.

9. Author's interviews with law enforcement officials, November 2009.

10. "Sahara Cocaine Plane Crash Probed," *BBC News,* November 17, 2008.

11. Jamie Doward, "Drug Seizures in West Africa Prompt Fears of al Qaeda Links," *Observer,* November 29, 2009.

12. Ibid.

13. Ibid.

BIBLIOGRAPHY

Books

Baker, Raymond. *Capitalism's Achilles Heel*. Hoboken: Wiley, 2005.

Benjamin, Daniel, and Steven Simon. *The Age of Sacred Terror*. New York: Random House, 2003.

Bergen, Peter. *Holy War, Inc*. New York: Touchstone Press, 2002.

Booth, Martin. *Opium*. New York: St. Martin's Griffin, 1996.

Cassara, John. *Hide and Seek*. Washington, D.C.: Potomac Books, 2006.

Charles, Robert B. *Narcotics and Terrorism*. Philadelphia: Chelsea House, 2004.

Coll, Stephen. *The Ghost Wars*. New York: Penguin Press, 2004.

Cooley, John K. *Unholy Wars*. London: Pluto Press, 1999.

Courtwright, David. *Forces of Habit*. Cambridge, MA: Harvard University Press, 2001.

Crile, George. *Charlie Wilson's War*. New York: Atlantic Monthly Press, 2003.

Davenport-Hines, Richard. *The Pursuit of Oblivion*. New York: W. W. Norton, 2002.

Docherty, Leo. *Desert of Death*. London: Faber and Faber, 2007.

Escohotado, Antonio. *A Brief History of Drugs*. Rochester, NY: Park Street Press, 1996.

Farah, Douglas, and Stephen Braun. *Merchant of Death*. Hoboken, NJ: Wiley, 2007.

Griffin, Michael. *Reaping the Whirlwind*. London: Pluto Press, 2001.

Hafvestein, Joel. *Opium Season*. Guilford, UK: Lyons Press, 2007.

Hanes, W. Travis, and Frank Sanello. *The Opium Wars*. Naperville, IL: Sourcebooks, 2002.

Haq, Ikramul. *Pakistan*. Lahore: Annoor Printers and Publishers, 1991.

Haq, M. Emdad-ul. *Drugs in South Asia*. New York: St. Martin's Press, 2000.

Haqqani, Hussain. *Pakistan Between Mosque and Military*. Lahore: Vanguard Books, 2005.

Hussein, Zahid. *Frontline Pakistan*. London: I. B. Taurus, 2007.

Hoffman, Bruce. *Inside Terrorism*. New York: Columbia University Press, 2006.

Lawrence, Bruce, ed. *Messages to the World*. London: Verso Press, 2005.

Lesser, Ian, Bruce Hoffman, John Arquilla, David Ronfeldt, and Michele Zanini. *Countering the New Terrorism*. Santa Monica: Rand Corporation, 1999.

Macdonald, David. *Drugs in Afghanistan.* London: Pluto Press, 2007.

Maley, William, ed. *Fundamentalism Reborn?* London: Hurst, 1998.

Marks, Howard. *Mr. Nice.* London: Vintage Books, 1996.

McCoy, Alfred. *The Politics of Heroin,* rev. ed. Chicago: Lawrence Hill, 2003.

———— and Alan Block, eds. *War on Drugs.* Boulder: Westview Press, 1992.

Mehta, Suketu. *Maximum City Bombay Lost and Found.* New York: Vintage Books, 2004.

Musharraf, Pervez. *In the Line of Fire.* London: Simon & Schuster, 2006.

Naím, Moisés. *Illicit.* New York: Doubleday, 2005.

Napoleoni, Loretta. *Terror Incorporated.* London: Penguin Books, 2003.

Nasiri, Omar. *Inside the Jihad.* New York: Basic Books, 2006.

National Commission on Terrorist Attacks upon the United States, Thomas H. Kean, and Lee Hamilton. *The 9/11 Commission Report.* New York: W. W. Norton, 2003.

Rashid, Ahmed. *Descent into Chaos.* New York: Penguin Books, 2008.

————. *Jihad: The Rise of Militant Islam in Central Asia.* New Haven, CT: Yale University Press, 2002.

————. *The Taliban.* New Haven, CT: Yale University Press, 2000.

Risen, James. *State of War.* New York: Simon & Schuster, 2006.

Rubin, Barnett R. *The Fragmentation of Afghanistan,* second ed. New Haven, CT: Yale University Press, 2002.

Schroen, Gary. *First In.* New York: Presidio Press, 2005.

Sifaoui, Mohamed. *Inside al Qaeda.* London: Granta Books, 2003.

Tenet, George. *At the Center of the Storm.* New York: HarperCollins, 2007.

Woodward, Bob. *Bush at War.* New York: Pocket Books, 2003.

Yousaf, Mohammed, and Mark Adkin. *The Bear Trap.* Lahore: Jang Publishers, 1992.

U.S. Government Documents

"Afghanistan: Foreign Secretary Mulls Over Afghanistan." U.S. Embassy (Islamabad) cable, October 1996. Barbara Elias, ed., *Pakistan: "The Taliban's Godfather"? Documents Detail Years of Pakistani Support for Taliban, Extremists,* National Security Archive electronic briefing book no. 227, National Security Archive/George Washington University (NSA/GWU hereafter), http://www.gwu.edu/~nsarchiv/NSAEBB/NSAEBB227/index.htm.

"Afghanistan, Iran, Pakistan Country Profiles." Office of Intelligence Drug Enforcement Administration, January 1992. Narcotics Collection, box 11, folder: Drug Trafficking/Pakistan. NSA/GWU.

"Afghanistan: Russian Embassy Official Claims Iran Interfering More Than Pakistan." U.S. Embassy (Islamabad) cable, November 30, 1995. *Pakistan,* Elias, ed., NSA/GWU.

BIBLIOGRAPHY

"Afghanistan: Taliban Rep Won't Seek UN Seat for Now." U.S. Embassy (Islamabad) cable, December 1996. *The Taliban File, 9/11 Sourcebook,* National Security Archive electronic briefing book no. 97, Sajit Ghandi, ed., NSA/GWU, http://www.gwu.edu/~nsarchiv/NSAEBB/NSAEBB97/index.htm.

"Afghanistan: Taliban Victory's Impact [excised]." National Intelligence Daily, CIA, September 30, 1996. *Pakistan,* Elias, ed., NSA/GWU.

"Afghanistan: U.S. Interests and U.S. Aid." Letter to U.S. State Department, 1992. Document collection of Peter Tomsen, former U.S. Special Envoy (Tomsen collection, hereafter).

"A/S Raphel Discusses Afghanistan." U.S. Embassy (Islamabad) cable, April 22, 1996. *Taliban File,* Ghandi, ed., NSA/GWU.

"Daily Muslim Article on Balochistan Heroin Seizure." U.S. Embassy (Islamabad) cable, December 1990. Narcotics Collection, box 30, folder: Pakistan/Afghanistan FOIA Documents. NSA/GWU.

"[excised] Believe Pakistan Is Backing Taliban." U.S. Embassy (Islamabad) cable, December 6, 1994. *Taliban File,* Ghandi, ed., NSA/GWU.

"[excised]/Pakistan Interservice Intelligence/Pakistan (PK) Directorate Supplying the Taliban Forces." From [excised] to DIA, Washington, D.C., [excised] cable, October 22, 1996. *Pakistan,* Elias, ed., NSA/GWU.

"Finally, a Talkative Talib: Origins and Membership of the Religious Students' Movement." U.S. Embassy (Islamabad) cable, February 20, 1995. *Taliban File,* Ghandi, ed., NSA/GWU.

"GOP Begins Cleanup of Smugglers Den at Sohrab Goth." U.S. State Department cable from Karachi consul, December 1986. Narcotics Collection, box 30, folder: Pakistan/Afghanistan FOIA Documents. NSA/GWU.

"Heroin, Guns and the War in Pakistan." Robert Oakley, U.S. Embassy (Islamabad) cable to Secretary of State, December 1988. Narcotics Collection, box 30, folder: Pakistan/Afghanistan FOIA Documents. NSA/GWU.

"Heroin in Pakistan: Sowing the Wind." CIA. Published in *The Friday Times* (Lahore), September 3, 1993.

"HFAC International Narcotics Control Task Force Hearings, May 22." U.S. State Department document, June 1986. Narcotics Collection, box 29, folder: Pakistan. NSA/GWU.

"IIR [excised] Pakistan Involvement in Afghanistan." From [excised] to DIA, Washington, D.C., November 7, 1996. *Pakistan,* Elias, ed., NSA/GWU.

International Narcotics Control Strategy Reports 2001–2007, U.S. State Department Bureau for International Narcotics and Law Enforcement Affairs, Washington, D.C.

"Meeting with the Taliban in Kandahar: More Questions Than Answers." U.S. Embassy (Islamabad) cable, February 15, 1995. *Taliban File,* Ghandi, ed., NSA/GWU.

"Monograph on Terrorist Financing." 9/11 Commission, August 21, 2004, http://www.9-11commission.go/staff_ statements/911_TerrFin_Monograph.pdf.

"Narcotics and the New Government." U.S. Embassy (Islamabad) cable, December 1988. Narcotics Collection, box 30, folder: Pakistan/Afghanistan FOIA Documents. NSA/GWU.

"Narcotics—FY 90 Budget." Robert Oakley, U.S. Embassy (Islamabad) cable to INM Assistant Secretary Ann Wrobleski, March 1989. Narcotics Collection, box 30, folder: Pakistan/Afghanistan FOIA Documents. NSA/GWU.

"The Narcotics Issue and Contacts with Politicians." U.S. State Department letter to U.S. Embassy (Islamabad), September 1988. Narcotics Collection, box 30, folder: Pakistan/Afghanistan FOIA Documents. NSA/GWU.

"Narcotics Production/Trafficking in Northern Helmand." U.S. Embassy (Islamabad) cable, June 1989. Narcotics Collection, box 30, folder: Pakistan/Afghanistan FOIA Documents. NSA/GWU.

"Narcotics Trafficking and the Military." Near East and South Asia briefs, CIA, January 30, 1987. Narcotics Collection, box 30, folder: Pakistan: Narcotics Control Preparedness. NSA/GWU.

"Narcotics Trafficking from Afghanistan." U.S. Embassy (Islamabad) cable, March 1989. Narcotics Collection, box 11, folder: Drug Trafficking/Pakistan. NSA/GWU.

"National Intelligence Daily." Director of Central Intelligence, CIA, May 1, 1998. This document has not yet been assigned to a collection. NSA/GWU.

"National Narcotics Intelligence Consumers Committee Report for 1985–1986." Afghanistan Collection, box 12. NSA/GWU.

"New Fighting and New Forces in Kandahar." U.S. Consulate (Peshawar) cable, November 3, 1994. *Taliban File*, Ghandi, ed., NSA/GWU.

"Pakistan: Countering an Expanding Drug Industry." Intelligence assessment, CIA, September 1988. Narcotics Collection, box 11, folder: Drug Trafficking/Pakistan. NSA/GWU.

"Pakistan." DEA country analysis, undated. Narcotics Collection, box 30, folder: Pakistan. NSA/GWU.

"Pakistan's Narcotics Control Program." Letter from Edward Fox, Asst. Secretary of Legislative and Intergovernmental Affairs, to the Chairman of the Foreign Affairs Committee, U.S. House of Representatives. Narcotics Collection, box 30, folder: Pakistan Narcotics Preparedness. NSA/GWU.

"Pakistan Support for Taliban." U.S. Embassy (Islamabad) cable, September 26, 2000. *Pakistan*, Elias, ed., NSA/GWU.

"Request for Afghan Opium Crop Figures." U.S. State Department cable to U.S. Embassy (Islamabad), October 1992. Tomsen collection.

"The Taliban: What We've Heard," U.S. Embassy (Islamabad) cable, January 26, 1995. *Taliban File*, Ghandi, ed., NSA/GWU.

"The Taliban—Who Knows What the Movement Means?" U.S. Embassy (Islamabad) cable, November 28, 1994. *Taliban File*, Ghandi, ed., NSA/GWU.

"TKO Proposal." [name exised] Islamabad Country Office, Drug Enforcement Administration, March 25, 1993. Narcotics Collection, box 30, folder: Pakistan. NSA/GWU.

U.S. Counternarcotics Strategy Afghanistan 2007. Thomas A. Schweich, UNODC, http://www.state.gov/documents/organization/90671.pdf.

"U.S. Engagement with the Taliban on Usama bin Laden." U.S. State Department summary, circa July 16, 2001. *Taliban File*, Ghandi, ed., NSA/GWU.

"Veteran Afghanistan Traveler's Analysis of al Qaeda and Taliban Exploitable Weaknesses." Defense Intelligence Agency cable, October 2001. *Taliban File*, Ghandi, ed., NSA/GWU.

"Visit of INM Assistant Secretary Wrobleski: Meeting with President Zia." U.S. Embassy (Islamabad) cable, September 1987. Narcotics Collection, box 29, folder: Pakistan. NSA/GWU.

"Worldwide Drug Threat Assessment: A Joint Intelligence Report." Committee on Narcotics Intelligence Issues. Document prepared by representatives from the DEA, DIA, U.S. Customs, U.S. Coast Guard, and the National Drug Intelligence Center. April 2000, http://jeremybigwood.net/FOIAs/FOIA .htm.

Reports and Studies

Alexiev, Alexander. "Inside the Soviet Army in Afghanistan." Santa Monica: Rand Corporation, May 1988. Afghan Collection, NSA/GWU.

Byrd, William, and Christopher Ward. *Drugs and Development in Afghanistan*. Social Development Papers: Conflict Prevention and Reconstruction. Washington, D.C.: World Bank, December 2004.

———, and Doris Buddenberg, eds. *Afghanistan's Drug Industry*. Vienna: UNODC/World Bank, 2007.

Curtis, Glenn E., and Tara Karacan. *The Nexus Among Terrorists, Narcotics Traffickers, Weapons Proliferators and Organized Crime Networks in Western Europe*. Washington, D.C.: Library of Congress Federal Research Division, December 2002.

International Crisis Group. "Afghanistan's Endangered Compact." Asia briefing no. 59, January 29, 2007, http://www.crisisgroup.org/home/index.cfm?l=1& id=4631.

———. "Central Asia: Drugs and Conflict." November 26, 2001, http://www .crisisgroup.org/home/index.cfm?l=1&id=1430.

————. "Countering Afghanistan's Insurgency: No Quick Fixes." Asia report no. 123, November 2, 2006, http://www.crisisgroup.org/home/index.cfm?id=4485.

————. "Pakistan's Tribal Areas: Appeasing the Militants." Asia report no. 125, December 11, 2006, http://www.crisisgroup.org/home/index.cfm?id=4568.

Katzman, Kenneth. "Terrorism: Near Eastern Groups and State Sponsors, 2001." Washington, D.C.: Congressional Research Service, September 10, 2001.

Maimbo, Samuel Munzele. "Money Exchange Dealers of Kabul: A Study of the Hawala System in Afghanistan." Finance and Private Sector Unit South Asia Region. Washington, D.C.: World Bank, June 2003.

Perl, Raphael. "The Taliban and the Drug Trade." Washington, D.C.: Congressional Research Service, October 5, 2001.

Porteous, Samuel D. *The Threat from Transnational Crime*. Canadian Security Intelligence Service, commentary no. 70, 1996.

Rabasa, Angel, Steven Boraz, Peter Chalk, Kim Cragin, Theodore W. Karasik, Jennifer D. P. Moroney, Kevin A. O'Brien, and John E. Peters. *Ungoverned Territories: Understanding and Reducing Terrorist Risks*. Santa Monica: Rand Corporation, 2007.

Rubin, Barnett R. "The Political Economy of War and Peace in Afghanistan." *World Development* 28, no. 10 (2000): 1789–1803.

————. *The Road to Ruin*. Center on International Cooperation, New York University, October 7, 2004.

———— and Abubakar Siddique. *Resolving the Pakistan-Afghanistan Stalemate*. U.S. Institute of Peace, special report 176, October 2006.

———— and Jake Sherman. *Counter-Narcotics to Stabilize Afghanistan*. Center on International Cooperation, New York University, February 2008.

———— et al. *Too Early to Declare Success*. Afghanistan policy brief. Center on International Cooperation, New York University, March 2005.

Sifton, John, and Zama Coursen-Neff. *Killing You Is a Very Easy Thing for Us*. New York: Human Rights Watch, July 2003.

Torabi, Yama, and Lorenzo Delesgues. "Afghan Perceptions of Corruption: A Survey Across Thirteen Provinces." Integrity Watch Afghanistan, February 2007.

United Nations Assistance Mission in Afghanistan. *Suicide Attacks in Afghanistan 2001–2007*. UNAMA, September 2007, http://www.unama-afg.org/docs/_UN -Docs/UNAMA%20-%20SUICIDE%20ATTACKS%20STUDY%20-%20SEPT %209th%202007.pdf.

United Nations Office on Drugs and Crime. "Afghanistan: Opium Survey, 2001– 2007." http:www.unodc.org.

————. *The Opium Economy in Afghanistan*. New York: UNODC, 2003.

Weiss, Martin, et al. *Terrorist Financing*. Washington, D.C.: Congressional Research Service, August 3, 2005.

Wilder, Andrew. *Cops or Robbers?* Kabul: Afghanistan Research and Evaluation Unit, July 2007.

Speeches and Testimony

Beers, Rand. "Narco-Terror: The Worldwide Connection Between Drugs and Terrorism." Testimony, Committee on the Judiciary, U.S. Senate, 107th Cong., 2nd sess., March 13, 2002.

Blair, Tony. "Prime Minister's Statement to Parliament on the September 11 Attacks." October 4, 2001, www.number10.gov.uk.

Braun, Michael. "U.S. Counternarcotics Policy in Afghanistan: Time for Leadership." Testimony, Committee on International Relations, U.S. House, 109th Cong., 1st sess., March 17, 2005.

Casteel, Steven. "Narco-Terrorism: International Drug Trafficking and Terrorism—a Dangerous Mix." Statement, Committee on the Judiciary, U.S. Senate, 108th Cong., 1st sess., May 20, 2003.

Cilluffo, Frank J. "Threat Posed by the Convergence of Organized Crime, Drug Trafficking, and Terrorism." Statement, Committee on the Judiciary, Subcommittee on Crime, U.S. House, 106th Cong., 2nd sess., December 13, 2000.

Costa, Antonio Maria. "Briefing to the Committee on International Relations." Washington, D.C., September 20, 2006.

Tandy, Karen. "Statement Before the Committee on Armed Services." U.S. House of Representatives, Washington, D.C., June 28, 2006.

Tenet, George. "Challenges in a Changing Global Context." Testimony, Select Committee on Intelligence, U.S. Senate, 108th Cong., 2nd sess., February 24, 2004.

———. "Converging Dangers in a Post 9/11 World." Testimony, Select Committee on Intelligence, U.S. Senate, 107th Cong., 2nd sess., February 6, 2002.

———. "Worldwide Threat in 2000: Global Realities of Our National Security." Statement, Select Committee on Intelligence, U.S. Senate, 107th Cong., 2nd sess., February 2, 2000.

Tomsen, Peter. "Statement on Afghanistan: In Pursuit of Security and Democracy." Speech before the U.S. Senate Committee on Foreign Relations, Washington, D.C., October 16, 2003.

Scholarly and Magazine Articles

Abbas, Hassan. "Pakistan Through the Lens of the 'Triple A' Theory." *Fletcher Forum of World Affairs* 30, no. 1 (Winter 2006).

"Afghanistan's Tribal Complexity." *Economist*, January 31, 2008.

Anderson, Jon Lee. "The Taliban's Opium War." *New Yorker*, July 9, 2007.

Bearak, Barry. "Unreconstructed." *New York Times Magazine*, June 1, 2003.

Beehner, Lionel. "Musharraf's Taliban Problem." Council on Foreign Relations, September 10, 2006, http://www.cfr.org/publication/11401/musharrafs _taliban_problem.html.

———. "NATO and the Afghan-Pakistani Border." Council on Foreign Relations, August 3, 2006, http://www.cfr.org/publication/11237/nato_and_the _afghanpakistani_border.html.

Behar, Richard. "Kidnapped Nation." *Forbes*, April 29, 2002.

Blanchard, Christopher M. "Afghanistan, Narcotics and U.S. Policy." Congressional Research Service, Washington, D.C., December 7, 2004, and May 26, 2005.

Burgess, Mark. "In the Spotlight: Islamic Movement of Uzbekistan (IMU)." Center for Defense Information, the Terrorism Project, Washington, D.C., http://www.cdi.org/terrorism/imu.cfm.

Carpenter, Ted Galen. "How the Drug War in Afghanistan Undermines America's War on Terror."CATO Institute, Washington, D.C., November 10, 2004.

Chouvy, Pierre-Arnaud. "Drugs and the Financing of Terrorism." *Terrorism Monitor* 2, no. 20 (October 21, 2004), http://www.jamestown.org/publications _details.php?volume_id=400&issue_id=3116&article_id=2368732.

———. "Narco-Terrorism in Afghanistan." *Terrorism Monitor* 2, no. 6 (March 25, 2004), http://www.jamestown.org/publications_details.php?volume_id=400& issue_id=2929&article_id=23648.

Dalrymple, William. "On the Long Road to Freedom Finally." *Tehelka Magazine* 5, no. 9 (March 8, 2008), http://www.tehelka.com/story_main38.asp?file name=Ne080308on_the.asp.

Felbab-Brown, Vanda. "A Better Strategy Against Narco-Terrorism." Audit of the Conventional Wisdom series, MIT Center for International Studies, Cambridge, Mass. January 2006, http://web.mit.edu/cis/pdf/Audit_01_06_Vanda .pdf.

Galen Carpenter, Ted. "How the Drug War Undermines America's War on Terror." Foreign policy briefing, CATO Institute, Washington, D.C., November 10, 2004.

Glassner, Susan, and Walter Pincus, "Seized Letter Outlines al Qaeda Goals in Iraq," *Washington Post*, October 12, 2005.

"A Godfather's Lethal Mix of Business and Politics." *U.S. News & World Report*, December 5, 2005.

Goodhand, Jonathan. "From Holy War to Opium War?" *Central Asian Survey* 19, no. 2 (June 1, 2000): 265–280.

Grare, Frederic. "Pakistan: The Myth of an Islamist Peril." Policy brief, Carnegie Endowment for International Peace, Washington, D.C., February 2006.

Hasnain, Ghulam. "Karachi's Gang Wars: Portrait of a Don." *Newsline*, September 2001.

Hersh, Seymour M. "The Other War: Why Bush's Afghanistan Problem Won't Go Away." *New Yorker*, April 12, 2004.

Hitz, Frederick. "Obscuring Propriety: The CIA and Drugs." *International Journal on Intelligence and Counterintelligence* 12, no. 4 (Winter 1999): 448–462.

Hussein, Zahid. "Narco Power." *Newsline*, December 1989.

Kaplan, Eben. "Terror's Twisted Money Trail." Council on Foreign Relations, New York, April 4, 2006.

Lifschultz, Lawrence. "The Death Toll of Educated Afghans in Peshawar Is Now More Than One Thousand." *Newsline*, October 1989.

———. "Heroin Empire." *Newsline*, July 1989.

Maass, Peter. "Gul Agha Gets His Province Back." *New York Times Magazine*, January 6, 2002.

McGirk, Tim. "Terrorism's Harvest." *Time*, August 9, 2004.

Powell, Bill. "Warlord or Druglord?" *Time*, February 8, 2007.

Rashid, Ahmed. "Afghanistan on the Brink." *New York Review of Books*, June 22, 2006.

Rubin, Barnett R. "Saving Afghanistan." *Foreign Affairs*, January-February 2007.

Rubin, Elizabeth. "In the Land of the Taliban." *New York Times Magazine*, October 22, 2006.

Sancton, Thomas. "Dispatches." *Time*, April 4, 1994.

Schweich, Thomas. "Is Afghanistan a Narco-State?" *New York Times Magazine*, July 27, 2008.

News Stories

Ahmed, Shafiq. "Taliban Accounts Frozen." *Dawn*, January 24, 2006.

Baldauf, Scott, and Owais Tohid. "Taliban Appears to Be Regrouped and Well-Funded." *Christian Science Monitor*, May 8, 2003.

Bergen, Peter. "The Taliban: Regrouped and Rearmed." *Washington Post*, September 10, 2006.

Bonner, Arthur. "Afghanistan's Other Front: A World of Drugs." *New York Times*, November 2, 1985.

———. "Afghan Rebel's Victory Garden: Opium." *New York Times*, June 18, 1986.

Braun, Stephen, and Judy Pasternak. "Long Before Sept. 11, Bin Laden Flew Aircraft Under the Radar." *Los Angeles Times*, November 18, 2001.

Brunwasser, Matthew. "The Embargo Buster." *Frontline*, PBS, May 2002, http://www.pbs.org/frontlineworld/stories/sierraleone/bout.html.

Burch, Jonathon. "Afghan Airport to Help Switch from Drugs to Fruit." Reuters, August 4, 2008.

Burnett, Victoria, and Mark Huband. "UK Trains Afghans in Anti-Drugs Drive." *Financial Times*, January 10, 2004.

Callinan, Rory. "Taliban Back in Drugs, Terror Business." *Australian*, May 31, 2004.

Chivers, C. J. "Dutch Soldiers Stress Restraint in Afghanistan." *New York Times*, April 6, 2007.

Chouvy, Pierre-Arnaud. "Licensing Afghanistan's Opium: Solution or Fallacy?" *Asia Times*, February 1, 2006.

Cole, Matthew. "Killing Ourselves in Afghanistan." *Salon.com*, March 10, 2008, http://www.salon.com/news/feature/2008/03/10/taliban/.

Coll, Stephen. "Anatomy of a Victory: The CIA's Covert Afghan War." *Washington Post*, July 19, 1992.

Constable, Pamela. "A Poor Yield for Afghan's War on Drugs." *Washington Post*, September 19, 2006.

Cooper, Helene. "NATO Chief Says More Troops Needed in Afghanistan." *New York Times*, September 22, 2006.

DeYoung, Karen, and Douglas Farah. "Infighting Slows Hunt for Hidden al Qaeda Assets." *Washington Post*, June 18, 2002.

Farah, Douglas. "Al Qaeda's Gold: Following the Trail to Dubai." *Washington Post*, February 18, 2002.

———. "Al Qaeda's Road Paved with Gold." *Washington Post*, February 17, 2002.

Gall, Carlotta. "Afghans Accuse U.S. of Secret Spraying to Kill Poppies." *New York Times*, February 27, 2005.

———. "Taliban Battle Afghan Forces in Drug Region." *New York Times*, February 3, 2006.

——— and David Cloud. "U.S. Memo Faults Afghan Leader on Heroin Fight." *New York Times*, May 22, 2005.

Ghani, Ashraf. "Where Democracy's Greatest Enemy Is a Flower." *New York Times*, December 11, 2004.

Guggenheim, Ken. "U.S. Official Says Taliban Behind Opium Surge." Associated Press, October 3, 2001.

Higgins, Holy Barnes. "The Road to Helmand." *Washington Post*, February 4, 2007.

Hollbrooke, Richard. "Still Wrong in Afghanistan." *Washington Post*, January 23, 2008.

Hsu, Spencer, and Walter Pincus. "U.S. Warns of Stronger al Qaeda." *Washington Post*, July 12, 2007.

Kaplan, David. "Paying for Terror." *U.S. News & World Report*, December 5, 2005.

———. "The Saudi Connection." *U.S. News & World Report*, December 15, 2003.

——— and Joshua Kurlantzick. "How a Terror Network Funds Attacks." *U.S. News & World Report*, October 1, 2001.

Khan, Noor. "Taliban Collected Taxes, Ran Heroin Labs, Had Own Judge in Afghan Town." Associated Press, December 12, 2007.

———. "Taliban Hang Three Alleged Afghan Informers." Associated Press, April 1, 2007.

Kroft, Steve. "Afghanistan: Addicted to Heroin." *60 Minutes*, CBS, October 16, 2005.

Lifschultz, Lawrence. "Inside the Kingdom of Heroin." *Nation*, November 14, 1988.

Lowinson, Joyce H., and David F. Musto. "Drug Crisis and Strategy." *New York Times*, May 22, 1980.

Makarenko, Tamara. "Central Asia's Opium Terrorists." *Wide Angle Productions*, PBS, http://www.pbs.org/wnet/wideangle/printable/centralasia_briefing_print .html.

Marquand, Robert. "The Reclusive Leader Who Runs the Taliban." *Christian Science Monitor*, October 10, 2001.

Mazzetti, Mark, and David Rohde. "Al Qaeda Chiefs Are Seen to Regain Power." *New York Times*, February 18, 2007.

McDowell, Patrick. "As Disruption from War on Taliban Ends, Traffickers Moving Big Heroin Shipments." Associated Press, March 3, 2002.

Meyer, Josh. "Al Qaeda 'Co-Opts' New Affiliates." *Los Angeles Times*, September 16, 2007.

———. "Pentagon Resists Pleas for Help in Afghan Opium Fight." *Los Angeles Times*, December 5, 2006.

———. "U.S. Anti-Drug Efforts in Afghanistan to Be Bolstered." *Los Angeles Times*, December 8, 2006.

Mintz, John. "15 Freighters Believed to Be Linked to Al Qaeda." *Washington Post*, December 31, 2002.

Moore, Molly. "NATO Confronts Surprisingly Fierce Taliban." *Washington Post*, February 26, 2008.

———. "Struggling for Solutions as Opium Trade Blossoms." *Washington Post*, March 21, 2008.

Mujahid, Islam, and Gretchen Peters. "Buddhist Relics Latest Casualties of Pakistan's Talibanization." ABC News, October 15, 2007, http://blogs.abcnews .com/theblotter/2007/10/buddhist-relics.html.

Peters, Gretchen. "Afghan War Flares Anew." *Christian Science Monitor*, April 6, 2003.

———. "American Voice on New Terror Video." *Christian Science Monitor*, October 29, 2004.

———. "Hostilities Flare Again in America's Other War." *Christian Science Monitor*, March 31, 2003.

———. "Opium Bumper Crop Seen to Benefit Taliban." ABC News and ABC News Radio, September 3, 2006, http://abcnews.go.com/International/Story ?id=2390033&page=1.

———. "Taliban Drug Trade: Echoes of Colombia." *Christian Science Monitor*, November 21, 2006.

———. "Taliban Stamping Out Hashish but Opium Production Continues to Flourish." Associated Press, April 14, 1997.

———. "They're Back: A New, Vicious Taliban Take Shape in Afghanistan; Opium Funds a New Type of Taliban Army." ABC News and ABC News Radio, June 27, 2006, http://abcnews.go.com/International/story?id=2124643&page=1.

———. "Violence Grows in Pakistan's Tribal Zone, Despite Army Presence." *Christian Science Monitor*, December 12, 2005.

———. "Weary Taliban Come In from the Cold." *Christian Science Monitor*, December 14, 2004.

Rashid, Ahmed. "Wages of War." *Far Eastern Economic Review*, August 5, 1999.

Rohde, David. "Overhaul of Afghan Police Is New Priority." *New York Times*, October 18, 2007.

Risen, James. "An Afghan's Path from U.S. Ally to Drug Suspect." *New York Times*, February 2, 2007.

Rupert, James, "A Pakistani Officer Wages Jihad Against U.S." *Newsday*, October 7, 2007.

——— and Steve Coll. "U.S. Declines to Probe Afghan Drug Trade; Rebels, Pakistani Officers Implicated." *Washington Post*, May 13, 1990.

Sciolino, Elaine. "U.S. Urging Afghan Rebels to Limit Opium." *New York Times*, March 26, 1989.

Scott Tyson, Ann. "Taliban Gains Forestall U.S. Troop Reductions in Afghanistan." *Washington Post*, September 22, 2006.

Sly, Liz. "Opium Cash Fuels Terror, Experts Say." *Chicago Tribune*, February 9, 2004.

Smith, Graeme. "Doing It the Dutch Way in Afghanistan." *Globe and Mail*, December 2, 2006.

———. "Talking to the Taliban: Globe Special Report." *Globe and Mail*, March 24, 2008, http://www.theglobeandmail.com/talkingtothetaliban.

Tohid, Owais. "Al Qaeda's Uzbek Bodyguards." *Christian Science Monitor*, September 28, 2004.

———. "Bumper Year for Afghan Poppies." *Christian Science Monitor*, July 24, 2003.

BIBLIOGRAPHY

Tolchin, Martin. "CIA Admits It Failed to Tell Fed About BCCI." *New York Times*, October 26, 1991.

"U.S. Designates Suspects in Pakistani Drug Lord's Ring." Associated Press, November 27, 2007.

Vaknin, Sam. "Hawala, or the Bank That Never Was." United Press International, February 2, 2002.

Witte, Griff. "Emerging Epicenter in the Afghan War." *Washington Post*, March 15, 2007.

INDEX